Temples of Sound

Jim Cogan and William Clark

Temples of Sound

Inside the Great Recording Studios

Foreword by Quincy Jones

CHRONICLE BOOKS
SAN FRANCISCO

Library of Congress Cataloging-in-Publication Data:
Cogan, Jim.
Temples of sound : inside the great recording studios /
Jim Cogan and William Clark.
    p. cm.
Includes index.
ISBN 0-8118-3394-1
1. Sound recording industry—United States—History.
2. Popular music—United States—History and criticism.
I. Clark, William. II. Title.
    ML3790 .C52 2002
    781.64'149'0973—dc21
        2002004425

Manufactured in China.

Design: Ph.D, www.phdla.com

Distributed in Canada by Raincoast Books
9050 Shaughnessy Street
Vancouver, BC V6P 6E5

10 9 8 7 6 5 4 3 2 1

Chronicle Books LLC
85 Second Street
San Francisco, California 94105
www.chroniclebooks.com

Front cover: Aretha Franklin belts it out, 1967.
Page 2: Ray Charles goes country, when country wasn't
    cool, at United Western Recorders, early 1960s.
This page: With a cigarette and the blues, Peggy Lee leans
    into the mic at Capitol's Melrose Studio, mid-1950s.
Back cover: Bob Dylan, recording "Like a Rolling Stone,"
    1965.

Contents

Foreword

BY QUINCY JONES

For many musicians of my generation, the experience of music started in live shows, then moved along to getting recorded in a studio. All the energy and excitement of the stage and the audience that we were used to is lacking in the controlled environment of a studio. At first, our task as musicians and arrangers was to use the technology to simply capture the magic of live music onto that little strip of tape. Later, as a producer, I had to learn to use the full potential of the technology to do things that literally hadn't been heard before.

My first time in a recording studio—after playing with combos and big bands in jook joints and dance halls—was like stepping into a space ship. But it wouldn't take long to realize that all those buttons and dials had power that could be harnessed. In a studio, the technology rides the music, and vice versa. We rode both all the way.

I've been privileged to work with the full spectrum of what the twentieth century had to offer in recording technology, from 78-rpm disks to DAT, from monophonic sound to 5.1 surround sound. I was on tour with Lionel Hampton's band in 1953 when Leo Fender handed Monk Montgomery a guitar-shaped bass to replace his upright. Monk and I broke the instrument into its first 10-inch jazz album, Art Farmer's *A Work of Art* on Prestige Records. Without that electric bass we wouldn't have the electric rhythm section, rock and roll, or the Motown sound. I utilized the first commercially recorded synthesizer in the sixties for the *Ironside* theme.

But you have to make sure the technology doesn't outpace the humanity. Some of the folks in this book, such as Bruce Swedein, Rudy Van Gelder, Tom Dowd, and Phil Ramone, were masters of using the technology to keep the music human. It didn't matter if a studio was a shiny, state-of-the-art outfit or a raggedy little room whose jerry-rigged equipment was held together with tape and whatever else was on hand: magic was laid down for the rest of the world to hear.

The technology only goes so far: the studio was where planned and unplanned collaboration happened. The genius of the musicians brushed against the genius of the engineers, producers, and arrangers. You could go in expecting one thing and come out with something entirely unplanned—and twice as good.

Temples of Sound brings me back to the days when the modern era of recording began. Maybe it's impossible to re-create the experience of being in the studio during the great takes; the cigarette smoke, the banter, the fights, the sleepless nights, the joy of hearing a playback that everyone knows is right because you can see it in everyone else's eyes. Maybe it's impossible, but this is the next best thing. Just listen.

— Quincy Jones, July 2002

Introduction

Recording music in the studio used to be a romantic endeavor. Between the late 1940s and the late 1970s, players by and large were all in the same space at the same time, along with an engineer, who was piloting the whole deal. The lights were low and ashtrays were as necessary and as plentiful as microphones.

Temples of Sound opens the door to some of the great rooms where the American soundtrack was recorded. Rooms where the sound from six instruments and three singers leaked into every microphone at the session—all five of them. Control rooms where the technology consisted of little more than duct tape and solder, applied to a badly designed console purchased from the radio station across town. Studios where the john doubled as the echo chamber. We tell the stories of the people who were there, making the music, recording it; creating art on the fly. Sometimes the records they made have distortion, contain a bad note, or suffer from other musical flaws, but they all possess that intangible thrill that keeps them fresh and alive—worth caring about decades after we first heard them on the radio or played them on a record player.

The original idea for this book was pure and simple: photos of great musicians in the recording studio. There's something about these pictures that's magic, something that's supremely cool. They capture intimate, private, unguarded moments—the moments when art is being created.

There's Aretha, hitting a high note in the studio. What song is it? There's Muddy Waters, eyes closed, acoustic cradled, raining down Delta beatitude. Or Dylan, inscrutable behind shades, or Nat "King" Cole, confident down to his toes. Mostly, we wanted photos where you could smell the cigarette smoke, where you saw a phalanx of microphones on boom stands, arrayed like cranes at an excavation site. Pictures where you could feel the buzz in the room, where the music filled the frame.

Although recording started in 1877 with Thomas Edison reciting a nursery rhyme into a tinfoil cylinder, it wasn't until the 1910s that recording devices—Victrolas and other assorted phonographs—proliferated in America. In fact, so great was the response to having music in the home, people who could not afford necessities such as an icebox were purchasing "talking machines."

By the mid-'20s, recording "went electric." Tinfoil cylinders evolved into wax cylinders, which in turn gave way to discs. The wars, particularly Word War II, slowed the progress of recording owing to the need for shellac, the primary compound of discs. However, the Second World War brought about an unexpected breakthrough; in an abandoned bunker in Germany, the allied forces unearthed a tape machine! Jack Mullins, one of the discoverers of this Third Reich wonder, brought the parts back to his home in San Francisco, modified it, and auditioned it for crooner Bing Crosby. When der Bingle realized he could tape his vocals instead of singing them live or recording on discs for his radio broadcasts, thereby enabling more flexible layering and editing—and longer recordings allowing more time for golf—the Ampex Tape Company was born.

Suddenly, in the studio of the late '40s and early '50s, it was tape, not discs, that captured the music, and the fidelity dramatically improved. For record buyers, twelve-inch long-play vinyl would soon replace the seven-inch 78. In the late '50s and early '60s, stereo, *true stereo*, slowly replaced mono and, for the first spectacular time, great echo and a new sense of space was heard on records. From the beginning of the era, recording pioneers like Les Paul, with "How High the Moon," and Bill Putnam, with "Peg 'o My Heart," were expanding the possibilities of recording, multitracking voices and instruments, and using artificial reverberation in an artistic as opposed to naturalistic fashion. Recording had entered the modern era.

Fueled by groundbreaking radio stations like WSM in Nashville, WDIA in Memphis, and, later, WVON in Chicago, the different regions, even cities, in the postwar-to-disco era may as well have been different countries. Just as the great chefs of the world create dazzling arrays of dishes out of the same basic food groups, the arrangers, musicians, and engineers likewise gave new twists to shared sources. From New Orleans to Memphis to Chicago, traversing northward up the mighty Mississippi, these practitioners crafted three vastly different responses to jazz, gospel, and blues roots. Trace elements of regionalism remain, but there's nothing today quite as diversely thrilling as when the Countrypolitan sound of Nashville, the second-line funk of N'awlins, the smooth Windy City soul of Chicago, and the surf harmonies of California came spilling out, one after the other, from the (AM) radio.

At the beginning of this era, there were perhaps a dozen men who recorded virtually all the songs on the radio. They were explorers and pioneers, the audio equivalent of the first NASA astronauts. Studio founders/engineers such as Tom Dowd in New York, Cosimo Matassa in New Orleans, and Joe Tarsia in Philly possessed the right stuff. They were among the artists/craftsmen/innovators/businessmen/music lovers who launched the new world of record making. That is to say, the old new world.

Recognition for these men and their role is long overdue—in fact, even on reissued classic recordings, the names of everyone from the photographer to the fourth trombonist are listed, while the guy who captured and crafted these pieces of art often goes uncredited. It's a very select crowd. Some are still working, some are retired, some are gone. Part of the thrill of creating this book was getting in touch with these American craftsmen, hearing their tales and recognizing why the records they engineered sound like they do.

We got to hang with Cosimo Matassa in the French Quarter and talk about Little Richard sessions. We talked to the Greta Garbo of recording, Rudy Van Gelder, about recording Miles and Monk in his parents' living room in Hackensack—while also working his day job as an optometrist. We visited "the man," Sam Phillips, founder of Sun Records, in his East Memphis home, and discussed sound and soul and slapback echo. Through all the war stories, what comes across is a shared joy at making music. They are the greatest generation of recording engineers, those who did it all in the studio—before MTV, recording schools, or computers.

All of these pioneers built their own studios, their own temples of sound. Thankfully, many of these rooms are still standing, if not fully functioning. Some, like Stax in Memphis, are gone. Others, such as Chess, Sun, Motown, and RCA B, are rightfully recognized as landmarks and are in use as museums. Today, walking into RCA B in Nashville, "Home of 1,000 hits," Western 3, where the Beach Boys classic *Pet Sounds* was recorded, or Chess Studio on Chicago's South Side, one can feel the vibe. As recording legend Al Schmitt, engineer for Sam Cooke, Frank Sinatra, Barbra Streisand, and Steely Dan, said, "All those souls [of recording artists] have congregated in those studios; that's what you feel when you walk in."

11

The fact that many of these places were little more than converted radiator shops (Sun Studio in Memphis) or fruit and vegetable refrigerators (J&M Studio in New Orleans) makes the recordings that came out of them, like "Great Balls of Fire" or "Blueberry Hill," all the more magical. Perhaps most significant, the studio provided a backdrop for more than mere hit making. It was a space, a sanctuary, where blacks and whites labored daily as artistic collaborators. We might take this dynamic for granted today, but there was a time when the American recording studio was virtually the *only* arena where this sort of cross-pollination was a matter of course. Think about it—you take a gospel-bred African American girl from the churches of Detroit, white musicians from south of the Mason-Dixon, and throw in a Jewish bohemian producer from Brooklyn. The result is "Chain of Fools."

Without a doubt, there are more terrific studios than those profiled in this book, but we endeavored to strike a balance, especially between genres, periods, and regions (the book rolls along like a music-filled road trip, from Hollywood to Miami). Simply put, we wanted to provide a snapshot of the middle part of the American Century, back when a bunch of talented people gathered in drafty, smoky rooms and created records that gave you pause, that gave you goose bumps.

Temples of Sound, then, is more than just a peek into the rooms where so much important music was made. It's an affectionate look at the people and the performances, the turmoil and the whatever-it-takes-but-make-it-happen philosophy behind the recordings we love. It's our ultimate hope that *Temples of Sound* enlightens as it affirms. If a nation's soul can somehow be glimpsed through its art, then turning these pages we observe, in an entirely new way, who we are.

A cooler-than-thou Dino croons away while a bevy of background vocalists (through the vocal booth window) lend support at a swingin' mid-1950s session at Capitol.

Capitol Studios
KING OF POP

Rock and roll may have ruled near the end of the decade, but the 1950s were really the golden age of pop. The era's tightly arranged and orchestrated pop confections (later relabeled "adult contemporary," then "easy listening," then "lounge") laid down the perfect soundtrack for the new prosperity and the extended leisure time the nation was enjoying after World War II. The record label putting out many of the best-selling—and best-sounding—records of the era was the relatively new Capitol Records, using a killer hand of artistic vision, technological know-how, and megawatt star power to trump its competition.

Indeed, Capitol's 1950s talent stable was the record-biz equivalent of MGM's screen roster of the '30s. Sure, Decca still had Crosby, RCA had Perry Como and Dinah Shore, and Columbia had Tony Bennett and Johnny Ray. But with the likes of Frank Sinatra, Nat "King" Cole, Peggy Lee, Dean Martin, Judy Garland, Nelson Riddle, Jo Stafford, Tennessee Ernie Ford, and June Christy, as well as the husband-and-wife teams of Louis Prima and Keely Smith and Les Paul and Mary Ford, Capitol fielded a team that was hard to beat. For a good ten years, Capitol was the undisputed king of pop.

Three vs. the Big Three

Three ambitious men founded Capitol Records. The first partner, and the company's first president, was songwriter Johnny Mercer, lyricist of such standards as "That Old Black

Magic," "I'm an Old Cowhand," "Hooray for Hollywood," "Jeepers Creepers," "Blues in the Night," and "Come Rain or Come Shine." The second partner was Glenn Wallichs, who owned Music City, on the corner of Sunset and Vine, the largest record store on the West Coast. The third partner, who served strictly as an investor in the company, was Buddy DeSylva, a former lyricist like Mercer, who became head of production at Paramount Studios.

In early April 1942, Capitol Records opened for business, setting up shop in a tiny, stuffy storefront at 1483 Vine Street in Hollywood. Capitol's first recording session was set for June 5, 1942, at Radio Recorders Studio at 7000 Santa Monica Boulevard. Radio Recorders opened in 1936 and quickly became the premiere recording studio in L.A. In fact, exactly one week before Capitol's first session, Bing Crosby was there crooning his original version of "White Christmas" for Decca. The song would go on to hold the title of best-selling single ever for nearly fifty years.

But whatever magic was in the studio that day must have followed Crosby out the door. Capitol's first record, "The General Jumped at Dawn," by Paul Whiteman's New Yorker Hotel Orchestra, was quickly pressed and shipped to stores just weeks after the June 5 session. The record flopped. And to make matters worse, only days after its release, James C. Petrillo, president of the American Federation of Musicians, made this announcement: "Records are killing off jobs for musicians. From this day on, no more will ever be made in the United States." The AFM recording ban—a squeeze play by Petrillo to force record companies to pay musicians royalties—was on.

Glenn Wallichs later wrote, "When Petrillo slapped his ban on all recordings shortly after our first release, we again thought we were licked. But it turned out to be our biggest piece of good fortune. Before the ban went into effect, we worked night and day turning out such tunes as "Cow Cow Boogie" and "G. I. Jive." When those tunes became popular, we were the only company that had recorded them, and dealers all over the country began to buy from us."

But as the AFM ban dragged on, Capitol had to get creative about finding new music to release. They searched for masters of unreleased material by independent producers or collectors who made records for their own enjoyment. Among the masters Capitol bought in 1943 were two songs: "Vom, Vim, Veedle" and "All for You" by the King Cole Trio.

Nat

Nathaniel Adam Coles was born in 1919 in Montgomery, Alabama. His family moved to the Bronzeville section of Chicago before he was five. Coles was winning amateur contests playing piano by the time he was twelve. By age fifteen his jazz band was headlining in nightclubs, and he dropped the "S" from his last name. Three years later, the "King" nickname began to stick. By then he was married, living in Los Angeles, and leader of the King Cole Trio with guitarist Oscar Moore and bassist Wesley Prince. His lightly swinging group quickly won acclaim as the three virtuoso jazzmen combined to make a pleasing sound that appealed even to non-jazz fans. Plus, Nat could sing a little bit. Early on, his voice was higher and decidedly more urban, or "jivey," than it would become later, but he already possessed a distinctive way of delivering a song, using clear diction and sly, sexy phrasing. The trio proved a popular draw at clubs on the West Coast, and, in July 1940—in a bit of "small world" foreshadowing—Glenn Wallichs invited them to play at Music City's grand opening.

Over the next two years, the King Cole Trio made records for the Decca and Verve labels. And in the fall of 1942, they recorded "Vom, Vim, Veedle" and "All for You" for a small African-American-owned company called Excelsior. These were the masters that Capitol bought and released in 1943. "All for You" made it all the way to number eighteen on the *Billboard* charts. When the AFM ban was lifted in November 1943, Capitol signed Nat to their maximum contract of seven years and also to their maximum royalty percentage, 5 percent.

The King Cole Trio's first recording session for Capitol was scheduled for November 30, 1943, at C. P. MacGregor Studios on Western Avenue. (Capitol would book the cramped MacGregor Studios for smaller sessions, reserving Radio Recorders when they needed space for more musicians.) It was a Tuesday afternoon session, lasting the standard union three hours, from 2:00 until 5:00. Johnny Mercer was on hand to produce the recordings, while John Palladino, who would be present for many of Capitol's greatest sessions, took charge of the engineering duties.

Four songs were selected for the session: "Gee Baby, Ain't I Good to You," "If You Can't Smile and Say Yes (Please Don't Cry and Say No!)," an instrumental jam titled "Jumpin' at Capitol," and a song Cole had written himself, "Straighten Up and Fly Right." The song was based on an old African American folktale, and Cole—the son of a preacher man—claimed he heard his father use it in a sermon.

> A buzzard took a monkey for a ride in the air.
> The monkey thought that everything was on the square.
> The buzzard tried to throw the monkey off his back.
> The monkey grabbed his neck and said, "Now, listen Jack!
> Straighten up and fly right."

The mix of jivey patter, a funny child's fable, and a swinging, relaxed groove proved irresistible. By April 1944, it had risen to number nine on the *Billboard* charts. From his very first Capitol session, Cole was on a roll. The hits kept coming.

In 1946 the King Cole Trio had its best year to date, scoring with Bobby Troup's classic "Route 66" and reaching all the way to number one with the romantic ballad "For Sentimental Reasons." But perhaps the trio's most significant hit of 1946 was their original reading of Mel Tormé's "The Christmas Song." This holiday chestnut rose to the number-three spot and hung around the charts long after the Christmas season was over. But what made it so important for the King Cole Trio was that it was the first time that strings were added to their basic instrumentation. It was a harbinger of things to come.

A year later Nat Cole would make his first recording without the trio—the first in which he didn't even play the piano himself. "Nature Boy" was handed to his road manager outside the Lincoln Theater in Los Angeles by Eden Ahbez, an odd-looking man with shoulder-length hair and a full beard, wearing leather sandals. Ahbez had grown up in an orphanage. As an adult, he began a personal spiritual journey, claiming to have walked across America eight times. He didn't own a home or have many worldly possessions. But he did have a song—and he wanted Nat Cole to sing it.

Once Cole got his hands on the writer's soiled and unsigned sheet of music, he quickly grasped its brilliance, even if others did not. He began to perform "Nature Boy" in clubs with the trio. But Cole wanted to record the strange song with a full arrangement—with strings. After a few months of talking about it, Capitol producer Jim Conkling finally gave in. "Nature Boy" became a number-one hit, and one of the biggest records of 1948.

The great success of "Nature Boy" effectively spelled the end of Nat Cole, jazz pianist, and the beginning of Nat Cole, pop vocalist. He would remain a jazz pianist at heart—and he is still respected as one of the most tasteful and accomplished players ever—but in the marketplace he was suddenly a pop crooner. Cole's next two hits, "Mona Lisa" and "Too Young," would quickly galvanize this perception.

Melrose Place

In the fall of 1948, Capitol Records purchased their own recording studio. The building at 5515 Melrose Avenue was formerly the home of radio station KHJ. Downstairs, at the front of the building, was Nickodell's bar, a regular stop for many of the jazz and classical musicians who recorded at Capitol. The lower level also housed two small studios, Studio B and Studio C. The latter studio saw the most work in the early days, as it was perfect for small group recording. Upstairs was Capitol's Studio A, originally built as a radio theater with audience and stage facilities. This is where the dance band and large orchestra recordings were made.

The music recorded in these studios set a new standard of rich, clean sound. The bottom end was fatter than on competitors' records, the high end clearer. Added to the perfectly balanced mid-range, the Capitol engineers created a breathtaking pallet of sounds.

Veteran engineer John Palladino described how Capitol achieved its superior sound to writer Charles Granata:

"The whole secret of Capitol's sound, and something that was given a great deal of attention, was the use of acoustic echo chambers. . . . We wanted to have control over the sound in a physically limited situation, like a small studio. The only way we could do that was to

18

concentrate on proper equalization, use the best mikes, and develop the best echo chambers [which were located on the building's roof].

"We'd get the newest and best microphones, speakers, and tape machines, but the boards [mixing consoles] were really simple, basically one step up from a radio board! Capitol designed the consoles, which were twelve position boards with rotary pots. There was basic EQ available on ten of the twelve channels, and I mean basic—two positions for high frequencies, two for low. At that point, on Melrose, we were using the Ampex 200 tape machine, running at thirty ips [inches per second—the speed of the tape passing through the machine. Faster speeds produce greater sonic accuracy]."

The Ampex 200 tape machines were an innovation. Previously, recordings were made on acetate discs. Capitol was the first studio to fully employ tape machines, which recorded a fuller range of sound than discs and allowed producers and engineers greater flexibility in editing and multitracking.

Two newcomers to Capitol would be among the first to take advantage of the studio's technology. In 1948 the comedy team of Dean Martin and Jerry Lewis was the hottest act in show business. In August of that year, they signed with Capitol and went into the Melrose Avenue studio for the first time on September 13. However, another AFM recording ban was in effect at the time. Capitol got around it by recording the musical tracks with a nonunion orchestra in Mexico. Dean and Jerry then put their vocals to the songs "That Certain Party" (on which Lewis's voice is accelerated to exaggeration while Martin's remains at normal speed) and "The Money Song." Neither side did well when the 78 was released in October. But Martin would soon have his first top-ten hit as a solo artist, "Powder Your Face with Sunshine (Smile, Smile, Smile)."

On a Saturday afternoon in March 1950, Cole entered the Melrose studio to record the song "Mona Lisa." Les Baxter's Orchestra played the arrangement—and Cole believed it was one of the best he'd ever heard. Like all Cole sessions, this one went off with hardly a hitch. "Mona Lisa" went to number one by June, sold more than a million copies, and won the Academy Award for best song from the now-forgotten film *Captain Carey, U.S.A.*

But what Cole didn't know at the time was who had really authored the beautiful arrangement for "Mona Lisa." He assumed orchestra leader Les Baxter did it. Actually, it was written by a young man named Nelson Riddle. When the song went to number one, Riddle was a little peeved that he wasn't getting any credit, but he chalked it up to experience. Eleven months later, Riddle wrote another arrangement for a Nat Cole session. The song, "Too Young," also went to number one. Again, Cole loved the arrangement. Again, all the credit went to Les Baxter. Now Riddle was getting upset.

Riddle and his wife attended a show that Nat was playing in Los Angeles. At the time, the Riddles were broke. Mrs. Riddle told her husband, "You are going to go to him and tell him that you wrote those arrangements." After Cole found out the truth, he confessed to Riddle, "I just thought you were the copyist because you were always running around fixing the notes in the fiddle section."

The first credited session Nelson Riddle arranged for Cole yielded another huge hit, 1952's "Unforgettable" (it would go to number one nearly forty years later when Nat's daughter, Natalie, dubbed her vocals on the original arrangement to sing a duet with her father). Though other Capitol artists were selling well, notably Jo Stafford, Peggy Lee, and Capitol president Johnny Mercer (Mercer had three number-one hits in 1945 alone), Nat Cole was the undisputed king of Capitol, selling some 15 million records from 1943 to 1952. After "Unforgettable," the two men would work together on 251 more recordings, and Riddle would handle the orchestrations for Cole's groundbreaking but short-lived 1956 TV show (the first prime-time variety series hosted by an African American). But as great as their collaboration was, Cole and Riddle probably would have made even more records together if Capitol hadn't signed another artist in 1953.

Frank

From the late 1930s through the World War II years, Frank Sinatra swooned his fans out of their bobby socks. First as the singer with Tommy Dorsey's Orchestra, and then as a solo act, Sinatra had become a pop music phenom, leaving scores of young women laid out in the aisles. The music world wouldn't see the likes of it again until Elvis in the late '50s and the Beatles in the '60s.

But as the '50s dawned, Sinatra had hit rock bottom. His personal life was a mess. Ava Gardner, his wife, the love of his life, and a woman considered by many to be one of the most beautiful in the world, was about to dump him. To make matters worse, his career had gone down the tubes. After the war, Sinatra's records suddenly sounded dated, remnants from a past that was gone forever. He couldn't buy a hit. Columbia Records, his label throughout the '40s, figured he'd finally run out of juice and cut him loose. Sinatra grew so depressed he slit his wrists. His suicide attempt—like so much else in his life at the time—was a failure.

At the end of 1952, Sam Weisbord, one of Sinatra's agents at William Morris, was shopping him around. Weisbord called Alan Livingston, vice president of Capitol's A&R (Artists and Repertoire) department. Would Capitol be interested in signing Frank Sinatra? Livingston thought it over. "Yes, I would be interested," Livingston replied. "You would?" answered the surprised agent. When Livingston announced to the Capitol sales force at their national convention that the label had just signed Sinatra, the loud response was "Noooo!"

But the salesmen would soon learn that Capitol's Sinatra was not the same old Frankie of the past. This Sinatra had been around the block a few times, was older, more bruised. He was still a crooner, but with an edge. Yes, he was angrier, but also more vulnerable. No longer a lightweight singing idol, the new Sinatra had the m.o. of a guy who might break down and cry, then punch you out for watching.

21

But above all else, this Sinatra was swinging. And the man who helped him swing more than any other was Nelson Riddle. They worked together for the first time on April 30, 1953, at the Melrose Avenue studio. The session had been originally scheduled with another arranger/conductor, Billy May. But May was unavailable. Riddle arranged two songs ("I Love You" and "South of the Border") in the Billy May style, much brassier and beat-driven than his own. Then he arranged two songs ("I've Got the World on a String" and "Don't Worry 'bout Me") in his own relaxed, swinging fashion.

At the session, Sinatra was told that Riddle was merely conducting for May. But when the singer heard "I've Got the World on a String" he recognized the different sound and asked, "Hey, who wrote that?" Producer Alan Dell replied, "This guy—Nelson Riddle." Sinatra smiled, "Beautiful!"

And beautiful it is. Hearing "I've Got the World on a String" today, it's hard to imagine that this was the first time the two had worked together. Frank slips into the song like he's putting on his favorite pair of suede loafers, first toying with the lyric, then once the rhythm kicks in, bouncing along with the beat like a guy who, well, really does have the world on a string.

Riddle would later say, "Most of our best numbers were in what I call the tempo of the heartbeat. That's the tempo that strikes people easiest because, without their knowing it, they are moving to that pace all their waking hours. Music to me is sex—it's all tied up somehow, and the rhythm of sex is the heartbeat."

One of Sinatra and Riddle's greatest album collaborations, *Songs for Swingin' Lovers*, is practically a treatise on the heartbeat tempo. Sinatra had the idea that he wanted sustained strings featured on the album, and Riddle obliged. Harry Edison's tasty, muted trumpet also offers wry commentary throughout. Perhaps the highlight of the album is the sublime interpretation of "I've Got You under My Skin." Sinatra, the perfectionist, did twenty-two takes of the song. Reportedly Riddle finished the arrangement in the car on the ride over, working by flashlight as his wife drove their station wagon to Melrose Avenue. As Sinatra and Riddle began the night's session, a team of copyists was furiously putting the arrangement on paper. When the musicians played the arrangement for the first time later that evening, it was as if they were playing something they already knew. When they finished, the hardened crew of studio players applauded Riddle.

Since the Melrose Avenue studio once served as a radio station, Studio A featured a stage and seating area originally used for live radio broadcasts. Now Sinatra invited guests to watch his recording sessions. The invitation-only concerts attracted a VIP crowd, and Sinatra seemed to feed off of the audience.

Arranger Billy May remembered a Nelson Riddle session during which Sinatra was in a bad mood, tense, and needling the conductor/arranger. He wasn't satisfied with one song in particular. After some twenty-eight takes, Riddle stopped the band. Sinatra was looking around the room, edgy and angry. The tension was thick. The room was dead quiet. Then,

from his position near the rear of the room, Sweets Edison hollered, "Shit, daddy, you can't do it no better than that." Everyone, including Sinatra, fell out laughing. From then on, when the air got too thick at a session, or if Sinatra demanded one too many takes, someone in the orchestra would merely shout out, "In the immortal words of Sweets Edison . . ." Sinatra always laughed.

Dean Martin tries to focus on the lyric sheet while pallie Frank Sinatra and pianist Ken Lane (to Frank's right) look on, ca. 1959.

The Tower

In the first half of the 1950s, Capitol Records was simply on fire. Nat "King" Cole and Frank Sinatra seemed to share a penthouse on the *Billboard* charts, with records constantly landing them in the top ten. Kay Starr and the husband-and-wife duo of Les Paul and Mary Ford also hovered around the top of the charts consistently (with Kay Starr hitting number one in 1952 with "Wheel of Fortune" and Les Paul and Mary Ford reaching the top spot twice with "How High the Moon" in 1951 and "Vaya con Dios" in 1953). Dean Martin went top ten with "That's Amore" in 1953. Tennessee Ernie Ford had one of the biggest hits of the decade when his "Sixteen Tons" went all the way to number one in 1955. Even Mel Blanc, the voice of nearly all the Warner Bros. cartoon characters, including Bugs Bunny and Yosemite Sam, had a top-ten hit as Tweetie Pie with "I Taut I Taw a Putty Tat," cowritten and arranged by Billy May.

But perhaps the label's most unlikely hit maker was comedian Jackie Gleason. While the "great one" was making television history playing Ralph Kramden on *The Honeymooners* and a

23

host of other characters on *The Jackie Gleason Show*, he was also making best-selling albums of "mood music"—background melodies for drinking cocktails and heavy petting. Though the comedian began making records as a lark, his efforts were not perceived as mere novelties by the record-buying public. His first album, *Music for Lovers Only*, held the number-one album spot for seventeen weeks in 1953, went gold, and stayed on the charts for more than two years.

Gleason racked up four number-one albums in two years, including 1954's evocatively titled *Music, Martinis, and Memories*. Though he couldn't read music, he still "wrote" many of his album's songs. He would convey the music he was hearing in his head to an arranger, often using graphic suggestions such as making the strings sound like "a man pissing off a high bridge." An example of the Gleason touch could be heard every week, as his "Melancholy Serenade" served as the theme song for *The Honeymooners*.

With the money rolling in, Capitol wanted to build a new corporate headquarters where all their offices, including the studio, could be in one building. Like everything else connected with Capitol, it had to be classy and modern, and it had to take advantage of the latest technology. The job of designing the building went to architect Welton Beckett, who had often dreamed of creating a round building. Now he had his chance.

Located just off the corner of Hollywood and Vine, the Capitol Tower became the world's first round office building and an immediate Hollywood landmark. The thirteen-story building opened on April 6, 1956. Contrary to legend, the round tower was not designed to resemble a stack of records. But the eighty-two-foot spire, resembling the spindle of a record turntable, added to that perception. In fact, it was nothing more than the final fifties moderne pièce de résistance. It has absolutely no practical purpose, although the red light at the top does flash H-O-L-L-Y-W-O-O-D in Morse code. Samuel Morse's daughter was even there at the opening-day ceremonies to flip the switch.

The "Stack-o-Wax" on the corner of Hollywood and Vine, not long after it opened for business in 1956.

Capitol's three new studios—Studios A, B, and C—were built on the tower's ground floor, in the building's rectangular base. The studios were "floating" rooms, meaning they were encased in a layer of asphalt-impregnated cork, which provided insulation from external vibration. Wall panels featured movable reflecting surfaces, using birchwood on one side to provide a hard sound and fiberglass on the other to create a soft sound.

But perhaps the studios' most stunning features weren't actually in the studios. They were buried twenty-five feet below the Capitol Tower's parking lot. The studios' four shock-mounted echo chambers (designed by Capitol recording artist and sound expert Les Paul), with ten-inch-thick concrete walls and twelve-inch-thick ceilings, were a technological marvel. Only the best microphones, such as the legendary, German-made Telefunken tube mics, were used in the large wedge-shaped chambers. For mono recordings, one chamber was used. Two chambers were employed for stereo recordings. Today, clients continue to book the Capitol Studios just to use these echo chambers.

25

The studio's first session actually took place before the tower was officially opened. Though the Capitol Tower was commonly referred to as "the house that Nat built," the honor of the first session fell to Sinatra. Oddly enough, he didn't sing a word. Instead, he conducted a fifty-six-piece orchestra for an album titled *Tone Poems of Color*, with several top composers writing odes to colors like "Gold" and "Magenta." But the balance of the room was off, and the musicians hated what they heard. The room had an incredibly dead sound.

Nelson Riddle joked that the building actually was a hell of an office building but nowhere that anyone would want to record music. The problems with the studios' balance took about a year and a million dollars to fix. The rooms were designed to sound like the studios on Melrose Avenue, and even after changes were made, many of the musicians still liked the sound at Melrose better.

Some, including Nelson Riddle, would insist that most of Capitol's best records were made at Melrose, and historically speaking, that may be true. But there were still many masterpieces made in the Tower studios, including one of Nat "King" Cole's very first dates in Studio A. Recorded in August and September of 1956, Nat's *After Midnight* album offered his fans a treat most had dreamed of for eight long years. He made one last album with the trio. Over the years, the personnel had changed. John Collins was now on guitar, and Charlie Harris played bass. Nat's good friend Lee Young (Lester's younger brother) contributed drums. In addition, each track offers a featured soloist, either "Sweets" Edison on trumpet,

26

Willie Smith on alto sax, Ellington veteran Juan Tizol on valve trombone, or the great Stuff Smith on violin. Each did a session of four songs with Nat (except Edison, who cut five).

The results, though without any hit singles, are among the finest perform-ances Cole ever recorded. His piano playing is a wonder, swinging, tasteful, and always inventive. You can practically hear the joy in his fingers as he cuts loose on "Just You, Just Me," "Caravan," and a playful remake of "Route 66." But the star of this show is Nat's voice. He's having a ball, stretching phrases, sending lyrics on a vocal roller coaster, sometimes dropping words altogether. "Get yours . . . on . . . Sssss . . .," he repeats teasingly before wrapping up with "Get your kicks on rooouuute Six-Six!" (instead of "sixty-six"). He also plays it straight on a couple of tunes, giving a soulful, introspective reading of "Blame It on My Youth." For Cole fans, it's the best of both possible worlds: the easy infectious swing of the trio featuring Nat's incredible playing, plus a vocal confidence and maturity he had yet to develop during the trio's heyday.

Sinatra also recorded a masterpiece at the Tower. In fact, many critics consider *Only the Lonely*, recorded in May and June of 1958, one of the greatest albums of all time. The emotions are bleak and searingly heartfelt, both from the singer, who still pines for his lost love (Ava Gardner), and from the arranger, who was in mourning (Riddle's mother and six-month-old daughter had both recently died from illnesses).

Opposite: The lights are low on Lou Rawls, ca. 1966, as he sings about the dark side of a dead end street.

Above: Looking like they just left the malt shop, the Beach Boys harmonize at one of their earliest Capitol sessions, 1961.

27

Sinatra didn't flinch at the assignment of reaching deep inside himself to pull out a vocal performance drenched in heartache. He even tackles Ava Gardner's favorite song, "What's New?" giving it a reading that raises goose pimples. But for most, the highlight of the album is the song that was originally the twelfth and final track on the record, Johnny Mercer's "One for My Baby." Sinatra told writer Robin Douglas-Home about how the brooding recording was made.

"We ended *Only the Lonely* with that song, and something happened then that I've never seen before or since at a recording session. I'd always sung that song before in clubs with just my pianist Bill Miller backing me, a single spotlight on my face and cigarette, and the rest of the room in complete darkness. At this session, the word had somehow got around, and there were about sixty or seventy people there: Capitol employees and their friends, people off the street . . . anyone. Dave Cavanaugh was the A&R man, and he knew how I sang it in clubs, and he switched out all the lights—bar the spot on me. The atmosphere in that studio was exactly like a club. Dave said, 'Roll 'em,' there was one take, and that was that. The only time I've known it to happen like that."

Sinatra would go on to make other great albums for Capitol, including the swinger *Come Dance with Me* (1960) with arranger Billy May, the bleak *No One Cares* (1959) with Gordon Jenkins, and the classy *Nice 'n Easy* (1960) with Nelson Riddle. But to many fans, *Only the Lonely* stands as the peak performance of an outstanding career. Surprisingly, for all its acclaim today, the album was not a hit back in '58, one of the rare Sinatra albums to not crack the top ten during the '50s. Still, at the first annual Grammy Awards held in 1959, the singer and the album were singled out. Frank Sinatra walked off with his first Grammy—for designing the year's best album cover for *Only the Lonely*.

Still Standing

The end of the 1950s was the end of the golden age of pop, and, by association, of Capitol Studios. Sinatra left Capitol in a huff in 1961 after they balked at backing him in his own record label. He eventually hooked up with Warner Bros. and started Reprise Records.

Nat "King" Cole had a top-ten hit in 1962 with "Ramblin' Rose" and followed it up with another top-ten, "Those Lazy-Hazy-Crazy Days of Summer," in 1963. But then the hits ended. He was diagnosed with lung cancer in December 1964 and died on February 15, 1965. He was only forty-five years old.

Capitol continued to thrive in the age of rock and roll with two of the hottest acts in the business—the Beatles and the Beach Boys. But the Beach Boys rarely recorded at the Tower, preferring Bill Putnam's United Recording Service on Sunset Boulevard. Capitol distributed the Beatles for their English parent company, EMI, which bought Capitol back in 1955. The Beatles never recorded at the Tower, working mostly at EMI's Abbey Road Studios in London.

Over the next decades stellar acts continued to enter the Tower studios: Bobby Darin, the Lettermen, and the Kingston Trio; Lou Rawls, Nancy Wilson, and Glenn Campbell in the 1960s; Natalie Cole (Nat's daughter), Linda Ronstadt, Peabo Bryson, and Anne Murray in the 1970s; Crowded House, Freddie Jackson, and Donnie Osmond in the 1980s. A lot of music came out of the Tower, but no one could say it was the same as it had been in its '50s heyday.

In the early 1990s it was "Hammer time," as MC Hammer recorded his platinum hits at Capitol. But perhaps the biggest event of that decade was when Ol' Blue Eyes himself strolled back through the Tower's doors for the first time in more than forty years. Producer Phil Ramone had coaxed him out of retirement to record a series of duet albums. It was one last hurrah. And there was no better place for it to happen.

For a moment, the clock was turned back. Sinatra stood in the middle of Studio A and belted out some of his greatest songs right there on the floor in front of fifty-five swingin' musicians (Sinatra rejected the "modern" convention of the vocal booth). If you squinted slightly, you were transported back to another time. And if you listened real hard after the music stopped, you could almost hear someone say, "In the immortal words of Sweets Edison . . ."

United Western Recorders
HOLLYWOOD'S SWINGIN'

"Let's hear that sound again."

A ukulele and harpsichord have melted together aurally in a smear that sounds like a mandolin being played in an ice factory.

"That's a good sound, that's a beautiful sound, but there's no top, or upper note," says Brian Wilson over the talkback mic in a voice pitched somewhere between a plea and a demand. "One more time, and I the want . . . the tempo should be—," he starts to snap his big fingers crisply into the talkback. "Bah-bah-bum, *snap!* Bah-bum-bum-uhh, *snap!* This is 'Caroline, No.' Bah-bum-bah-bah *snap!* Bah-bah-bum, uh, SNAP, ready now, two and . . ."

The gang of session players, numbering a dozen or so, is right there, trying to feel what the big kid in the striped T-shirt hunched over in the control room is feeling. You wonder if any of those assembled in the studio that day realized that this would be about as good as it would ever get. It was 1966. They'd congregated in the smallest room of the hottest pop recording studio, United Western, in the hippest music scene going, Los Angeles. The players were in thrall to the man whom today they compare to Mozart. They'd canceled other sessions to be at United Western Recorders to make an album that people still play, now and forever—the one true enduring pop masterpiece, *Pet Sounds*.

The intimacy of the room, combined with the number of players blowing into each other's mics, created a unified whole, a sweet conspiracy of sound. After the trial and error of

Brian directs the orchestra in Western 3, 1966. "He heard the whole deal, like *that*," said Beach Boy brother Carl.

producing his brothers and cousin on the first two Beach Boys albums, Brian Wilson was, by 1966, trying to top John Lennon and Paul McCartney, Burt Bacharach and Hal David, and Phil Spector and Jack Nitzsche all by himself. Only the best instrumentalists in Los Angeles were used. Some, like Leon Russell and Glen Campbell, had become recording stars in their own right. "Brian set everyone up playing pretty much live and balanced in the room," says engineer Mark Linett, who remixed the *Pet Sounds* box set for stereo. "It's why you can hear him saying things [on the talkback mic] like 'Move a little closer' or 'Play a little louder,' things you almost never hear today. It's a lost art, really."

The first recording studio, Thomas Edison's coach house in Menlo Park, New Jersey, was quite literally a laboratory. Many great recording studios were churches in past lives, but nobody ever used the studio as both lab and church the way Brian Wilson did in 1966.

"Brian was working so intensely, like if he didn't get these ideas out right now, he'd lose them," said guitarist Billy Strange some thirty years later.

These days, Brian Wilson is regarded with a mixture of awe and patronizing pity, but once upon a time in the mid-'60s, he marshaled his gifts to make music that has changed, and possibly saved, a life or two. Whether ballad or rocker, it's music of perfection and grace. And just about all of it—the perfection and grace part, at least—was made in Hollywood at 6000 West Sunset Boulevard, in Western Recorders 3. Wilson had always felt something about that room. It's not as big as Western 1 or 2, and not nearly as large as the showpiece, United A, where Sinatra did "It Was a Very Good Year," or United B, where Ray Charles stunned everyone with the country-soul smash "I Can't Stop Loving You." But that's just what he liked about it. It had always been a place where he could do his work, where he was in control.

Engineer Chuck Britz, who had recorded and mixed virtually all the Beach Boys' hits, had become a sort of surrogate dad. Brian's real dad would sometimes come around the studio, but he just put everyone on edge. His brother, the sweetly soulful Carl, was by his side in early 1966 during sessions for *Pet Sounds*. Together, Carl and Brian, just a couple of kids from the sticks, would pray before *Pet Sounds* sessions, actually pray, for a hit. Those prayers were and were not answered.

One of the surprises one sometimes encounters when entering recording studios is the jarring disconnect between the sonic scope of the records and the size of the room where those records were made. Certainly, in the case of *Pet Sounds*, the feeling is disbelief, whether willfully suspended or not. The room dimensions of Western 3 are a mere fourteen by thirty-four. The equally cozy control room housed a Bill Putnam–designed Universal tube console, a Scully 288 four-track, and a pair of Altec 604Bs for playback monitors. The tape that caught the music was Scotch 201/203.

Brian set up the musicians in 3 like an orchestra, not a rock band. Hal Blaine, the most popular drummer in town, sat front and center in the room, with little baffling. Basses were to his right, and behind them was an organ. Horn players were lined against the right wall, facing the center. Closest to the control room was the guitar section, all in a row, with the amplifiers facing Hal's kit. The baby grand faced the control room as well, with a tack piano and second organ behind it along the left wall. Percussion was spread wall to wall along the back, facing the control room. Strings were generally overdubbed, but if they too were cut live, they would be baffled off in the back of the room.

"Brian knew basically every instrument he wanted to hear and how he wanted to hear it," said engineer Chuck Britz. "He called in the players one at a time, which was very costly. Brian would work with that instrument until he got the sound he wanted. The process often took hours."

Session player Don Randi remembers: "One time the session went so long, that Glen Campbell, Hal Blaine, and a couple of us started eating pistachio nuts and throwing the shells on the floor of the studio. By the time [Brian was ready for us] the entire carpet was a solid red."

Although *Pet Sounds* remains the most mythical recording to emerge from United Western, it has pedigreed competitors. In the same room, Western 3, the Mamas and the Papas created enduring pop masterpieces of their own, like "California Dreamin'" and "Monday, Monday." Frank Sinatra moved into offices upstairs above the reception area when he left Capitol to form his own label, Reprise, in 1960. All of his Reprise recordings, including standards like "It Was a Very Good Year" and "Strangers in the Night," were done here.

United Western Recorders has arguably been the scene of more hit records—from the 1950s to right now—than any other studio in America. The list is overwhelming: Nat "King" Cole; Barbra Streisand; Whitney Houston; the Rat Pack of Dino, Sammy, and Frank; Bing Crosby; Ray Charles; the Stones; Elton John; Eric Clapton; Tom Petty; R.E.M.; k.d. lang; Bonnie Raitt; and on and on. No other studio has won more technical excellence awards, and no studio has garnered as many Best Engineered Grammys as this complex of studios on Sunset Boulevard.

But we're getting ahead of ourselves. . . .

By '66, Brian Wilson was unquestionably the kingpin of an L.A. music scene that had recently exploded, beating his mentor Phil Spector at his own game. Spector had invited him to sit in on some sessions. Spector didn't realize that the big kid was sponging all he heard. "I kind of learned everything he was doing," Brian would recall years later. "I think I maybe picked up more than he thought I would." Armed with this knowledge, Wilson would become the first rock producer to use the studio as a discrete instrument.

Classic Beach Boys records like "Wouldn't It Be Nice" and "The Warmth of the Sun" possess huge block chords with saxes, bass harmonicas, maybe accordions, carrying you—yes, like a wave—on that delicious downbeat. He would use three basses—two electrics with different tones, along with an upright, for the fattest low end ever heard on pop records. He also learned from Spector how two tones—say, a banjo and a harpsichord—would form a third, less recognizable, yet deeper, more gorgeous tone. Spector would never use a banjo, however,

33

and his records, which are every bit the Wagnerian opuses rock critics have proclaimed, simply do not possess the clean muscle of Wilson's work.

If *Pet Sounds* is the pinnacle of what a pop record can be, that album's pinnacle is most certainly the last track, "Caroline, No." Using flutes, bass flute, saxes, harpsichord, ukulele, guitars, basses, drums, and a gorgeous vibraphone, the backing track is all mellow confection. It's sweet in the best sense, never saccharine, owing to the timelessness of the composition, which contains the most heartbreaking chord changes of any three-minute pop song before or since. The message is one of portent, of a loss about to happen. When Brian sings in an achingly pure voice, "Where did your long hair go?" it does what the best art is supposed to do—it cuts to the heart without the brain interfering. He doesn't insult the listener. Instead of merely singing of a love grown up, grown hard, you realize that on a deeper level he's really talking about himself. Deeper still, you realize he's talking about the times. Brian Wilson knew. In effect, he was saying, "This is it. It's all—sweetness, innocence, beauty for beauty's sake—gone."

Guitarist Billy Strange, whose shimmering twelve-string guitar glosses *Pet Sounds*, gives the most succinct reason why this music, these recordings, have gained importance over the decades: "There was never a man more dedicated to his craft than Brian Wilson. It was simple. If he wasn't happy with what he heard, he wouldn't let it come out until it was perfect. His love for the music and the process by which he creates it were, and still are, a marvel to behold. Very simply, he is one of the most talented human beings who ever walked into a recording studio."

City of Angels

Since the late '40s, the country's premier studio musicians have migrated west to Hollywood. Whether playing on film scores, television scores, clubs, or cartoons, this is where the action, and the money, is. New York's Brill Building, the songwriting factory where so many early-'60s hits were born, was on the wane, and the studios back east were perceived to be full of character, perhaps, but hardly state-of-the-art.

By the mid-'60s, L.A. was the place for pop. "You could walk down the halls at United Western and you'd hear the Beach Boys in 3, the Mamas and the Papas in 2, the Righteous Brothers [over there], Dean Martin would be in 1, it was amazing" says Allen Sides, who in 1977 would take the reins as owner of United Western, renaming the studios Ocean Way. Fresh-faced baby-booming renegades like Sam Cooke, Phil Spector, John Phillips, and Brian Wilson became the vanguard of new pop sounds.

The studios of the '50s, lashed to labels like CBS, RCA, and Capitol, seemed somehow stodgy and stultifying to this new breed of artist. By the late '60s, "some of those studios had become like old-folk's homes," says Allen Sides. Autonomy was demanded and granted on an unprecedented level. These new artists wanted to work in the studios they wanted to work in,

34

far from corporate glare. Both CBS and Capitol were still cutting tracks, but rarely were they cutting edge. Most of the new breed was gathering at one of three spots: Gold Star (Spector), Sunset Sound (Turtles, the Doors, Brasil '66, Buffalo Springfield), or United Western (the rest).

How did this complex of studios start? Why are these rooms considered to be among the best sounding ever? Why have they gone virtually unchanged from their original design?

The answer is Bill Putnam.

The Mamas
(Michele Phillips
and Cass Elliot)
and the Papas
(Denny Dougherty
and John Phillips)
sing sweetly to RCA
77 ribbon mics at
Western 3, 1967.

With the exception of guitarist and recording innovator Les Paul, no one had the renaissance scope encompassing music and technology that Bill Putnam did. "My dad and Les Paul, who was a family friend, used to tease each other and say, ' You were the first, No you were,'" says Putnam's son, Bill Jr.

Such "firsts" include overdubbing multiple voices onto tape, the first use of artificial reverb, the first vocal booths, the first half-speed mastering, the first use of delay lines in the studio; in short, these two men did more to bring recording and its technology into the present than practically everyone else combined. Putnam himself was a songwriter, inventor of the modern recording console, producer, mixer, studio designer, singer, and businessman proficient in the art of the deal. "He even tuned the pianos," says a still incredulous Allen Sides. "He did so many things well, it's scary."

35

United Western Recorders: Hollywood's Swingin'

By 1957, Putnam had pretty much conquered the audio world. His UREI product line of recording gear and his custom Universal consoles were being used by the top studios. He had built the "grand palace" back home in Chicago, Universal Recording, "one of the most magnificent rooms ever," according to longtime engineer Bruce Swedein. It was in Chicago that he attracted music royalty such as Duke Ellington, Count Basie, Nat "King" Cole, Sarah Vaughan, and Quincy Jones, becoming the first engineer to truly be on equal footing with the stars he recorded. Hollywood friends like Bing and Frank, however, were putting a bug in his ear: "Work out here with us; you'll mop up." Besides, they probably were tired of having to fly him out to the West Coast for every gig.

Putnam sold his interest in his beloved Universal Recording back in Chi-Town, and, with the backing of Crosby and Sinatra, first purchased the United Studio complex. After a while, he acquired Western (United Western consisted of two complexes, at 6050 and 6000 Sunset Boulevard, separated by a parking lot). He was able to incorporate some new ideas, such as expanding the control rooms ("They used to rightfully be referred to as 'booths,'" says Sides) while retaining the large, open, and mellow sound of Chicago's Universal A.

"They both [Universal and United Western] are very similar," states Bruce Swedein, who's engineered more sessions in both places than anyone. "They both bear Bill's stamp. Of course, they both sound gorgeous."

Putnam was the spirit, the chain-smoking life force, behind United. With his UREI offices located above the reception area, the distance between tech lab and studio was as short a throw as possible. He did it all, occasionally even flying out to handle the sound for some of JFK's shindigs. When Frank Sinatra is your pal, anything is possible.

An often overlooked attribute of engineers and producers is the incredible people skills it takes to handle artists, record label "suits," girlfriends, hangers-on, whatever. Not surprisingly, Putnam excelled at this as well: "Besides everything else, he was also an amazing diplomat," says Sides. However, when dealing with the Chairman of the Board, things could get dicey, baby. For an example, Sides relates the following:

"Bill was Sinatra's first choice, but Bill was getting busier and busier. Finally, Frank said, 'Look, I'll put you on a retainer.' It was an absurd amount of money. Bill did this for a while, even putting a three-track [recorder] in Frank's home in Palm Springs. Bill would get calls from Sinatra at two in the morning about some mixes or something. Finally, Bill gets another call at 2 A.M. and he hears, 'It's Frank.' Putnam says, 'Frank who?' and hangs up. They remained friends."

36

Another Putnam tale exemplifies the shrewd operator he could be:

"In the late '50s, [virtually] none of the labels were interested in stereo. It was all still mono. They were cost conscious; they thought [mixing down to] stereo was a waste of time.

But Bill could see the potential. So, at that time he started to feed his mixes to two separate control rooms: one for mono, the other stereo. He built up an amazing backlog of [stereo] material. When stereo hit big in '61 or '62, none of the record companies had any catalog. But Bill did—about two and a half years' worth. It was a lot of material. Understand that United Western was doing about two hundred thousand a month in studio billing; that's roughly a million a month now. So the record companies came to Bill and said, 'We'll pay you for the tape [of the closeted stereo mixes].' And he said, 'No, you can't pay for the tape, but if you repay me all the studio time that was used in the last two and a half years, you have a deal.' And they did. They wrote him a check for the whole thing."

United and Western were separate entities, used by two different crowds: United was the preferred room of the older, more established stars—the Rat Packers, the Nats/Bings/Franks and Rays; Western attracted the Brat Packers—the Wilsons and Phillipses of the day. Both camps competed for studio time with the likes of Fred Flintstone and Yogi Bear, as Hanna-Barbera 'toons helped keep the studio humming around the clock. Both United and Western were very similar in layout and design, however.

United had been the first Putnam project, with Western a virtual clone three years later. United boasts two large rooms: A (approximately forty-five by sixty-five by twenty-two) and the slightly smaller B, while Western had the mammoth 1 and the slightly smaller 2. Each had a third, smaller room, as well as assorted dubbing suites and mastering rooms.

In a town with a history of studios and sound stages, this one broke the mold for what a full-service music studio could be. The staff assembled at UW was the stuff of legend. Besides engineer/producer Bones Howe (Elvis, the Fifth Dimension, the Mamas and the Papas), who had emigrated from Radio Recorders, three of Putnam's protégés from here would emerge as the top engineers from the '60s through the '90s: Wally Heider (whose Western 3–inspired studio became the rage for the nascent L.A. rock scene), Lee Hershberg (the dean of L.A. engineers in the '60s and '70s, as well as the first digital engineer in the '80s), and Allen Sides, who would soon begin to emulate the man he refers to as a father, the same guy Bruce Swedein calls "the father of modern recording."

The Punk Meets the Godfather

Allen Sides was a young hi-fi snob who happened to run a very successful studio in Santa Monica on a street called Ocean Way. He became enamored with what Putnam was doing in Hollywood after hearing the Rat Pack on a Nelson Riddle–arranged soundtrack album, *Robin and the Seven Hoods*. In the late '60s, he took a lateral position as runner (read: gopher) at Western. "I wasn't a very good runner," he now says.

One day while on an errand, he happened across a storage facility that was housing all the old gear being mothballed by United Western. "Racks and big tables full of Universal limiters, consoles, everything," he says. He offered the caretaker (a Putnam crony) six thousand dollars for the whole lot. This was classic tube gear that had cachet even then, gear that now is considered almost priceless. "That guy didn't really know what he had," says Sides dryly. "In two days I sold enough to cover my check." Putnam found out about this audacious coup and decided to give the kid a look-see. Despite the score-of-years age difference, and despite having been one-upped, Putnam recognized a soul mate. They became friends and partners, buying up studios in the '70s and '80s like corporate raiders.

Brother Ray Blurs the Lines

Pet Sounds wasn't the only revolutionary album recorded during these years at United Western. In the early '60s, there wasn't a whole lot going on in music. The jazzers and the rockers from the previous decade had either lost touch or changed gears. The British Invasion was still a couple of years away. Recording artists of the day were safely ensconced within the boundaries of prescribed genres. Except one: Ray Charles.

Charles's vast talent has long been considered a national treasure, yet people have a hard time placing him alongside other protean innovators such as Miles Davis or Marvin Gaye. When you see him now, say, performing the national anthem, it is very much a Mount Rushmore moment. It is easy to forget that once, like Brian Wilson, he too was a firebrand, the guy who, by merging gospel, jazz, and blues, single-handedly invented soul. Maybe it's because he has always been out there, making such high-water music, that we don't fully know what to do with his massive legacy. Maybe it is because he delights in confounding labelers, delights in making music that is borderless by design. Maybe it's because he refuses to be a tortured artist, preferring, like his mates George Jones and Willie Nelson, to simply be a troubadour.

"Those guys are my kind of guys. I mean, they're ordinary people and we're into each other. See, I like ordinary people. I don't like nobody with something up their ass," says Ray today.

Ray was already an established star by the time the sessions for his new album were booked for United B in 1962. "What'd I Say," "Hallelujah I Love Her So," and other sanctified shouters had been smashes for his first label, Atlantic, but now he had joined up with ABC/Paramount for newer, fresher sounds—and full, eventual ownership of all his material. To challenge the suits at ABC, and to challenge his own musical wanderlust, he decided to go country when country wasn't cool. The album title, *Modern Sounds in Country and Western Music*, was as clinical as it was hip. But the music was unlike any heard before. It was country all right, but country had never sounded so smooth, so soulful, so doggone jazzy.

Brother Ray and A&R man Sid Feller had assembled the top pros in B. Engineering the sessions was the owner of United, Bill Putnam himself. His assistant was the guy who would go on, in two years' time, to engineer all the great Sinatra hits of the '60s ("Strangers in The Night," "That's Life," and perhaps the finest Sinatra Reprise album, *Francis Albert Sinatra and*

39

Antonio Carlos Jobim): Lee Herschberg. The studio was pregnant with strings, rhythm section, horns, and the omnipresent early-'60s choir of guys 'n' gals. It was in this setting that Brother Ray reconfigured country and showed us yet again how silly labels of all types are. ("You take country music, you take black music, it's exactly the same goddamn thing," Ray once told Peter Guralnick.)

With the snare drum brushed in lazy circles, the choir sweetening the chorus, and strings padding the verses like God's own gauze, Ray comes at the listener from a place that sounds like a church stuck smack-dab in the middle of a cotton field.

The song that ignited the public was "I Can't Stop Loving You," a cover of the Don Gibson classic. Black listeners were challenged by Ray to accept a music called "country." White listeners were challenged to accept music called country being played by a black man. This was a social experiment as much as a musical experiment.

Unlike Brian Wilson's experiment with *Pet Sounds*, however, which wouldn't go gold for decades, this was an experiment that swept the country like a panic. Three weeks after its release, it had sold three hundred thousand copies. The next week, the figure skyrocketed to seven hundred thousand, including some that had been sold to people who didn't even own a record player, according to *Billboard*.

For these sessions, the choice was to cut everything live to two-track, mixing the instruments, voices, and heavenly reverb from the custom chamber into a stereo cocktail that goes down as smooth as a mint julep on a summer's day. The console was a custom Universal, but according to Mark Linett, an engineer familiar with them, there was a distinct sonic advantage to a live, as opposed to mixed, track: "One of the failures I've always felt about those consoles of the early '60s is that there was sometimes a real distortion problem. The live to two-track, three-track, and mono stuff always sounded fantastic, but when they started mixing it through the board they definitely lost a lot of the fidelity."

The album, cut live in the studio by two mavericks, Charles and Putnam, helped further establish United Western, and it earned Putnam a Grammy nomination for Best Engineered Album of the Year, 1962. Alas, as fate would have it, he lost out to another genre-bending phenomenon, the Chipmunks.

In 1977, Allen Sides took over the ownership of United, followed by Western, just as his mentor had. It continued through the next decades, as Ocean Way Recording, to be the premier studio for classic pop like Barbra Streisand's *Broadway* and *Evergreen* albums, Natalie Cole's "Unforgettable," and Whitney Houston's "I Will Always Love You," while also hosting its share of rock hits up to the present. In fact, right into the new millennium, engineer producer Jack Joseph Puig has had the old United A booked solid, recording or mixing such bands as Green Day and No Doubt onto platinum plateaus. Today, the control room is tricked out in a swirl of psychedelic swathing, complete with candles and lava lamps; vintage Putnam Universal consoles stand in proud relief alongside more contemporary "tools."

40

Sides recently sold the old Western portion of the complex to computer whiz Rick Adams. Renamed Cello, the studio hosts a staff of gracious industry vets who honor the Western legacy. Like the present Ocean Way just next door, it continues a tradition of nearly a half-century of great record making.

"His ears should be in the Smithsonian": Brian Wilson, listening to his masterwork, *Pet Sounds,* in the control room of Western 3, 1966.

Coda: The Pet Sounds of Banana and Louie

"Chuck, can we bring a horse in here, if we promise not to screw anything up?"

Chuck Britz knows the first rule of recording: go with the damn flow. With Brian Wilson this rule had to be followed inside and outside the studio. Still, even Britz is momentarily flummoxed. "I . . . beg your pardon?"

Wilson explained to Britz that this next bit was going to be the part that went *after* the last track. Chuck was used to this sort of logic. And so Brian ushered into Western 3 not a horse, but his two pet beagles, Banana and Louie, for an a cappella barking session to close *Pet Sounds*.

At the end of an album of odd meters, uncommonly pretty chord changes, impeccable vocal stacks, courageously vulnerable lyrics, and paradoxical instrumentation comes the most improbable denouement: Banana and Louie barking while the doppler sound effect of a passing train is heard rising, and then . . . falling. The dogs seem to be chasing the train, which seems to be chasing the sun, which seems to be chasing tomorrow.

With that, Brian Wilson, the Orson Welles of rock, drew the curtains to a close.

41

Sunset Sound
STRANGE DAYS

As we initially approach Bruce Botnick's cottage studio, it feels like a stolen moment from *Apocalypse Now*. High up in the hills of Ojai, a quaint community of fragrant orange groves and haciendas just inland from Santa Barbara, Botnick is comfortably ensconced in his home studio compound. Music is heard seeping through the walls.

For all the culture-defining hits he engineered at Sunset Sound in Hollywood—his dossier of pop/rock icons includes the Turtles, Brasil '66, Buffalo Springfield, Love, Herb Alpert, the Beach Boys, Randy Newman, Jackson Browne, and Neil Young—he will be forever linked to the timeless recordings he made with the Doors.

He's to be interviewed with extreme prejudice because (a) there has never been anything quite like the Doors' exotic blend of blues, jazz, and beat poetry; and (b) decades later, the music sounds more muscular, more vital, than when it was made. Through the door, a familiar sinewy guitar is heard. Latin flourishes on cymbals. Sinister keyboard, yet it too is familiar. Finally, standing outside looking in, we see Botnick approach. As he opens the door, a voice—the voice of the Lizard King himself—positively curdles out of the studio monitors screaming a beat mantra that no one's yet heard, over and over: "Money's better than soul, money's better than soul, money's better than soul, money's better than soul. . . ."

Goose-bump shit.

Botnick's no Colonel Kurtz, however. A diminutive, barefoot man in shorts who's

Bruce Botnick at the custom tube console designed by Alan Emmick, ca. 1965.

wearing glasses, he appears not even remotely horrified. For most of the 1960s, Botnick was arguably the hottest engineer at a very hot time in a hot town. These days he engineers scores for films by Steven Spielberg and James Cameron. He reflects on then and now with maybe a hint of nostalgia, but with nary a trace of sentimentality. He is a soft-spoken and thoughtful man who resonates with the self-assuredness of one who has been there. He is gracious, but will not suffer fools. His story, as much as anyone's, embodies the L.A. ethos of "go with it." He knows he was part of a special time and place, and, while he appreciates the past, he has no time to wallow in its mire.

Ray Manzarek, the Doors' keyboardist, says simply, "Bruce was the *perfect* engineer for the Doors."

"I started—directly after high school—at Liberty Records recording studio on the very first transistor consoles that were ever built," Botnick recalls. "But when Liberty decided to get out of the studio business, having their own room, I lost my job and I went on the street looking. One of the first places I went, besides wanting to either work for United or to go to work for Capitol—which I couldn't get—was Sunset Sound Recorders, and I met with [owner] Tutti Camarata and his assistant Gypsy Ballou. I talked for a long time about big bands and recording, microphones, different things like that, and they gave me a shot.

"What impressed me right away about Bruce," recalls Camarata, "wasn't only his ears—which were very good—but his willingness to work; he was very diligent, always."

44

Botnick continues, "I used to live there. I mean, I had nothing else to do in my life. Nothing else I ever wanted to do when I got that job. I would do commercials starting about eight in the morning until lunchtime for Midas Muffler and different people, and then after lunch I would do children's albums with Tutti. We would do story tellers, or Annette Funicello or whatever, and then in the evening I would do my rock and roll, and I would finish it at three or four o'clock in the morning, go to sleep on the couch, take a shower there and just do it [again]. And I didn't care. I was having a great time and that went on for years."

The Doors, er, Doors. Robby Krieger, Ray Manzarek, Jim Morrison, and John Densmore during the recording sessions for the Doors' first album, 1967.

Sunset Sound is unique among the essential studios in that while most studios help birth a variety of musical genres, over a forty-year span Sunset has maintained a strict regimen of rock. All things rock. A short list of jams that have been kicked out of here includes the Rolling Stones' trifecta *Beggar's Banquet*, *Let It Bleed*, and *Exile on Main Street* (mostly overdubs and mixing); Prince's *Controversy*, *Dirty Mind*, *Purple Rain*, and *1999*; Van Halen's *oU812*; Zeppelin's *Led Zeppelin II* and *Zozos* (you know, "Stairway to Heaven"); and Walt Disney's *Bambi*. That's right. This place, in the heart of what is now known as the Media District, started out as a spot in which old Uncle Walt could do his Mouse music. Sunset had the sweetest of intentions, it really did.

Understand that in 1962, when owner, bandleader, and founder Tutti Camarata dreamed up this place, there was no such thing as rock and roll. Not really; not anymore. Rock was on furlough. But the '60s were about to become *the* '60s, and in L.A., it was all happening down at the strip, as in Sunset Strip. The band that would transform Sunset Sound studios was a self-contained tribe of film-school dropouts and jazzers from Venice Beach called the Doors. Named after an Aldous Huxley book, *The Doors of Perception*, these guys did not fool around. Playing ten-minute oedipal rages bathed in Latin and jazz swirls, nobody on the strip had seen anything like this. Suddenly, pop songs like the Turtles' "Happy Together"—recorded

45

in the same period, at the same studio, by the same engineer—seemed like they'd come from a whole 'nother epoch.

Tutti

Tutti Camarata was Walt Disney's director of recording during the late '50s. At one point, Camarata asked Walt, who was famous for his integration of media departments, why he didn't have an in-house recording studio. Walt's enigmatic reply? "I'd rather be a client." Camarata took the hint. After sussing out locations, he settled on the perfect spot: a former auto-repair garage on Sunset Boulevard, just a few doors down from United Western.

The floors were slightly tilted—the motor oil had to drain from the cars, after all—and Tutti intuited that this would bode well for the acoustics. "I had some people I trusted for those sorts of things [acoustic design] check the place out. They thought it looked good," he says simply. No studio worth its salt has parallel surfaces, since the sound waves tend to bounce back into themselves, resulting in a mire of "standing waves."

Tutti took the plunge and hired a brilliant audio designer named Allan Emmick to craft custom tube consoles as well as a one-of-a-kind echo chamber. Soon, the Mouse That Roared came to Camarata's new shop to create the scores and soundtracks for films such as *101 Dalmatians*, *Mary Poppins*, *Bambi*, *The Jungle Book*, and loads more. Sunset became known as a great sounding room that featured quality gear.

But for all the success that Camarata was having with advertising jingles and Disney soundtracks, it was the fortuitous combination of the bourgeoning Sunset Strip scene just a few miles down the road at the Whiskey a Go-Go, along with the addition of Botnick in 1963, that set Sunset on its way. (When asked directly how much of Sunset's '60s success should be attributed to Botnick, Camarata doesn't equivocate: "All of it.") It was largely on the strength of Botnick's work that Sunset Sound gained its early rock credentials. "When I arrived there," Botnick says, "Tutti took me to see a session in progress, and I had never seen a studio like this. This was, like, ultramodern in its approach. The console was set in, like, a big parson's table, except the front was sealed. And the console was set into it. So it was flush, and it was a solid panel with fourteen inputs and a selector to busses, one through three [each "buss" relates to the tracks on the multitrack tape]. There were volume controls for the control-room monitors or studio monitors. There were four big meters, for left, center, right, and for mono. You could switch the metering to either be mono, stereo, or three-track. So you could do 'live' in stereo, stereo/mono, mixing, and go to three-track [a modified Ampex 351] as your backup. It [the custom board] didn't have any equalizers built into it. Alan was of the mind that EQ really wasn't that important. The choice of microphones, where you put it, was more important. The patch bay was down to the right and you were sitting [practically] inside the console and the electronics were inside. Everything that you did on the console, you patched [connected via cables], which was the standard in those days."

46

It is axiomatic that the bond between assistant and engineer never really loosens. No matter if the assistant is today a revered engineer himself—as with Bruce Swedein and his mentor Bill Putnam. True to this code, Botnick is even now somewhat awed by Camarata.

"Tutti invented the isolation booth. Period. It was his idea. [As Tutti]: 'Why are we always having the singer in the same room with the band and we can never get the band sounding the way we want it to sound?' So Tutti Camarata, in the history of recording, should be given credit for that isolation booth. Period.

"At the end of the studio was the mastering room where we had our Neumann lathe [where master acetates were cut], and one day he said to me, 'You know, I think we should turn this into an iso booth. We could put strings in there.' And that happened. The minute that happened we became the place on the planet to record. It was a really wonderful time, because, at the same time I was doing the Doors, I was doing Brasil '66, I was doing the Turtles, Love, Van Dyke Parks—*Song Cycle*—that was a great album. I loved doing that one. And that trumpet player—what's his name? Chet Baker. Those were good recordings. Lots of fun.

"A lot of stuff walked in the door because we were hot. People came. We had all these iso booths and we could do all kinds of amazing things. We had a small eight-inch speaker in the corner of the iso booth [that] I fed the rest of the band through, and I had three microphones in there for the strings, and they would listen to what was coming out. We didn't use headphones in there. So we left the leakage, which was OK, but I got such separation. Used to do lots of dates with Jack Nitzsche [Phil Spector's arranger who also contributed to early Neil Young solo records as well as such Rolling Stones classics as "Get Off My Cloud" and "Satisfaction"] where we'd have four violins, one viola, and one cello, or he would double it; it would be eight, two, and two. Sometimes it got up to twenty strings in a room that wasn't too much bigger than up to here [gestures to indicate approximately an eleven-by-fifteen-foot area]. I mean, it was sardines in a sausage. I did a thing with Randy Newman [Newman's wonderful debut album on Reprise] that his uncle Alfred Newman conducted just before he died, and we had fifty-five pieces between the studio and that iso booth."

Much of the success of Sunset was the result of Camarata's insistence on custom-made, quality gear. Botnick, who has a fully digital console in his home studio today, talks about the uneasy cross fade between the early Alan Emmick—designed custom tube boards and the next generation of custom-designed solid-state consoles: "Having lived in the room as long as I did [Botnick was the Sunset staff engineer from 1963 to 1968] when all of a sudden one day—and Tutti, in his infinite wisdom, didn't go out and buy consoles; he always made his own—they took out the tube consoles and put in the solid-state console. Which gave us all the flexibility we were looking for, [but] right in the middle of a session—in the middle of an album—it changed. All my sound went away. The openness; the punch. I might as well have been recording at another recording studio. I didn't know what I was listening to. It was shocking. That's when I learned about solid state."

47

Along with Joe Tarsia's Sigma Sound in Philadelphia, Sunset is among the last few remaining family-owned major recording studios in the country. Like Sigma, the father has passed the reins to his son, in this case Paul Camarata. Paul has kept the business running admirably, upgrading each of the three rooms and even acquiring the Sound Factory, a complex that is minutes away. The one room that has remained virtually untouched is Studio 1, where Botnick recorded every Doors studio album except *L.A. Woman*, as well as Buffalo Springfield, Love's cult hit *Forever Changes*, the first two Neil Young solo LPs, Randy Newman, Tim Buckley, chunks of *Pet Sounds* and "Good Vibrations," and pretty much the rest of the heady L.A. music of the day. Botnick reflects on what made Studio 1 so special: "A lot of great music has been recorded there and it's just a good room that musicians used to love to play in. And it had great leakage [the bleed of one instrument's sound into another instrument's microphone]. That's one of the things that made [it]. That's like Universal Recorders [Bill Putnam's Universal A in Chicago].

"The studio was very interesting, because the floors were concrete with asphalt tile on them. The walls were brick with panels of absorbent materials spaced six feet apart. The ceiling was pretty low. I don't think it was more than eight feet, nine feet. . . .

"The best rooms are not dead rooms. They just have great leakage that you can work with. We didn't have the isolation [between instruments]. We all had to do things live in those days, [so] leakage, the quality of the leakage, was very important, and that separated the studios. If a room didn't have good leakage, people didn't work in them."

Meditation Room

It wasn't only the sound of the studio itself that was crucial, but the sound—in an era before digital effects processors—of the echo chambers. Botnick, who in his intelligence and quasi-hippie jazziness reminds you of a West Coast Rudy Van Gelder (interestingly enough, the only engineer that Botnick inquired about in his interview for this book), seems to hold a special place in his sonic soul for Sunset's chambers: "That chamber that Alan Emmick designed and built was just extraordinary. I used to go in there and just meditate, go in the chamber right off the control room. Open the control-room door and walk right in.

"[The echo chambers are] rectangular with different angles, and they're built inside of a block wall. They are all wood, framed, stuffed, and with about three or four layers of drywall that have been glued and screwed and maybe about twenty or thirty coats of resin over it. So it felt like a wooden room. You could go in there, sit and turn off the light, and think you were in the biggest wooden room you've ever been in. Just sitting in it."

Reminded of Botnick's penchant for reverberant meditation, Ray Manzarek laughs, "That's absolutely true! Bruce would take a break—we'd be wondering where he was—and he'd be in that damn echo chamber! Only a sound guy would do that."

"It had a meat locker door on it," continues Botnick, "And, to show you how unique

these things are—and I really believe that it has something to do with longitude and latitude and zenith—think of it—we duplicated a chamber next door to it; I mean, we literally tried to do it and [get it] down to the millimeter and could not come close. It didn't have the reverb [decay] time, it didn't have any of that, so we wound up tearing it down. The best studios were happy accidents, I guess.

"At Sunset Sound, we had a really great selection of microphones. In fact, the echo chamber had RCA 44s [warm, smooth ribbon microphones that had contributed to the mellow "crooning" quality of vocalists such as Bing Crosby, who sang radio broadcasts using them] in the chamber. That really did contribute to the sound in the chambers. When they took those microphones out, it didn't sound as good. So when I went back there [as a freelancer] to do mixes, I always put the RCA 44s back in."

It was an era in which AM radio ruled, before consultants and demographers reined in the playlists. Botnick reflects on the differences between then and now.

"You used to be able to identify a recording when you heard it on the radio—to know where it was recorded and what record label it was on—according to the sound. But you can't do that anymore. You always used to know the sound of a Columbia record because of the sound. It was great, because I loved doing different kinds of music. Radio in those days was not 'narrowcast.' You turned on a station like they had here, KFWB, and you'd hear Frank

The control room for Sunset 1, birthplace of records by Buffalo Springfield, Brasil '66, Herb Alpert, Sam Cooke, the Turtles, the Beach Boys, James Taylor, the Doors, Joni Mitchell, Louis Armstrong, and Annette Funicello.

49

Sinatra followed by the Doors. I mean, we had all these influences. You mixed influences. They worked. There was a DJ there at KFWB, B. Mitchell Reed, and he used to come to our sessions all the time, and I could call him up and say, 'B, I just finished a mix and I would like to hear it on the radio.' And I would cut him a ref [reference copy], take a messenger up there and he'd call me up and say, 'When we come out of commercial at one o'clock, listen,' and then it would be there and we could hear it. One time. Never announced, never. We used to do that with Doors stuff, Love, everything. Just to hear if the mix worked on the radio.

"We'd go in our cars in the driveway of Sunset Sound and listen. I would also have a transmitter set up to a compressor, one of those Radio Shack transmitters, and we'd go out to the car and hit the play button."

Strange Days

So what about the guys from Venice Beach, the film school dropouts and wanna-be jazzers who took rock to another level? The Doors' music has been mythologized ad nauseam, with Oliver Stone's eponymous flick and Barney Hoskyns's excellent, edgy book *Waiting for the Sun* adding fuel to the fire that started with Jerry Hopkins's *No One Gets Out of Here Alive*. Botnick somehow makes it all sound so casual.

"Jac Holzman [the president of Elektra Records] was from New York and he didn't know where to record out in L.A., so he asked [his label's first singer-songwriter artist, Tim Buckley], 'Where should I go to record, Tim?' and he said, 'Oh, there's this kid over at Sunset Sound Recorders. That's a good place.' So Jac did a deal—thirty-five dollars an hour, which is what the studio used to cost—and they booked in. Actually, it was Jac's wife who told him to sign the Doors. I didn't know who they were until they walked in the door. I wasn't thinking. I was just doing it. Just going with it. I'd never heard anything like them, but we were the same age. It was my music. My background was jazz and classical. It wasn't Elvis Presley and Memphis rock and roll. So when they came in, I thought, 'Hey, this is very cool,' and I just responded to what I was hearing."

Manzarek recalls the maiden session the Doors had with Botnick as getting off to a less-than-auspicious start: "I remember, we went into the control room for that first playback, and it just didn't sound right—too 'trippy psychedelic'—not in-your-face enough. Bruce, to his credit, knew it wasn't happening. So he told us, 'Let me have a night to work on this.' He worked—I mean, all night—and we came back the next day. Bruce hit 'play,' and it was there—the Doors sound. From that moment on we never looked back."

"We did the whole album [the self-titled first album with "Light My Fire"] in six days, which was not unusual," says Botnick. "You'd expect to go in anywhere from one to six days and the album was done." With tongue firmly in cheek, he adds, "Only later on did we discover the fun of dragging it out. They were playing at the club, at the Whiskey, and then they would come and record. All we had to do was get a performance. The only thing that we did overdub

[was], we doubled some voices. We did overdub a bass, which was [session pro] Larry Knetchel doubling Ray's [Manzarek's bass] part, but beyond that, that was it.

"Paul [Rothchild], the producer, would say, 'That's a good take. We don't have to go any further,' or 'Let's do another one.' But we didn't, that whole album, none of the voices, of Jim's vocals, are overdubbed. They're all live. Everything you hear is live, except for the [occasional] doubling, of course. It's when we got into *Strange Days* on an eight-track that we started to go crazy." Manzarek relays the possible reasons for this: "Paul Rothchild took us into the control room at Sunset and showed [guitarist] Robby Krieger and I this beast of a machine. He explained to us that we now had *twice* the tracks to play with. Robby looked at me, and I looked at him, and we both rubbed our hands together and said, 'Let's get to work.'"

When asked about the infamous Dionysian shenanigans and the psychedelic hijinks that allegedly took place at Sunset—you know, the booze, the drugs, the fire extinguisher (in Stone's film, an out-of-control Jim Morrison is seen emptying the contents of a fire extinguisher all over everything)—Bruce remains at room temperature. "Jim was peaking on acid. He went to the church across the street. He had an epiphany, and I don't know; you'll have to ask him. Next time you see him," he says wryly, "ask him." He has, apparently, been down this road before.

But, come on, the fire extinguisher? The Oliver Stone in us wants to know. "Yeah, he did spray it on certain things in the studio, but he didn't do the console. The control room was locked, so he couldn't hurt the control room. He would have had to break the window. That he didn't do. There were reports, it has been said, that he threw a television through the window. He did not. It was my TV. It was tuned to a Dodger game, and it was facing into the control room and he bumped up against it, and it fell on the floor. But it still works. I still have it."

Botnick still produces the occasional Doors reissue, but only for the right reasons—a new format, for example—as opposed to simply rehashing what was already cast nearly perfectly in rock. "For instance; on this last Doors stuff that we just put out about a year and a half ago [1999], I went back and remastered everything. Went back to the original two-track masters, but I transferred them to 96k/24 bit [high-resolution analog-to-digital converters], and then we mastered analog. On the first album, we had left certain words out because we couldn't cross the 'fuck' barrier; there were certain words you couldn't use. So I went back to the four-track master of the first album and pulled off his vocal and put the two-track up on my Sonic Solutions [digital work station], took his [Morrison's] part and put the words in, just overlayed it in. Nobody realized that. Like in 'Break on Through'; instead of saying 'She gets high, she gets high,' he went, 'She gets, she gets.' So I put the 'highs' in. Or in the middle of 'The End,' where we took out this whole thing he was doing, going 'fuck, fuck, fuck,' we [originally] took all that out. I put it in, but I layered it in, and we mastered it. So that's the kind of stuff I will do, but I won't try to re-create it. It's too hard. I'll just sit there forever and just be going back and forth trying to match levels. And what for? So I can make it clear? Who cares?"

51

Botnick shares his thoughts on why records from that time feel different.

"You always had to set up your own session. Align your own tape machines. Do your own maintenance. I mean, I know nothing technically. I do not know the workings. I knew how to align a machine; they showed me: 'Don't do this; it stops working.' But in those days, we all mastered our own discs, cut our own vinyl, and because of it we learned [to be] . . . I'm not going to say better mixers, but it made us know what would work when it hit the cutting room. So you had to learn different things and, being that I could cut my own disc, you could see if you were in trouble or not [with problematic levels or frequencies]. I think things were better than they are today from the standpoint that we did things live for the most part. And so we had a better picture in our minds of what it was supposed to sound like. Whereas today a lot of times it is one instrument at a time, and my hat goes off to these guys, that they are able to assemble a whole mix.

"One of the reasons I stopped doing a lot of pop records was because I got fatigued. An album that should have taken two or three weeks to do would take eleven months or longer, and I just ran out of enthusiasm. To me, recording should be a lot of fun. You should be able to enjoy the ride and by the time of the end of the recording you [should] still know why you were doing it.

"The performance is 100 percent of everything in my book. That's what it's all about. That's why it's very difficult to go back and remix anything, because there are so many different reasons why things sounded the way that they did. Sometimes I wish I could be there. Not physically younger again—which is always a wish. But physically—to be in that space again. And it's like going back to these tapes that you just heard, that I was just mixing from 1969. And I can't do it that way anymore. It's like we've talked for years about, 'Well geez, should we go back and remix the old albums and make them better?' And I keep going, 'No,' because I'm not the same person now that I was then. I've gone through a lot in my life. It's a record of the time, and who I was and where I was. The food I ate, the girl I was making love to. You know? Whatever."

Exile on Sunset:
Mick wails, Keith
waits, 1972.

Temples of Sound

RCA B
HOME OF A THOUSAND HITS

You're driving across country, and you're searching the dial. At some point in the trip you inevitably come across an oldies station playing music that's not quite pop, but not exactly country. Light and smooth, familiar, the music feels secure in itself. Like an old friend, it's reliable and steady. Like an ice-cold beer, it's predictable yet undeniably refreshing. If you find yourself in the middle of the road and in the mood for music that's impeccably performed, produced, and recorded, you'll leave it stuck to that frequency and let the miles ease by. And if you happen to stop in at a diner or roadhouse where there is a jukebox that doesn't take paper, chances are you'll hear more than a few songs that were recorded at RCA B in Nashville, because from 1957 to 1977 they had more chart-topping "cool" country hits than anyplace else.

And just because they do country in Nashville, don't assume they did country at B. Fact is, the "A Team," the cadre of Nashville studio pros who played together—day in, day out, literally, for those twenty years—forged a whole new breed of sophisticated country music over the course of some fifteen thousand sessions. Mathematically speaking, that's about fifty thousand songs. RCA B produced a soundtrack that America calls its own: Roy Orbison's "Only the Lonely"; Don Gibson's "I Can't Stop Loving You"; Bobby Goldsborough's "Honey"; Sgt. Barry Sadler's "Ballad of the Green Berets"; Jim Reeves's "He'll Have to Go"; Charley Pride's "Is Anybody Goin' to San Antone"; Dolly Parton's "I Will Always Love You"; Al Hirt's "Java"; the Everly Brothers' "All I Have To Do Is Dream"; and Elvis's "It's Now or Never."

With just a U47 tube mic between them, Phil and Don Everly work out their patented close harmonies at RCA B in 1960.

These are just a taste of the broad range of smashes that were matter-of-factly cranked out on a daily basis.

The plaque on the door to RCA B reads, "Home of a Thousand Hits." As usual in Nashville, it's being modest.

Way Back

Country music's origins can be traced to the folk and ballad tradition of the British Isles from as far back as the eighteenth century. In America, this "string music"–so called because of the preponderance of string instruments such as banjos and fiddles–coupled strong melodies with storytelling, which in turn was subtly influenced by the field blues of the plantations. Two towering giants credited with founding what we know of as country music are the Carter Family, whose song "Will the Circle Be Unbroken" is regarded as the cornerstone of country, and the "Singing Brakeman," Jimmie Rodgers, whose "blue yodeling" made him the first true country star.

As with so many other regions and styles, such as the R&B promulgated by WDIA in Memphis or the soul music explosion ignited by WVON in Chicago, it was a radio station that fanned the flames of country music in Nashville. In this case, the station was the legendary WSM, founded with the insurance money of the Hay family (the call letters stand for "We Shield Millions"). What the "King Biscuit Time" broadcast did for Sonny Boy Williamson and Delta blues, the "Grand Old Opry," broadcast on WSM, would do for Roy Acuff, Earl Scruggs, and, well, you name 'em. To this day, the Grand Old Opry–now a venerable media conglomerate–is the requisite star-making venue for country.

In the 1930s and into the '40s, genres of music were, er . . . generic, such as "jazz" or "blues." By the '50s, however, that had drastically changed. Genres funneled into subgenres such as "Chicago Blues" or "West Coast jazz." The tines of country music had multiplied to take in bluegrass, as personified by Bill Monroe; honky tonk, such as the legendary Hank Williams; the "western swing" style of Bob Wills and his Texas Playboys, in addition to traditional country, best exemplified by performers like Acuff. Thanks to WSM and the Opry, country was not only competing with jazz, swing, and pop, it was selling better than all the others in the South, where most of the country artists came from and where the majority of them performed. Hank Williams, who was to the honky tonk what Sinatra was to the saloon, wasn't merely a country phenomenon but an across-the-board star. When he died at age twenty-nine, from too much sad and fast living, in the back of his Cadillac on New Years' Day 1952, just as his song "I'll Never Get Out of This World Alive" climbed the charts, country lost its most original voice since Jimmie Rodgers. And America lost one of its greatest songwriters ever.

With the death of Hank Williams, country music had no performer capable of crossing over to a wider, more mainstream audience. But something else had occurred that would cause country to rethink itself: the invention, in the mid-'50s, of the teenager.

56

On a sultry Memphis night in the middle of 1954, Sam Phillips and Elvis Presley took an old Bill Monroe country waltz, "Blue Moon of Kentucky," and kicked it in the hindquarters, thus creating, on the spot, rockabilly. This fusion of country and "hillbilly," laced with the sweat of rhythm and blues, was yet another strain of what would rapidly come to be called rock and roll.

The Country Gentleman

In sharp contrast to its unruly Tennessee cousin, Memphis, rock in Nashville was welcomed like a virus. Besides being repulsive to the jazzers and the swingers and to practically everyone over twenty, this greasy new kid on the block was especially dreaded by the practitioners of country music, who feared it would wipe country—and country record sales—into oblivion. To compete, the brain trust in Nashville would have to come up with a new sound, a new approach to country. Bye-bye, banjo; fiddle, meet violin.

Enter the "Country Gentleman," Chet Atkins. That's "Mr. Guitar" to you.

The late Chester Burton Atkins was born on a small farm near Knoxville, Tennessee, in 1924. Born into a musical family, Chet's primary early influence was his older brother Jim, himself an accomplished guitarist. Revered by subsequent ax masters as George Benson, Dire Straits' Mark Knopfler, and the late George Harrison, Chet showed his intense desire to play at an early age; the "strings" of his first instrument, an old ukulele, were actually wires he had pulled from a screen door.

Nashville musicians of the old school, such as the A Team, to a person, credit Chet, along with bandleader and studio owner Owen Bradley, with being the ones who put their town on the musical map, making "Nashville" synonymous with "Music City USA."

"It was Chet—Chet and Owen—who did it, they really did," says Owen's brother Harold, himself a Nashville—and recording—legend, credited as the most recorded guitarist of all time (since 1949, his guitar can be heard on over one hundred thousand songs, and still counting). "Chet and Owen would not, in later years, ever receive an award by themselves. They would only accept an award if the other was there to share in the credit." Then he adds, as most musicians in Nashville do, "We're really like a family down here . . . I miss Chet." He pauses, then adds, "I have two of Chet's guitars. I wouldn't part with them for all the money in the whole world."

By the late '40s, Chet was making a name for himself as a guitarist, having played on such country classics as "Jamabalya" and "Your Cheatin' Heart," by Hank Williams. After moving around playing radio gigs in various markets such as Knoxville and Chicago, Chet firmly planted himself and his wife (the sister of Jethro Burns, of Homer and Jethro fame), in the budding Nashville scene of 1950. His calm sense of authority and shrewd musical judgment caught the attention of the RCA Victor suits in New York. He rapidly scaled the ladder at RCA, from artist to A&R scout and finally to producer. His surprise 1955 hit, "Mr. Sandman," was evidence that he could not only produce, he could sell.

Jim Reeves looks to the heavens behind a Telefunken 47 in RCA B, ca. 1961.

Soon, RCA wanted Chet to work with the hottest stud in their stable, Mr. Wiggle and Shake himself, Elvis Presley, who was not enamored of going to New York's RCA studios to record. In a supreme example of irony, Chet—who disliked not only rock and roll (he proclaimed it a passing fad) but its pelvic protagonist—was asked to work with Elvis. Hence, it was his guitar spikes that snaked through early Elvis rockers like "Heartbreak Hotel" and "I Got Stung." Encouraged by the results (money), RCA headquarters in New York wanted to put Chet in charge of producing Presley; and why not work at their very own studio? At the time, in the late '50s, Nashville had only one other studio in town (the first great Nashville studio, the Castle, was out of business by this time). That "other" studio, quite literally a stone's throw from B, was the Quonset Hut, operated by Owen Bradley, who in fact encouraged Chet to forge ahead and open the studio that would come to be known around town as "Little Victor."

The Quonset Hut is, in truth, as revered today in Nashville recording lore as much as RCA B. B had a wider range of artists, such as Perry Como, Al Hirt, Don Gibson, the Everly Brothers, Bobby Goldsboro, Barbra Streisand, the Monkees, Jerry Reed, Eddy Arnold, Willie Nelson, Charley Pride, Dolly Parton, Roy Orbison, and, of course, the King. Bradley's Quonset Hut, however, undoubtedly had more traditional country hits—as opposed to B's amalgamated country/pop/rock smashes—most importantly, the timeless, gracefully soulful records made by Patsy Cline.

58

Temples of Sound

Presley and Atkins, however, simply did not mix. Elvis, always supremely self-aware, no doubt sensed Chet's musical condescension. Unwilling participants in an arranged marriage, the two future legends quietly parted company in the studio as the '60s began. (Although they never crossed swords in any overt way, each perhaps cast too great a shadow on the other. Besides, Elvis was always the de facto producer of his music.) The pastel cinderblock building in the quiet residential neighborhood off of 16th Avenue, which they had largely put on the map, would become the birthplace of The Nashville Sound. This was where country crossed over. In fact, 16th Avenue was soon to be dubbed Music Row.

"Bill Milttenburg [RCA's chief engineer and recording manager] drew the plans for the building out on a dinner napkin," recalled Chet in his autobiography. In a mere four months, at a cost of $37,515, the "house that Chet built" was completed. The building measured a quaint 65 by 150, with offices occupying a single-story front. The business end, which housed the studio and the control room, had a second story, where the echo chamber lived. By November of 1957, B was ready to roll.

The A Team

The Nashville Sound, sometimes referred to as the "countrypolitan" sound, of the '50s, '60s, and '70s is familiar: pleasant melodies sung by singers who are up front in the mix, surrounded by strings, vibes, piano, guitars, and a choir of backing vocals. And although they may seem a world apart, RCA B's formula sound has more in common with Motown than with any other recording community. Both cultures had a self-described "family" feel. Both crews kept the focus on the singer and the melody. Like Motown, the singers could, in fact, be easily interchanged. Most significantly, both Nashville and Motown possessed a supremely talented core group of studio pros who displayed an uncanny shorthand that translated on tape to a smooth, metronomic swing. In fact, like the Motown crew, these players often created more than arrangements. In many cases, their playing—and the freedom they were given in playing—contributed substantially to a song's composition.

Where Motown had the "Funk Brothers," Nashville had the "A Team." The nucleus of that team consisted of Murrey "Buddy" Harmon on drums; Bob Moore on bass (usually upright); Hank "Sugarfoot" Garland (credited with creating a subgenre known as "Hillbilly Jazz") and Harold Bradley on guitars; Floyd Cramer tickling the ivories; and backing vocals arranged by either Anita Kerr or the omnipresent Jordanaires, led by Gordon Stoker. The A Team actually designed an ingenious shorthand coding system based on numbers.

"There were no charts, as such," says Bob Moore, who estimates that, over the course of four decades, he played his bass on close to a hundred thousand recordings. "We would just call out numbers, which related to notes." This may be the reason why the records we have heard all these years sound so seamless, so effortless. It also helps explain why so many records were cut so quickly. Sessions at B were held at 10 A.M., 2 P.M., and 6 P.M. every day.

Among the myths of rock, perhaps none is more unfair than the portrait foisted upon pop culture of Elvis Presley as a bloated mama's boy who'd rather eat a fried banana sandwich than make timeless music. In fact, Elvis was a great musician; a perfectionist who, as stated earlier, actually produced all of his records himself, except, interestingly, any records he ever made in Memphis with either Sam Phillips in the '50s or Chips Moman in the late '60s.

The Beatles had Abbey Road. Sinatra had Capitol (first Melrose Avenue, then the Tower) and United Western. Elvis had three studios in which he made the bulk of his best music: Sun, from 1954 to 1955; Radio Recorders (a historic L.A. studio most famous for Bing Crosby's "White Christmas") from 1956 to 1957; and RCA B, where he fashioned classic rock, gospel, and pop . . . as well as the '60s soundtrack swill to which he was contractually bound.

"Probably the reason that B got such a wide range of artists, especially the pop and rock stuff, is because of Elvis," says Harold Bradley. "Everyone [rock and pop artists] wanted to go where the hits were."

B, especially in its first decade that spanned 1957 to 1967, is where the hits were. And even though RCA built a brand spankin' new place designated Studio A in 1964 ("A big ol barn," chuckles Bradley), Elvis, after a brief fling, returned to the Priscilla of studios. He had huge success with pre-army singles made at B such as "I Got Stung," "A Fool Such As I," and "A Big Hunk o' Love," but it wasn't until he returned home from that bogus hitch in the army that the singer, the band, the studio, and, finally, the engineer were all in sync.

"Bill Porter, in my opinion, is the guy who should get most of the credit for the sound of Studio B," says boyhood friend and A Team bassist Bob Moore. "He changed the sound of the room when he got in there [approximately 1959]. It was not a great-sounding room at first; none of us cared for it that much until Bill took over."

Yes, Bill Porter. His name will probably never be mentioned in the same breath as Phil Ramone, Rudy Van Gelder, or Al Schmitt, and that's too bad. Too bad because, on the strength of the recordings he made for Roy Orbison, the Everly Brothers, Chet Atkins, Jim Reeves, Don Gibson, and Elvis, he should go down as one of the most exceptional mixers ever. (And his work, such as the pop-opera gems made by Orbison like "Running Scared," should never, repeat *never*, be remixed.) Porter changed the acoustics, the console's electronics, and the reverberation of B. "He was also the easiest engineer in the world to work with," says Gordon Stoker of the Jordanaires. "Bill was one of us; he was part of the family," seconds Moore.

Speaking from his Missouri home, Porter explains how he changed the sound of the room. "Tommy Strong [Porter's assistant] and I went out and bought these acoustical tiles, twenty-four inches wide and four feet long. We cut those up into sections of three and made triangle tents out of them. We hung them from different heights around the ceiling, and it solved so much of the problem [washy, muddy acoustics] that musicians would come in during playback and say, 'My God, it's never sounded so good in here before.'

"They called those tents 'Porter's Pyramids.' The room took on a neutral characteristic, so the signals from the instruments were basically clean. We found dead spots where the standing waves [sound waves that double back on themselves] canceled each other. Then we marked X's on the floor where we needed a lot of mic [level], so we'd get minimal mic leakage. For our sound source we beat on a tom-tom to get a low-frequency, resonant-type sound, then we'd move the mics around."

Listening to those classic tracks, such as recordings by the Everlys or Orbison, one is startled to hear the pristine clarity, the delicious presence. And regardless of the sound system on which these early '60s nuggets are heard, they sound not only cleaner, but better balanced—with more fully realized lows and mids, and smooth, round highs—than any records of the day. Or any day.

"Oh, man, Bill had such a presence on his tracks," said Harold Bradley. "I don't know exactly why that was, except he took such great care in his work."

Of all the great sessions that Porter and the others took part in, virtually all of the participants regard the Elvis sessions as special. "He had such an unbelievable charisma" is a sentiment heard more than once. In addition to charm, Elvis sessions were different in another important way: there was no clock. In a town that was—and still is—very methodical, Elvis simply did not care about time. The feeling was all-important. It helps, of course, when the session fees are not coming out of the artists' percentage of record royalties (ah, that sly Colonel Parker).

Gordon Stoker, who speaks of Elvis in the manner in which a father might speak of a son lost in battle, sets up what it was like to ride with the King: "He'd get into the studio at around seven at night, for a six o'clock session. If he was hungry, he'd order out for Krystal burgers, then we'd eat and go sit with him around the piano. He liked to get warmed up with old spirituals, gospel stuff. This would help him get relaxed. After a couple of hours, we'd get around to recording. The thing that was so amazing was, after hearing an acetate [demo versions of songs that were played on acetate, as opposed to vinyl, records], he'd hear that version once and he would have it down. He was very musical in that way. He would always kid around, but once it came time to record, he was all business."

Porter would be behind the glass, jockeying an RCA radio station tube console with twelve mic inputs and four outputs (tracks) that, in turn, would feed an Ampex two-track mixdown machine. (They had three-track in the early '60s, but Porter preferred the sound of the stereo two-track stuff. The three-track was, for him, merely backup.)

Another hallmark of the Porter B sound is the luminous echo. Although the studio had an echo chamber, it was rarely used. Instead, a German-made EMT 140 echo plate was used. For Porter, the echo plate was paramount to his sound. "We kept the plates chilled," he explains. "The air conditioning was very chilly up in that room. The cold air contracts the metal and the sound [of the plate] is a little bit brighter."

61

Nowhere is this more evident than on Roy Orbison's otherworldly pop masterpieces. With the exception of "Oh, Pretty Woman," most of his great hits, like "Crying," "Blue Bayou," "In Dreams," "Running Scared," "It's Over," and "Only the Lonely," were recorded by Porter, with the A Team, at B. For these sessions, the room was packed to the rafters with strings, rhythm section, percussionists, and back-up singers.

Orbison had started out with Sam Phillips at Sun. Phillips tried to make him another rockabilly cat and even had a hit with a bopper called "Ooby Dooby." Roy, however, had other intentions. Part pop, part ballad, part opera, his records can perhaps best be categorized along with Brian Wilson's *Pet Sounds* as "high pop," music that is almost too good, too artful, for the genre. This is clear from dizzying tracks such as "Running Scared" and "It's Over." In these two-and-a-half minute psychodramas, we eavesdrop on a world where fear and desire shift unpredictably. With Porter controlling the ether of the plates, and Moore and Harmon playing like Ravel's coachmen, Orbison—a sweet, soft-spoken soul—stands in the spotlight, afraid to take the glare, too obsessed to keep quiet even one minute more.

"If you listen to most pop records of that period," says Porter, "most of the records have a very limited dynamic range [from quiet to loud], maybe three or four decibels. On 'Running Scared,' we approached it like it was a classical piece. It's amazing, that song has a dynamic range of twenty-four db [decibel]. 'Dynamic' and 'Roy Orbison,' however, have never been mentioned in the same breath.

"Roy was so shy, he didn't hardly project at first; Chet [Atkins] had me sing right behind his ear for support," says Gordon Stoker. "Roy knew what he wanted," says Buddy Harmon. "Unlike the Elvis stuff, which was loose, Roy's sessions were carefully figured out in advance." Still, the players were allowed to contribute. "The drum pattern on 'It's Over,' I just came up with that on the session," he says of the signature snare riff.

Although many great pop, country, gospel, and rock tracks were cut at B, few can rival the sheer beauty of the Orbison cannon.

The Fade Out

By the mid-'70s there had emerged a silent power struggle between the musicians' union and the crew at Little Victor. In classic union fashion, there were people performing myriad superfluous duties that pissed off people with common sense. Things came to a head in 1977. The all-powerful union threatened to close down B if the union employees could not perform their "duties." The folks at B decided the union was bluffing. They weren't.

Today, RCA B, the little cinderblock studio that turned out a staggering 60 percent of the *Billboard* Country chart hits from 1957 to 1977, is owned by the Country Music Hall of Fame. The studio is now a museum. But for many of the A Team, the conviction remains that the room should be reopened, dusted off, and let loose to make cool country once more.

Stax
MEMPHIS SOUL STEW

Nothing can give more hope, create more happiness, or cause more heartache than a dream. Jim Stewart had a dream. As the 1940s segued into the 1950s, Jim Stewart, a mild-mannered, bespectacled bank clerk, was living a quiet, rather unremarkable life in Memphis. He'd moved there in '48, right after graduating from high school, leaving behind his childhood home on a farm in Middleton, Tennessee, near the Mississippi border. He got a job at Sears, then at the First National Bank. Then he got drafted into the army. After his two-year hitch ended in 1953, he was back in Memphis and back at the bank.

By then, a dream was beginning to haunt him, but he didn't know exactly what to make of it. All he knew was the dream had something to do with making music. When he was a kid, his folks had given him a fiddle, which he'd learned to play by ear while listening to the Grand Ole Opry on the radio every Saturday night. He knew in his heart he'd never be a great musician, but he loved to play, and he loved music.

Hope

After his return to Memphis in '53, Stewart and his fiddle joined up with disc jockey Sleepy Eyed John and his country swing band, the house band at a Memphis club called the Eagle's Nest. In August 1954, this local kid named Elvis started coming by with two other guys to play a few songs during intermission. Elvis had just made a record with Sam Phillips down at the Sun Studio right in town, and it was getting some play. By late October, Elvis had outgrown the

Eagle's Nest as his record, "That's All Right, Mama," flew up the Memphis charts. Then the record hit nationwide. And that's when Jim Stewart's dream began to take shape.

As far as Stewart knew, Sam Phillips couldn't play squat, but he still could make a hit record by recording someone else. Hmmm. . . . Stewart used the G.I. bill to get a B.A. in business management (he minored in music). By 1957, he was ready to take the first steps toward making hit records himself. He and two partners threw in three or four hundred dollars each to launch a new record label called Satellite (Russia's *Sputnik* was all over the news). His first studio was a two-car garage. His gear consisted of a portable tape player and some cheap microphones. He pressed three or four records, but he couldn't get them played on the radio or stocked in stores. Just like that, Satellite's seed money was gone, with nothing to show for it.

Stewart grew frustrated, but he was certain of one thing: making records was indeed what he wanted to do. Now, if only he could get his hands on some better equipment, specifically an Ampex 350 tape recorder. It cost thirteen hundred dollars—way too rich for his blood. He appealed to his sister, Estelle Axton, asking her for a loan in exchange for partnership in the company. Twelve years Jim's senior and a married mother of two, Estelle also worked in a bank (Union Planters). And, like Jim, she was a big music fan, but she preferred pop to country. When Jim approached her with his proposition of getting into the music business, she was intrigued.

Estelle eventually convinced her husband to take out a second mortgage on their house. With the money, Jim and Estelle bought out Satellite's two original partners and purchased the coveted Ampex 350. Now they needed a place to record.

A barber friend of Jim's had a vacant store in Brunswick, Tennessee, about thirty miles northeast of Memphis. The empty shop was little more than a wooden shack in the middle of a tiny country town. But a small band of dreamers, including Stewart, Estelle, and guitarist Chips Moman, who played on several of Satellite's early efforts, tried their best to convert it into a hit factory. It was not to be. The shop, an empty room with wooden floors that bounced sound, made a horrible studio. And the problems weren't confined to inside the building. Train tracks ran some forty yards away and, right on cue, a diesel would rumble by, ruining a take.

But history of sorts was still made there. So far, the handful of records put out by Satellite were either in the rockabilly or country/pop vein. Then, in the spring of 1959, Jim Stewart recorded his first black group, the Veltones. And the record, *Fool in Love*, wasn't half bad. In fact, it was good enough to get picked up by Mercury Records for nationwide distribution. Satellite received an advance of five hundred dollars. Once released on Mercury, *Fool in Love* sank without a trace, but for Jim and Estelle, it offered the first faint whiffs of success.

66

Perhaps it was this vague but intoxicating scent that awakened them to the reality that if they were ever going to make it in the music business, they had to leave Brunswick. To be successful, they needed to move their operation back to Memphis, where the talent was. They

began their search with two types of buildings in mind: an abandoned church or an abandoned theater. These structures would certainly be large enough for their needs, and were usually designed with some thought to acoustics.

Chips Moman, who had become Stewart's trusty lieutenant, found the abandoned Capitol Theater at 926 McLemore Avenue, in a predominantly black Memphis neighborhood. Moman loved black music and purposely hunted for studio sites in African American parts of town (Memphis was still strictly segregated in 1959). The rent was 150 dollars a month, nearly half of Jim Stewart's monthly salary at the bank. It was a big risk. But his dream had grown big, and it was so real now, he could practically touch it. He and Estelle signed the lease and got down to the work of transforming a cavernous movie house into a professional house of music.

Every day after everyone had finished their regular jobs, the old theater bustled with activity straight out of an Andy Hardy movie ("Hey! Let's build a studio!"). As part of the lease agreement, the seats were ripped out before the Satellite crew moved in, though some of the studs that had held them down remained and had to be sawed off. The space was huge, the ceiling reaching twenty-five feet at its highest point. Stewart and Moman erected a zigzag false partition, cutting the theater's total area in half and creating a studio space of forty by forty-five feet. Estelle sewed acoustical drapes, which Jim and Chips hung with great care. Hammers pounded and saws buzzed. A recording booth was built on the theater stage. Carpets were laid on the floor and a drum stand was hastily constructed. They called in "professionals" to hang burlap baffling on the ceiling, but that was it. Everything else was handmade and done on the cheap.

As a result, the studio maintained some rather quirky features. For one, the control booth incorporated one of the theater's original speakers—a huge monster that took up an entire wall—which was cranked up for bone-rattling playbacks. Another odd design element was the studio's floor, which, since this was an old theater, sloped down toward the stage. Stewart wouldn't spend the money to level it. This eccentricity actually worked in the studio's favor, since it meant the room had no surfaces that were directly opposite each other, thus preventing soundwaves from bouncing into one another.

Perhaps the most important alteration made to the old Capitol Theater was turning the candy stand in the lobby into the Satellite Record Shop. This was Estelle's brainchild, opened even before construction on the studio was finished, and it played a huge part in the studio's earliest days. First, it served its original purpose of bringing in some quick and much needed revenue. Second, it attracted the local kids, becoming a favorite teen hangout and quickly establishing the new tenants as part of the community. Third, the shop gave the studio management insight into the latest music trends so they could study what was selling, what the latest dances were, and ultimately what made a hit. Finally, the shop served as a talent magnet. Many young musicians would hang out there mulling over records, including one high school prodigy named Booker T. Jones, who showed up at the store every day after school and on Saturdays, hanging out for hours and catching snatches of the music escaping from the studio. He would buy one record a week, just enough, he would say, to be let back in.

With the record store in business, Stewart and his crew continued hammering the last nails into the studio. Before it was even up and running, Rufus Thomas—a true character in a city full of characters—ambled into the building. Thomas was a DJ at the impossibly popular WDAI, the first all-black radio station in the South. He also recorded the first certified hit on the Sun Records label, "Bearcat"—an answer to Big Mama Thornton's blues shout "Hound Dog" (later made immortal by that guy who sang during intermissions at the Eagle's Nest). A friend had tipped Thomas off that something was going on down at the old Capitol that he should probably check out. When he got there, he was surprised to see Stewart, the mousy guy who had come by the radio station shopping the Veltones' *Fool in Love*. Now Thomas had some songs he was looking to record. One was a duet with his eighteen-year-old daughter, Carla.

So, in the summer of 1960, Jim Stewart turned on the Ampex 350 and made his first recording in his new studio, "'Cause I Love You," sung by Rufus and Carla. The pick-up band on the session included Thomas's son, Marvell, on piano, and sixteen-year-old Booker T. Jones playing a prominent baritone sax.

When the record came out, it quickly sold five thousand copies in the Memphis area alone. Word leaked out up north to Jerry Wexler at Atlantic Records that this might be a platter to jump on—quick. Wexler listened to the record, liked what he heard, and fronted Stewart five thousand dollars to distribute "'Cause I Love You" on Atlantic. The money was a godsend; Estelle and her husband had taken out yet another mortgage on their home, and that, too, was almost gone. Under Atlantic's Atco label, the record went on to sell another thirty or forty thousand copies. A contract was drawn up by Atlantic for a deal to distribute all future records by Rufus and Carla Thomas. In addition, Stewart and Wexler made a handshake agreement giving Atlantic first refusal to distribute all future Satellite recordings. It was a perfect situation for Stewart, who didn't want to bother with that end of the business anyway.

It was almost too good to be true. The first recording out of Stewart's quirky, patched-together studio was a hit—particularly in the Memphis, Atlanta, and Oakland markets. The horn-rimmed bank clerk couldn't have been happier.

Happiness

Jim Stewart may have still had a thing for country swing, but musically, the success of "'Cause I Love You" rocked his world. Like a true believer, he saw the light and experienced a sincere and thorough rhythm and blues conversion. With only a handful of exceptions, everything recorded at 926 McLemore Avenue would have its roots in black music.

Though Jim Stewart recognized Rufus Thomas as a genuine personality, he felt that Carla was the real breakout talent. She had a sweet, soulful voice and a pure, open way of singing. She was also a budding writer, penning a perfect piece of teenage poetry called "Gee Whiz"

69

when she was just sixteen. ("Gee whiz, look at his eyes/Gee whiz, how they hypnotize. . . .") It would be her next recording.

Stewart wanted to go all out on this one. He had the Veltones come in and do background vocals. He hired a three-piece string section, led by his own violin teacher, Noel Gilbert, who played first violin with the Memphis Symphony. He even went to the extra expense of hiring a composer to come up with a string arrangement.

They all met on McLemore Avenue on a sticky August day in 1960. Oddly enough, the old theater had no air-conditioning (the unit was taken out before the building's sale to Stewart, who never replaced it). The session was called for two o'clock. But when the hour arrived, the arranger—and, more important, his arrangement—were no-shows. As the minutes ticked by, Jim Stewart, already a nervous man, got more and more nervous. He had three union musicians on the clock and he really wanted to keep the session from going overtime. At 2:30 the arranger still wasn't there. Stewart called him up. No answer. Everyone was sitting around. Waiting. Jim jumped in his car and floored it to the guy's house. He pounded on the door. Finally the man answered, looking bedraggled. He'd obviously been sleeping. It turned out he'd had a late gig the night before and had totally forgotten about the session. He also hadn't written the arrangement.

Stewart hopped back in his car and drove like crazy to the studio. It was now around three o'clock. He ran into the studio, grabbed his fiddle, and showed Noel Gilbert what he

70

wanted played—whole notes under the verses. At the bridge he told Gilbert to just doodle around by himself. Gilbert showed the other violinists what they had to do. The minutes ticked by. Stewart was beyond panic.

When the tape finally started to roll, it was past five o'clock and the string players were getting time and a half. Stewart, acting as engineer (as he would for nearly all the sessions in the early years), opened up the mikes and slated the song. And then, in a day plagued by disaster, there was suddenly magic. Carla's vocal couldn't have been sweeter. The strings played simply behind her, giving the perfect accents. After all the craziness, one take and *boom*—the session was over.

Days later, Carla Thomas was headed up to Nashville to begin her freshman year at Tennessee A&I. After a slow start, "Gee Whiz" began running up the charts during her second semester, eventually cracking the top ten on *Billboard*'s Pop and R&B charts. It was Satellite's biggest success so far, but the label would produce few hit records as quaint and sweet as "Gee Whiz" again. They were about to go in another, more muscular direction. The label's next hit, "Last Night," would help steer that change. The song was credited to the Mar-Keys, a group of R&B-loving white teenagers whom Jim Stewart knew of, but didn't particularly care for because he thought they were sloppy and sounded too unpolished. In fact, the only reason the Mar-Keys got anywhere near his studio was because their tenor sax player was his nephew, Packy Axton, Estelle's son. Stewart believed Packy was wild, irresponsible,

Opposite: Jim Stewart shows off his way-cool swinger pad office at Stax, 1966.

Above: No one worked the phones like Stax president Al Bell, shown here ca. 1966.

71

Stax: Memphis Soul Stew

and spoiled. At least Steve Cropper, the group's leader and guitarist, made himself useful by working with Estelle in the record shop and helping Chips Moman maintain the studio equipment. And, like Booker T. Jones, Cropper also wormed his way into playing some sessions.

In reality, few of the actual Mar-Keys played on the catchy instrumental. Cropper was left off because the song didn't need a guitar. The band's bassist and one of Cropper's best buddies, Donald "Duck" Dunn, was on a fishing trip with his dad. One of the song's writers— who was not a member of the band—played piano. Only Packy Axton on tenor sax and Wayne Jackson on trumpet (he would later form half of the Memphis Horns) were real Mar-Keys. The rest of the musicians were local players—and they were all black. Among them was saxophonist Floyd Newman, who gives voice to the song's title on the record ("Aaaah, last night!").

Jim Stewart made a quick dub of the song and dropped it off at radio station WLOK on his way up to Nashville. He and Moman, who cowrote "Last Night," were recording Carla Thomas's *Gee Whiz* album there in sessions scheduled around her classes. In the meantime, WLOK played the dub. Each time they played it, people called in requesting that they play it again. Customers walked into the Satellite Record Shop asking for copies of it—but there were no copies, only the dub being played on the radio.

After a few weeks up in Nashville working on Carla's album, Stewart and Moman had basically forgotten about the simple instrumental. But Estelle Axton hadn't forgotten, and she saw Stewart's lack of interest as tied directly to his lack of affection for her son. She confronted her brother and begged him to release the record. She pleaded with him. It didn't work. She turned on the waterworks. Jim was unmoved. Finally, she cussed him out. He'd never heard her use such language. Stewart put the record out.

After Jim consented to prepare the record for release, a horrible discovery was made. The first sixteen bars of the master tape had been mistakenly erased. With fingers crossed, Stewart and Moman dived into the garbage cans, hoping to retrieve a snippet of another take that they could substitute for the missing bars. Eventually they settled on a piece of tape that had a sound that closely matched the rest of the song and spliced it on the master. Estelle Axton heard the splice every time she listened to "Last Night."

Once it was out, the record became an instant classic, doing even better than "Gee Whiz" by breaking into *Billboard*'s top five on both the R&B and Pop charts. And though no one was aware of it at the time, "Last Night" provided a formula for success. Common ingredients would include the casual mix of black and white musicians, a bottom-heavy groove, a whiplike snare, and ensemble horn punctuation, with an organ weaving through the mix, tying it all together. The next hit record to come out of the studio (minus the horns but with Cropper's guitar) cemented the formula that served as the foundation of the "Memphis sound." But before that happened, changes swirled around 926 McLemore Avenue.

Perhaps the biggest change stemmed from the success of "Last Night." An unknown label on the West Coast notified Stewart that they had already appropriated the name Satellite

Records. Still, they were willing to sell him the name for a nice sum. Stewart, who hated the name anyway, let them have it, and he and Estelle substituted a new name, Stax, combining the first two letters of their last names: Stewart and Axton. After its initial release on Satellite, "Last Night" was rereleased as the first-ever recording on Stax Records.

Not long after the name change, Chips Moman stormed out of the Stax organization after a heated dispute with Jim Stewart over money and promises that he felt had not been honored (he wanted full partnership equal to Estelle's). Steve Cropper moved into his slot and ran the studio. David Porter, an aspiring writer from the neighborhood, began splitting his time between bagging groceries at the Jones Big D supermarket across the street (where many members of Stax's growing family parked their cars) and taking over Cropper's duties helping Estelle in the record shop. Most significantly, a house band was forming with Cropper on guitar, Booker T. Jones on keyboards, Lewie Steinberg on bass (who would be replaced by "Duck" Dunn in 1964), and an accomplished drummer brought in to Stax via Jones's recommendation, the incomparable Al Jackson. So great was Jackson's contribution that, to this day, Steve Cropper credits him as being the foundation of much of the label's success. "People ask me about what made the Memphis sound," he says, "and I tell them it was Al Jackson. Without him the whole thing just kinda falls apart." Jackson had the hardest snare pop in the business, a sound he emphasized by placing his heavy billfold on the drumhead to deaden the sound, creating the distinctive Stax "thud." His taste, according to Duck Dunn, was nearly flawless, and the band always followed his lead.

In the summer of 1962, this band was backing rockabilly cat Billy Lee Riley ("Red Hot," "Flying Saucer Rock and Roll"), who was in the Stax studio cutting a few sides. But the session was flat, and it ended early (Cropper claims the singer never showed up). With Riley gone, Cropper, Steinberg, Jones, and Jackson started to jam on a slow blues. Stewart's ears pricked up, and he asked the guys to start over from the top. The musicians didn't know the tape was running. When they finished, Stewart invited them in to listen to the playback. After a couple of plays, they all agreed the tune was good enough to release. Now they needed a B-side. Cropper remembered a groove Jones had been playing in the studio about a week before. The musicians went back and worked on it for a half an hour or so, then gave Stewart the signal to roll. They did two takes and that was that.

When Cropper heard the playback of the second tune he knew it was a hit. But Stewart liked the slower blues better. He ordered dubs made on both tunes. The next morning, Cropper went over to the Phillips Recording Studio where Scotty Moore, Elvis's original guitarist, made two acetates of each song. Cropper listened to them over and over that afternoon, and he knew, more than ever, that he was right: the second song, the faster one, was the hit. He quickly developed a plan to convince Stewart.

"I took it down to a friend of mine [DJ Rueben Washington] over at WLOK," Cropper recalled. "He had a drive-time [morning] slot. I said, 'Man I've got something for you to listen to.' He had another record going and he put mine on another turntable and he played about, I don't know, maybe the intro and half a verse, and he said, 'Wait a minute,' and he backed it up, turned the other record off, and started spinning mine. He played it four or five times in a row. It was funny. We were dancing around the control room and believe it or not, the phone lines lit up, like we were going to give away a Cadillac or something. I guess we had the whole town dancing that morning."

By lunchtime Stax knew it had another hit, but they didn't have a title for either song or a name for the band. For the slow blues, Estelle came up with the name "Behave Yourself." The other side, the hit side, was really funky. What was the funkiest thing they could think of? Bassist Lewie Steinberg suggested onions—funky onions. Cropper thought funky onions might leave a bad taste with buyers, but he knew people liked to eat green onions. And so, Stax Records put out "Green Onions" by a new group they called Booker T. and the MGs (originally intended as an homage to the British sports car, but when that company made it clear they didn't want their name associated with a soul band from Memphis, the group quickly claimed it stood for "Memphis Group"). It went straight to number one.

At the same time "Green Onions" was funking out its competition, Stax scheduled a session by what was billed as the hottest act to come out of Macon, Georgia, since Little Richard—a group called Johnny Jenkins and the Pinetoppers. But although they had an exciting stage show, the band just wasn't cutting it in the studio. During a break in the session, Al Jackson struck up a conversation with the guy who had driven the band to Memphis that day. He said that besides driving and carrying equipment, he usually sang a couple of songs with the Pinetoppers during their live gigs. He was hoping to maybe record something of his own if there was time.

When Stewart felt he had all he was going to get from Jenkins, there were forty minutes of studio time left. Jackson suggested they give the driver/singer a shot. Moments later, a very nervous Otis "Rockhouse" Redding (his current nickname) stepped up to the mic and barely managed to force out the words to his self-penned blues, "These Arms of Mine." Fireworks did not shoot from the sky when he finished, but at least Stewart felt like he had something to salvage the session. "These Arms of Mine" came out on the new Stax subsidiary, Volt Records. It went to number twenty on the R&B charts. Johnny Jenkins and the Pinetoppers soon vanished from the scene, but Otis Redding was about to emerge as a soulful force of nature.

With a good stream of hits pumping from down south, Jerry Wexler and Atlantic Records were ecstatic about their distribution deal with Stax. Wexler was smitten not only with the sound but also with the way the records were made. Booker T. and the MGs would come into the studio and, as Wexler said, "like four cabinetmakers or four plumbers . . . hang up their coats and start playing music in the morning." This, he believed, was really the way to make music.

Wexler couldn't get enough of the Memphis Sound, so in 1963, when he grew impatient for the newest Carla Thomas release, he started making calls from his office in New York.

74

Stewart told him that the equipment was down. Wexler thought he was getting the runaround and sent Atlantic's ace engineer, Tom Dowd, down to Memphis to check it out.

Dowd, who'd kept Atlantic ahead of the recording curve throughout the '60s, was appalled by what he found at the Stax studio. The equipment was indeed not working, but Dowd discovered that it had never been properly maintained. The New York engineer asked for a few simple parts to be flown in from New York, bought a screwdriver at a local hardware store, and overnight had the board and tape recorder working better than ever before. Stewart and Cropper gaped at him with their mouths open like they would at a magician. Just then Rufus Thomas (he of the impeccable timing) walked in and asked what was going on. They told him the equipment had just been repaired. Great, said Thomas. He just happened to have a new tune that needed to be cut right away. A few hours later Dowd walked out of the studio to catch a plane headed to New York with the master of Thomas's "Walking the Dog" under his arm—a song soon to become a top-ten Pop and R&B dance favorite.

As the hits mounted, the Stax family continued to grow. Young Isaac Hayes was brought in to play keyboards while Booker T. Jones went off to get his music degree at Indiana University. Al Bell, a former WLOK DJ, took over promotion. His charismatic presence energized the vibe around Stax. Plus, his connections in the radio world helped spike Stax's sales.

With the addition of Bell, an African American, Stax was now a thoroughly integrated company, not just in the studio but also in the front offices. In 1965, this type of casual racial harmony was unusual anywhere in the country, and absolutely unheard of in the South. Estelle Axton, whom David Porter dubbed "Lady A," said, "We never saw color. We saw talent. That was what was so great about being there."

If anyone doubted that a rare interplay was going on at Stax, they needed to look no farther than the company's musical heart and soul, Booker T. and the MGs. Half white, half black, they worked together seamlessly. Booker T.'s organ provided musical color. Cropper's distinctive, stinging guitar riffs added the flourishes and details. Duck Dunn's bass held down the rhythm, a throb that was felt more than heard. Al Jackson's drums were the hard-driving anchor, dictating the tempo. Together they played on hundreds of records, backing practically every Stax act, playing on nearly all the company's hit records.

The atmosphere at Stax was beyond laid back. The doors were virtually wide open, and anyone could walk right in. This was the atmosphere into which "Double Dynamite" Sam (Moore) and Dave (Prater) first entered in 1965. Jerry Wexler had caught their electrifying stage act in Miami, signed them to Atlantic Records, and "loaned" them to Stax, meaning Sam and Dave recorded there exclusively and all of their records came out on the Stax label. Jim Stewart knew nothing about Sam and Dave and tossed them off to his youngest and least-experienced writing team, Isaac Hayes and David Porter. At the time, Sam and Dave were in fact nothing more than a couple of scuffling entertainers. They had been given two bus tickets from Miami to Memphis. No way were they prepared for what they were about to see.

They took a cab from the bus station to Stax. Outside they met David Porter, who was talking to Packy Axton. Sam and Dave introduced themselves, and the four men talked for five or ten minutes. While they talked, Sam Moore noticed a man in his early twenties approaching them wearing a yellow flowered shirt and chartreuse high-water pants that revealed pink socks stuck in white straw loafers. But what was most amazing to Moore was that the guy was bald—a very odd thing twenty years before Michael Jordan made the look fashionable.

The multitalented Steve Cropper works on a mix at Stax, ca. 1966.

Sam and Dave went inside and met Jim Stewart, who looked just like what he was—a bank clerk. Stewart asked them if they'd met David Porter. They said yes, they'd met him outside. That's when Isaac Hayes, the bald guy with the green pants and pink socks, entered the room. Sam and Dave practically lost it right there when Stewart informed them that this was the guy who would be writing and producing their records.

But "Double Dynamite" had nothing to fear. Hayes and Porter poured their souls into the Sam and Dave productions, creating a writer/producer/artist combination for Stax on par with Lieber and Stoller with the Coasters at Atlantic or with Burt Bacharach and Hal David with Dionne Warwicke at Scepter. At sessions, the musicians would huddle around the piano where Hayes sat and worked out the chords as David Porter polished his lyrics.

One day in 1966, as everyone was standing around the piano, Porter excused himself and went to answer nature's call. The minutes passed and Hayes grew restless. "David, get

77

back in here!" he yelled. A muffled reply came from the men's room: "Hold on! I'm comin'."
Something about that answer hit Hayes in the musical funny bone. When Porter returned to
the piano, Hayes had an idea for a song. Isaac started playing some chords. David scratched
down some words on his legal pad. Before too long, Sam and Dave's first number-one record,
Hold On! I'm Comin' was born.

But their biggest hit would come the next year. "Soul Man" is possibly Isaac Hayes's
hottest arrangement, the horns and the rhythm section tweaked to a fever pitch. Steve
Cropper says that Hayes and Porter asked him to help them on the introduction, which
turns into a music lesson of tension and release. Cropper's plaintive bell-like guitar licks
are cut off by a muscular horn line, then Al Jackson's drums get the thing galloping off like
a runaway horse.

One of the greatest moments on any Stax record comes in this song's first chorus. Sam
and Dave incant, "I'm a soul man!" and the horns answer with a strong Hayes flourish. Then
Double Dynamite repeat, "I'm a soul man!" and this time Cropper's guitar cuts through the
mix with single notes that push the tension. Hayes had asked Cropper to give him some
"Elmore James," referring to the great bottleneck, or "slide," blues guitarist. Cropper didn't
have a metal slide on him, so instead he used a metal Zippo cigarette lighter. After he picked
four chilling, naked notes, Moore was electrified. "Play it, Steve!" he shouted. It only happened that one time on that one take, and the line is now immortal. Just another tremendous
performance cut live in the dusty old theater on McLemore Avenue.

Sam and Dave recorded some of the most incendiary music to come out of the Stax studio. But in this house, there was room for only one king, and that was the Big O, Otis Redding.
Steve Cropper says, "Otis was just everybody's big brother and best friend, and everyone
wanted to play with him. You just knew it was gonna be fun." In the winter, when the studio
was so cold that the Memphis Horns usually wore their coats during sessions, Otis still worked
up a sweat. In the summer when the room was stifling, Otis stripped to the waist and wailed
on, dripping buckets of sweat.

Redding wrote a lot of his material and paid special attention to the horn lines. Like
many at Stax, he couldn't read music, so he would sing the horn lines to the players with the
fervor of a gospel preacher. Trumpet player Wayne Jackson portrayed Otis as a soul revivalist
to writer Rob Bowman in his excellent history of Stax, *Soulsville, U.S.A.*: "He loved the horns.
He would run from his vocal mike down to where the horns were and go [sings the horn line
from 'I Can't Turn You Loose'], shake his fist at you, and be singing those parts, and it was just
electrifying. He'd just get right in front of you with that big fist up in the air and strut and sing
that stuff at you and you were just foaming at the mouth. He'd just have you so excited. We had
to calm him down, sometimes. That was pretty much the way he went about inspiring us. We
just played exactly what he was singing and that would be the horn line for the song. We were
strictly painting a picture for him to dance in."

Jim Stewart said simply, "Otis Redding was like a magic potion."

In 1965, Redding headed one of the most high-energy sessions ever at Stax when he cut his solid soul masterpiece, *Otis Blue*. Redding was between gigs and came off the road just long enough to record the album in a single, sweat-drenched twenty-four hours. It started, as usual for Stax, at ten in the morning and ran into the afternoon. After a short break, everyone was back at it until around eight, when many of the musicians had to work club gigs. The session resumed around two in the morning. By ten, they'd finished up, and Otis was back on the road the following day.

Otis Blue contains two of Redding's greatest compositions—his signature song, "Respect," and the classic "I've Been Loving You Too Long." It also has tremendous versions of two songs by his idol, Sam Cooke, "Shake" and "A Change Is Gonna Come." At one point during the session, Otis stepped out briefly to get a physical for a life insurance policy. That's when Steve Cropper got the idea of recording the Rolling Stones' "Satisfaction." Cropper got a copy of the record from the record shop, played it for the band, and they worked up a Memphis-style arrangement. When he returned, Redding barreled through the vocal, pronouncing "faction" as "fashuh."

As far as Cropper knew, Redding had never heard the song before. But when he finished with it, many people thought the Stones must have copped it from *him*.

In spite of his undisputed royalty at Stax, Otis had yet to score a number-one record. Jerry Wexler complained repeatedly that he thought Redding's vocals were always buried too deep in the mix. It was his usual complaint about all Stax recordings, but Redding's vocals were mixed even deeper than most. On "I Can't Turn You Loose" he sounds like he's shouting to get out of Al Jackson's bass drum. When Wexler would complain about not being able to hear the lyrics, though, Stewart would just tell him, "You have New York ears and we have Memphis ears."

Other than that, the relationship between Atlantic and Stax continued to run smoothly. In 1965, Wexler gave Stewart the heads up that Atlantic might be sold. Stewart then decided that, in order to protect his deal with Atlantic, he should have his handshake distribution deal set down in writing. Not long after the *Otis Blue* session, the contract was written up and signed. Stewart didn't bother having a lawyer look at it. He barely read it himself. He trusted Wexler, and after nearly six years in business together, it seemed like a mere formality anyway.

With this detail out of the way, the future looked bright. Otis Redding enjoyed tremendous success on his tour to England and France in 1966. The next year, a huge package tour, the Stax/Volt Revue, with all of the label's top acts, invaded Europe. The Beatles sent their limo to meet them all at the airport. Fans screamed. Everyone, including Booker T. and the MGs, Sam and Dave, Carla Thomas, and, of course, Otis Redding, was treated like a superstar. On their return, Redding and Booker T. and the MGs made a groundbreaking appearance at the Monterey Pop Festival. The Memphis Sound was exposed to a whole new audience—"the love

crowd," as Otis called them. Not long after that triumph, Sam and Dave's "Soul Man" became the biggest hit on Stax to date: number one R&B, number two Pop. And at the end of November 1967, Otis Redding was in the studio with a new song— a song he proclaimed would be his first number-one hit. All in all, 1968 looked like it was going to be a great year for Stax.

Heartache

On December 9, 1967, Otis Redding was in his private jet, flying with several members of the Bar-Kays (his backing band and the musical heirs to Booker T. & the MGs) from Cleveland to a gig in Madison, Wisconsin. It was snowing badly. All commercial flights had been grounded, but Redding was determined to make the show—and he almost did. The plane crashed in Lake Monona, just outside of Madison.

Steve Cropper was on the road with Booker T. & the MGs that day, snowbound in an airport in Indiana. Dave Porter, who sometimes sang with the group, went to call the office to tell them they were stuck and didn't know when they'd get back. When Porter returned from the call, Cropper remembers, "He was white as a sheet. And I mean that. All the color was drained from his face." When Porter told the group the news, they went numb. Similarly, everything at Stax froze. Redding's death affected Jim Stewart so deeply that he said he was never again the same person.

80

When Cropper finally got back to Memphis, Jerry Wexler was already calling for a new release on Otis Redding. Hours before Redding's body was even recovered, Cropper was mixing the song Otis predicted would go to number one, "Dock of the Bay." "It was tough," said Cropper. "Maybe the toughest thing I've ever done."

Stax had recently gone four-track, so Cropper could work with several separate tracks of Redding's vocals, adding tear-stained guitar licks and the sound effects of waves and seagulls. He sent "Dock of the Bay" to Jerry Wexler (who had delivered Redding's eulogy at the funeral services in the Macon City Auditorium). With his "New York ears," Wexler sent it back. For the hundredth time he complained the vocal was buried too deep in the mix and demanded Cropper remix it. "No way," says Cropper today. "No way I could remix that record."

The song was a big change of pace for Otis. It starts with him strumming an acoustic guitar over sound effects Cropper added of waves and seagulls. His vocal comes in soft and wistful: "Sittin' in the mornin' sun/I'll be sittin' when the evenin' come. . . ." For years, his hoarse pleading had earned him the nickname "Mr. Pitiful." But this record was less bluesy. More pop. All soul. True to Otis Redding's predictions, "Dock of the Bay" became his first number-one record—the first Stax release to go number one on both the Pop and R&B charts.

Stax released "Dock of the Bay" and the Sam and Dave smash "I Thank You" on January

Another ear-splitting, bone-rattling playback as heard through the monster movie theater speaker (at rear) in the control room in 1967. Sam Moore, Isaac Hayes, Booker T. Jones (mostly hidden), Andrew Love, Wayne Jackson, Dave Prater, Jim Stewart (seated at the board), and Steve Cropper.

81

Stax: Memphis Soul Stew

8, 1968. Days later, Warner Bros. bought Atlantic Records. Now, as laid down in the contract, Stax had six months to decide if they wanted to continue their distribution deal with Atlantic. Stewart felt Atlantic was not offering Stax enough financial incentive to continue the relationship. After Stewart's attempts to renegotiate the deal failed, a horrible truth was discovered. A clause buried deep in the contract that Stewart signed with Atlantic gave the bigger company the master recordings of the entire product they distributed. The cold reality began to sink in. Stax was a record company without a catalog. All of their labor over the last eight years belonged to someone else.

In the end, the difficult decision was made to break with Atlantic. That meant that everything by Otis, everything by Sam and Dave, even the hits by the label's heartbeat, Booker T. and the MGs, was no longer owned by Stax. The company virtually started from scratch after negotiating an agreement to become a subsidiary of media monolith Gulf and Western. But at least they would own what they produced.

The sale was to take place in May, a few weeks after the distribution deal with Atlantic officially ended. But on April 4, another event would rock Stax, and the nation. Just blocks away from the studio, Martin Luther King Jr., was assassinated on the balcony outside his room at the Lorraine Motel. It was a location the Stax family knew intimately. On particularly hot days, musicians were known to take a break and cool off in the Lorraine's pool. The motel's fried chicken and catfish, favorites of Dr. King's, were also loved by the Stax crowd. Artists who came to Stax from out of town frequently stayed at the Lorraine. That something so horrible could happen there was unthinkable.

"I don't wish death on anyone, but I wish that had happened anywhere but Memphis," Cropper says today. "Memphis was the coolest city in the world, man. I wouldn't have wanted to grow up anywhere else than there. That [King's assassination] changed everything."

The night of the assassination, black musicians had to escort Steve Cropper and Duck Dunn to their cars through an angry mob that had spilled into the streets. Dunn left his bass inside, and the next day he and his wife June drove back to retrieve it.

"I got out and June waited in the car while Isaac [Hayes] came over to talk to me," Dunn told Peter Guralnick. "All of a sudden these cop cars pull up, cops jump out and pull out their guns. They thought these black guys were doing something to hurt us because we were white. Pulling shotguns on Isaac. You want to see someone feel like an idiot? Well, it was our fault because we weren't supposed to be down there—they had helicopters and shit flying around, this was an area that was off-limits, but this was where we lived and worked, we were trying to act like everything was normal. And the next day, having to go down and face that shit—I mean, the cops jumped in because we were white. It makes you feel like shit."

Jim Stewart believed that King's assassination "kind of put a wedge" in the company. People that had worked side by side for years were now suspicious of one another. Al Bell agreed that "racial sensitivity" became heightened. Outside the building, tensions ran even

82

higher, as African Americans living in the neighborhood surrounding Stax began to show resentment to many of its employees—both black and white—that the company wasn't giving back more to the community.

Once, its doors had been literally wide open to anyone who came by, but now Stax was a locked-down operation—even to some of its employees. A new security system was installed. Barbed wire appeared around the parking lot. Sam Moore was threatened at gunpoint by one of the neighborhood gangs. Guns were even distributed to several employees. Morale plummeted. People started to leave. Booker T. was the first to go, in 1969. Cropper left in '70. Booker T. and the MGs' last Stax album, *Melting Pot*, came out in 1972. It was recorded in New York City.

But there was an upside. Under its new ownership by Gulf and Western, Stax would go on to new sales heights with artists like Isaac Hayes (with his smash albums *Hot Buttered Soul*, *Shaft*, *Black Moses*), Johnny Taylor ("Who's Making Love," "Jody's Got Your Girl and Gone"), and the Staple Singers ("[If You're Ready] Come Go with Me" and "I'll Take You There"). Even Rufus Thomas would enjoy another dance-craze renaissance ("Do the Funky Chicken," "Do the Funky Penguin," "The Push and Pull"). But the magic—indeed, the dream—was gone.

Estelle Axton allowed herself to be bought out of the company in the late '60s (she would later produce one hit in the mid-'70s, the novelty smash "Disco Duck," for her own small record company). Jim Stewart left the company in the early '70s, leaving the reins to Al Bell. But financial difficulties caught up with the company, and in 1975 Stax went bankrupt. Federal marshals seized the old theater that housed the Stax studio. Ironically, the bank that forced Stax into bankruptcy was Union Planters, where Estelle Axton once worked. In 1980, Union Planters sold the building to a church for ten dollars. Eight years later, it was demolished.

For years the site of 926 McLemore Avenue was a weedy, broken glass-filled vacant lot with a historic marker proclaiming it as a civic landmark. Now a group called the Stax Foundation is building a museum on the lot. Headed by longtime Stax employee Deanie Parker, and with the support of all the Stax alumni, the Stax Museum of American Soul Music and the Stax Music Academy is being built with loving care. Outside, its design is patterned after the original building, including an homage to the theater marquee. Inside, Stax studio A is re-created down to the finest detail, sloping floor and all. For generations to come, the museum will tell the incredible story of Stax—and bear witness to a dream that was bigger and brighter, and in the end, much sadder, than anyone could have ever imagined.

Sun Studios
MECCA FOR REBELS

Even if Elvis Presley had never so much as set foot in Sun Studio's tiny storefront at 706 Union Avenue, in Memphis, Tennessee, Sun and its visionary owner Sam Phillips would still rank as one of the most important forces of twentieth-century music.

Sun Records, the Memphis Recording Service (a.k.a. Sun Studio), and Sam Phillips are forever linked because of the records Phillips made in this former radiator shop. More than merely the songs, however, it's the sound and the performances contained on those records that continue to thrill. No other studio can claim the seminal blues, pop, and rock legacy that Sun boasts. Starting at the dawn of the 1950s, clear through the end of that pivotal decade, Phillips/Sun alchemized Howlin' Wolf, Little Milton, Rufus Thomas, Junior Parker, B.B. King, Elvis Presley, Jerry Lee Lewis, Roy Orbison, Charlie Rich, Johnny Cash, and Carl Perkins into icons.

In 1940s America, the kind of music that was being recorded was mostly proper and familiar, and the recording process was likewise proper and professional. The goal wasn't merely to capture a performance. Implicit in the recording process was the desire to buff the music to a high gloss. Sam Phillips reached for sandpaper. Through mic movement, a preacher-style blend of exhortation and cajoling, and the studio's acoustic characteristics that made the loud even louder, Phillips fostered a fit-to-burst sound in an atmosphere where poor whites and blacks could let loose the music that was way down inside of them. This fortuitous combination of gifted misfits and the maverick vision of Phillips, who spurred his charges to get raw and real in the studio, seared tracks like "Whole Lotta Shakin' Goin' On," "Red Hot," "Rocket 88," and "Baby Let's Play House" into our consciousness.

Memphis

Culturally and musically, Memphis in the late '40s and early '50s was a petri dish. This damp and humid river town has always been secure in its craziness. Producer and Memphian Jim Dickinson, whose credits include Ry Cooder, the Rolling Stones, and Bob Dylan, summed it up in a 1997 interview: "It was a shock for me, when I left Memphis, to see how unhip the rest of the world was. Memphis celebrates the individual. All the success that's come from Memphis has been individual success."

In 1950s America, you would be hard pressed to find an individual more hellbent on transmuting the genres than Sam Phillips. In Memphis, he had company. Disc jockey Dewey Phillips, although no relation to Sam, had a kindred firebrand desire to mix it up. Nowhere else did whites at this time publicly play what was called "race music," the rougher, embryonic R&B that was just being heard in juke joints. (It was Dewey Phillips who broke Elvis's "That's All Right Mama" on his *Red, Hot and Blue* radio show in 1954. And it was Dewey who partnered with Sam to put out Joe Hill Louis's "Gotta Let You Go" on the short-lived *Phillips* label in 1950.) There never was a disc jockey quite like Dewey Phillips. He gave no thought to advertisers or market share or to anything, really, except the record he was spinning—back to back to back, at times—with utterances such as, 'Aw, this record flat-out gets *gone!*' Blacks and whites alike tuned into his show with religious zeal. It was through this same *Red, Hot and Blue* show, ironically, that Elvis heard so much of the music that would shape his tastes.

But it wasn't just a city of crazy white guys. Memphis has always had a more urban—let's just say black—presence that distinguished it from, say, Nashville. After all, this is where the first all-black radio station, the legendary WDIA, originated. Beale Street, with its host of blues bars, loomed large in this mid-South town. Out of these two quarters came true originals: Rufus Thomas, B.B. King, Roscoe Gordon, and dozens more.

After a childhood that was part Faulkner, part Dickens, Phillips began his professional music career in radio. Starting out in small southern markets such as Muscle Shoals and Decatur, Alabama, Phillips moved up to Nashville before landing a job at WREC in Memphis in 1945. While at WREC, he metamorphosed from an announcer of music into a mixer of music, recording big bands for the CBS network from the storied Peabody Hotel in downtown Memphis. "I was working like, fifteen to eighteen hours a day, because I did all the big band broadcasts. Two and a half years before that I never thought I would ever *see* a big band."

Phillips had felt the need for more: more money for his family, more opportunities for his musical lust to be sated. Just as important, he felt an inchoate urge to get the raw "gutbucket" music he heard oozing from Beale Street. He knew it was ripe to explode; with his radio and mixing experience providing the foundation, he figured maybe he could be the vessel "these poor white and black folks" needed to get across. On the outskirts of downtown Memphis, he spotted a one-story storefront, formerly home to a radiator-repair shop. "After two years of looking, it was ideally [located]. I mean, east and south and north, and that way, you reached most of the people, and certainly the people I was looking for. When they came to town, it'd be easy to find. Beale Street was half a short block from the east end of [Union]," says the seventy-eight-year-old Phillips, in a voice that is at once syrupy and Pentecostal.

"I took that studio and I was so proud to get this little old storefront building. I walked in there and you would have thought God had delivered heaven to me."

On the second day of the 1950s, the Memphis Recording Service was open for business. "I knew how much work it was going to require, and I knew I didn't have any money and all that stuff, but anyway, in less than a week I was working, and I didn't have the money to hire a contractor or, really, any carpenters. I did hire one carpenter part time, I had to have *some* help on, but I did that and built that studio like it is now.

"I also knew that when I opened it up we'd record anywhere, anything, anytime. I meant that, but I had to have some kind of idea of how I was going to pay the rent and everything, and not impose on my salary from WREC. I often was asked at that time, 'What in the world are you all building a recording studio [for] and who you going to record?' and so forth and so on and on. I said, 'Well, man, I'm going to record anything I can.'"

Soon he was cutting not so much "anywhere, anything, anytime," but blues, music that hadn't been heard on disc much beyond the seminal field recordings of Alan Lomax's Folkways Recordings. Artists such as Howlin' Wolf or B.B. King have become such mainstay musical forces that their music feels as though it has always been around. In fact, there were fewer than a handful of places in the country where a black man could even think of making a raw blues recording. A few of these places are chronicled in this book. What sets Sam Phillips apart from people like Cosimo Matassa and Rudy Van Gelder, though, is that while they, of course, documented performances faithfully, Sam distorted, slapped, and tickled that shiny mono tape while seducing performances from artists they didn't even know they could give.

"When [Sun] first started," recalls Phillips, "every black artist played nothing but gutbucket blues. When they came in they saw this white man behind the glass; well, they just knew that I wanted another Count Basie or whatever. We established in a hurry that if they didn't give me some of what *they loved*, then they weren't gonna get any time of mine."

He tried different techniques on different combinations of players and instruments. "I'd say, 'Well, I tell you, we need the drum kind of in one spot, and just kind of get it as close to the way you work and the way you play off in sound, and feel each other if you can.' I love to move mics around. I don't like a standard setup. I mean, on stage they always played loud. I said, '*I don't want you to play studio volume.* I want to be able to let you play as close to what sounds natural to y'all.'"

87

There is a bit of a myth that the blues didn't get electrified until the musicians from the Delta migrated up to Chicago in the late '50s. While this is as hard to nail down as when the first true "rock" record was cut, there were a few of like-minded folks looking to crank up the blues. Howlin' Wolf [a.k.a. Chester Burnett] was the common thread between the Delta, Sun, and the Chicago Blues. Like other black artists that Sam cut at 706, the Wolf recorded fewer than a handful of tracks. But these are vital recordings in the development of rock. Even now, Phillips gets excited talking about the Wolf, whose music, Sam has famously said, "is where the soul of man never dies."

"The Wolf played like he was in a show. He liked to stand, and he'd start to wiggle his head, like, side to side. I needed a unidirectional mic [one that picks up 360 degrees] to get at him. His voice—which is still amazing to me—had these overtones. Man, I wish I could have done more [recording] on him."

From 1950 through 1952, Phillips recorded groundbreaking tracks on Junior Parker and the Wolf and others, such as "Rocket 88," by Jackie Brenston and Ike Turner (yet another disc considered by many to be the first "true" rock and roll record), and leased them out to labels such as Chess in Chicago and Modern in Los Angeles. This never sat too well with Sam—"I'm not saying they were bad people, but they stood for things I didn't stand for"— and he started the Sun Record Company in 1952.

Phillips had always been a worker. Supporting his mother, a deaf aunt, two kids, and a wife while still mixing big bands for CBS *and* starting a new studio from scratch, the "any-where, anything, anytime" ethos had worn Phillips down to the point of a nervous breakdown. In 1951, he underwent electric shock treatment. Undeterred, he debuted the Sun Recording Company in 1952 with the moody instrumental "Driving Slow," by Memphis saxman Johnny London. With hits by Bobby Blue Bland and Little Milton, among others, Sun quickly became a beacon for anyone with a feel for overamped, razor-edged blues.

Elvis

As stated earlier, Memphis was (and is) a town proudly populated by oddballs and misfits. Yet, even for Memphis, Elvis Presley was not standard issue. Born in Tupelo in a classic shotgun shack, Elvis was the mama's boy who would sneak into the Shake Rag section of town to listen to the old bluesmen. When the teenage Elvis and his parents moved into the not-quite-projects Lauderdale Court Apartments in midtown Memphis, Elvis would sit and play his guitar for anyone who would listen. Like all great artists, from Armstrong to Prince, Elvis was a sponge of a musical scholar, soaking up all he heard: Mario Lanza, the Statesmen, Ma Rainey, Roy Hamilton, you name it. Musically, not much flew beneath his radar.

88 By now most everyone knows the story of how, in 1954, this nineteen-year-old truck driver came to 706 Union to record a song, ostensibly as a gift to his mother; how Marion Keiser, Sam's assistant at that time, recorded the nervous young white man who dressed and

sounded black. (When she asked him whom he thought he sounded like, he replied unselfconsciously, "I don't sound like nobody." Man has rarely been this eloquent.) Knowing Phillips's oft-quoted remark, "If I can find a white man who sounds like a black man, I'd make a million dollars," Keiser made a note, then told Phillips about the strangely good-looking boy with the long sideburns.

Phillips helms the RCA console, surrounded by tantalizing stacks of Sun master tapes, 1954.

Intrigued by what he heard, Sam paired Presley with a couple of locals, bassist Bill Black and guitarist Scotty Moore. Moore, already an accomplished session hand, was impressed with the boy's voice, timing, and surprisingly vast knowledge of music. In July 1954, Presley, Moore, and Black went into the Memphis Recording Service for a trial run. After playing around with different styles for days, the trio suddenly "cut up" during a break with an old tune, "That's All Right Mama," playing it with a mixture of hillbilly honk and blues that sounded unlike anything–*anything*–that had ever been heard before. Phillips, half listening in the control room, lifted his head like a man who's just heard his lottery number called.

"What the hell y'all doin'?" asked Phillips, intrigued. "We don't know,"came the equally intrigued response. "Well, back it up to where I can get in [to start recording] and let's get it."

Thus spake Sam Phillips. From this moment on, our world would slant on a different axis.

Soon after this session was completed, Dewey Phillips "broke" the record, which could not be pressed fast enough to satisfy the demand, and that was only in Memphis. Suddenly, a new species inhabited the earth–the Elvis impersonator.

89

Presley and Phillips would make only nineteen tracks together. Among the most astonishing recordings in pop history is a union of these two souls, feeling their way in the dark new world of the studio. The recording isn't among Elvis's most familiar, but it's probably best that way. On "Blue Moon," the old chestnut gets a makeover that doesn't quite sound like it was performed or recorded by earthlings. With just a clip-clop rhythm beneath, the nineteen-year-old Presley makes a mournful lunar plea that is embedded in a swirl of gossamer echo. Both men would go on to greater heights, but neither one would ever hover above us like this again.

The Sound

But what of the Sun Sound? A lot of it had to do with volume. Lots of volume in a very small room. Producer Jim Dickinson made an interesting point: "Beyond a question of a doubt, the room is really the thing. That room sound is still special. It has to do with that old asbestos square acoustic tile, which covers everything but the floor. Sam made the flat ceiling into these kind of V-shaped rows with the acoustic tile and straight pins. When you speak, you can feel the air pressure in the room. The more volume that you put into that room, the more the midrange compresses. It's sort of like the Phil Spector principle of putting too much in too small a space. [When the sound gets loud] the room acts as a compressor."

"Any time that you can do a thing where you have an automatic natural *blend*, it is absolutely much better," adds Phillips. "It keeps it out of the pure mechanical world, and now that's what we're getting into. After I discovered my slapback echo [where a sound source, i.e., a vocal, is fed into the record head of a tape machine, then played back a split second *after* the vocal], I found usually that it gave a type of liveness that was very difficult [to capture]. I never went for, back then people wanted a fairly dead studio, and I wanted to keep it as live as I could and still be able to handle it in there and be able to let each of the members of the band work."

Phillips did most of it—the studio design, the producing, the engineering, the distribution—by himself. Although he possessed a modicum of electrical knowledge, Phillips utilized ingenuity in an inverse proportion to money: "Sure, there were better engineers than me electronically, but I couldn't buy a limiter to cut my masters with, so I built a limiter and a compressor. A little later on when I couldn't buy me a board, I had this little Presto four-input [console] and knew that I just needed a little more room. I saw an ad in one of the trade papers that there was a RCA70 D board used, so I called the engineer up there and I said, 'How much do you want for it?' and he said 'Five hundred dollars.' Well of course, that was a lot of money too, but I got that damn thing down here and all the electrolytic capacitors for the amps for the program amplifier and the alternate program amplifier monitor, they were just *cooked*, really. Well, I had that thing up and running in a week's time and that damn thing, it was just so perfect for what I needed.

"I knew my control room; so [when] I built my own cabinet [speaker] and angled it, I played with that thing till it got to the point where it was telling me the *truth*, and I knew."

90

As for microphones, the very best German-made Telefunkens were out the question. The two staples were mics made in America, by RCA and Shure. "God, I was so proud to have a [RCA] 77D, and I had a Shure 56S, and I had a old Altec black pencil [mic]. It was the only power [condenser] mic that I had. They were good microphones, but they were very omni-directional and I had to be careful with a chamber [room] so small."

Recording at Sun meant maybe two or three or five players in an eighteen-by-thirty-three-foot room, all playing loud. The sound is swimming around, again, because of the lack of space. Phillips is in the control room and the door is open to the studio. ("I didn't have a talk-back mic in the control room. Didn't want one. I wanted to stay close to the performers in the room.") With only a single (mono) track of tape, he captures the sound, the perform-ance, and the vibe that he and this shoebox-of-a-room helped create. There is no isolation on any one instrument. With the highly compressed sound and the leakage, the bleed from the guitars, drums, pianos, and two or three other instruments suddenly becomes an orchestra. If the mood of the song warrants it, he throws this type of tape-delayed echo—"slapback," onto the singer's voice. The result is primal, yet otherworldly.

This can best be heard in a song that today, right now, continues to electrify: "Great Balls of Fire"—two and a half minutes of sexual audacity by a fire-and-brimstone piano demon named Jerry Lee Lewis, one of the crop of young turks who came to record at 706 Union as though it were mecca. In one of the most infamous recording sessions in rock history, Jerry Lee and Phillips, both perhaps feeling the distilled spirit of the divine, engage in a verbal tus-sle over good and evil as represented by the Bible and rock and roll, respectively. Phillips, who always yearned to emulate the silver-tongued southern lawyers he had witnessed as a teen, got in a little practice while the mono tape rolls:

LEWIS: The blinded eyes are open.

PHILLIPS: Jerry . . .

LEWIS: The lame were made to walk.

PHILLIPS: Jesus Christ . . .

LEWIS: The crippled were made to walk.

PHILLIPS: Jesus Christ, in my opinion, is just as real today as he was when he came into this world.   .

LEWIS: Right. Right. You're so right you don't know what you're saying about it . . .

PHILLIPS: Now listen, I'm telling you out of my heart, and I have studied the Bible a little bit . . .

LEWIS: Well, I have too. I've studied it through and through and through and through and through. I know what I'm talking about.

PHILLIPS: Listen, when you think you can't do any good, to be a rock and roll exponent . . .

LEWIS: You can do good, Mr. Phillips, don't get me wrong.

91

Killer smiles: The
devil and the
preacher conspire to
make rock history
in Memphis, 1957.

PHILLIPS: Wait a minute, now, when I say do good . . .

LEWIS: You can have a kind heart . . .

PHILLIPS: I don't mean, I don't mean . . .

LEWIS: . . . you can help people . . .

PHILLIPS: You can save souls.

LEWIS: No, no, no. How can the *devil* save souls? What are you talkin' about? *Man, I got the Devil in me!* If I didn't have, I'd be a Christian.

On and on this went into the night, before they resumed and made rock history, with "Great Balls" soaring to number two on the *Billboard* Top Forty.

By 1956, others, such as Johnny Cash, Roy Orbison, Carl Perkins, and Charlie Rich, fell under the tutelage of Phillips. But it was Elvis, always Elvis, who will be forever linked to Sun and Phillips. Phillips, riding a streak of individual discoveries that has not been equaled to this day, perhaps thought that another Elvis would saunter into Sun—who could blame him— and when Carl Perkins recorded "Blue Suede Shoes" for Sun in 1956, Phillips thought he had found him. (For all the legend associated with Sun Records, very few of the recordings made much money. The chief reason is as nebulous as it is unglamorous—the lack of broad, efficient distribution such as Capitol or Columbia employed.) With Elvis getting more popular each day, RCA and Colonel Tom Parker approached Sam with an offer he could not refuse: to sell

92

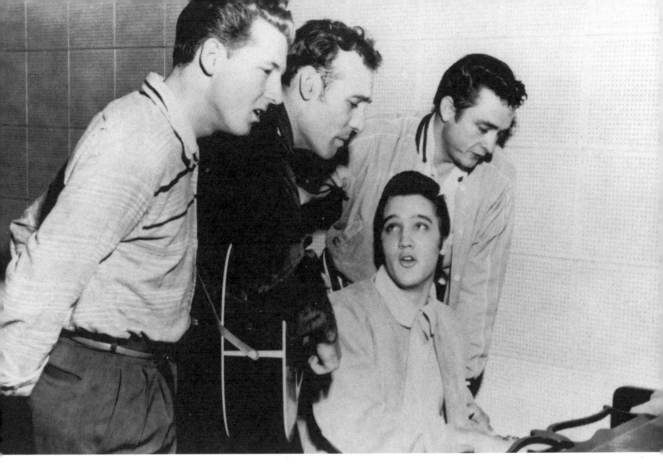

Elvis's Sun contract for the unheard-of sum of thirty-five thousand dollars. Sam, in debt, figured he would be able to recapitalize to the extent that he could finally go national, like Columbia and Capitol. Perkins, a solid songwriter, would be the next Elvis. Phillips let Elvis go to RCA. History tells us that neither Carl Perkins nor anyone else would be the next Elvis.

In all these years, Sam Phillips has put a brave face to the fallout of this decision. In interview after interview, he resolutely denied any doubts about this choice. Today, however, as he reclines in bed, battling a nasty bout of bronchitis, there are trace elements of regret.

"I really believed that it ["Blue Suede Shoes"] was going to be big. I really did, but you never know. Till this day, you don't know. But I knew that I just couldn't miss this one."

He continues: "Oh, man. We parted. I wouldn't have sold his contract, and he almost didn't OK it. The man almost did not OK it. And if it hadn't been for the element [in the contract] with Mrs. Presley, that old Parker–Tom–put in, I'm here to tell you he would *not* have left Sun, and he would have been just as big or bigger."

None of the recording artists and engineers of this era could have imagined the fame and legend that would grow up around them through the years. Sally Wilbourn, Sam's wife and assistant since the late 1950s, puts the Sun Studio Myth into perspective. "People don't realize. They talk about those records from Sun and the studio on Union, but you know, at that

The "Million Dollar Quartet" (Jerry Lee Lewis, Carl Perkins, Johnny Cash, and by-then Sun alum Elvis) harmonize around the piano, ca. 1957.

93

time, nobody thought it was anything special. In fact, by 1959, we couldn't wait to get out of there, because it was so small. And there was no air-conditioning."

Phillips continued to work, of course. In 1958, he built a then state-of-the-art studio around the corner from Sun called the Phillips Recording Service, which registered some hits of its own, such as the frat-house classic "Wooley Bulley," by Sam the Sham and the Pharoahs, and "Lonely Weekends," by Charlie Rich.

By 1960, the rock and roll that Sam Phillips helped forge seemed unseemly. The records, and artists, of the day were figuratively airbrushed to accommodate a new frontier, a new decade. Phillips, perhaps his heart broken, perhaps wanting to have more to show for his labors, spent less and less time in studio. In the psychedelic, confused days of 1969, Sun was forgotten. Sam sold his interests in Sun, which he'd "built with [his] own little hands," to Shelby Singleton. Phillips acquired radio stations and, in his fashion, he went from one American institution to another: not too long after he sold Elvis's contract to RCA, he invested in a small hotel chain with the quaint name of Holiday Inn.

After years of mistaken identities such as a scuba shop and a garage, Sun Studio, at 706 Union Avenue, was restored to its rightful self in 1982. Rockers the world over, from U2 to Tom Petty, from Bonnie Raitt to Def Leppard, continue to make pilgrimages to Sun in an effort to soak up the magic the space possesses.

Across town, in swank East Memphis, the still-mesmerizing Phillips accounts for his success with his "talent for seeing in people things that, a lot of times, I don't think they knew they had themselves. Now, that sounds like a profound statement, and it is. God gave me the best set of ears, I believe . . . and I just had different ideas."

Above: Anything, anywhere, anytime. Whether you wanted metal processing or sonocastic sound, the Memphis Recording Service was the place.

Opposite: 706 Union, the former radiator-repair shop that changed music history.

94

J&M
COSIMO'S FACTORY

New Orleans inhabits its own separate universe. Its rich mix of French, African, Native American, Caribbean, pirate, Yankee, Southern, Cajun, and Creole influences creates a cultural gumbo duplicated nowhere else. It's what puts the extra spice in New Orleans cooking, the extra frill in its French Quarter architecture, and the unique and undeniable funk in its music.

The wild sounds of the great Allen Toussaint as a teenager at Cosimo's, ca. 1958.

In the years before the Civil War, slaves were often allowed to congregate in a field on the edge of the city. This area became known as Congo Square, and Sunday afternoon dances with drums and African string instruments became joyful celebrations. Following the Civil War, new sounds started to develop here. Drummers mixed Caribbean beats with military marches. Horns began to imitate the shouts and moans of the sanctified church. At funerals, bands accompanied the bereaved to the cemetery playing slow, mournful dirges. But after the burial, the musicians "got happy" and made a joyful noise as they paraded through the streets. As they passed by, onlookers fell in line behind the procession of mourners, forming a second line of revelers, carried along by the loose-limbed, easy-rolling rhythms. The music proved irresistible, possessing the potent brew that later came to be known as funk (pronounced "fonk" in N'awlins).

The music developed into ragtime, blues, and jazz. It spread north with the migration of African Americans to urban meccas like New York and Chicago, passing through Memphis and St. Louis along the way. The teens and '20s witnessed a steady procession of musical prophets emanating from New Orleans: Buddy Bolden, Jelly Roll Morton, Sidney Bechet, King Oliver, Kid Ory, and, of course, the man who gave life to modern music, Louis Armstrong.

But to find true fame and fortune (and of these early innovators, only Armstrong found much of the latter) all these artists had to leave New Orleans. Though the city had plenty of great musicians, it had no music industry—meaning record labels or even recording studios— until after World War II, when Cosimo Matassa opened the J&M Recording Service.

In 1945, Matassa, the son of Italian grocer and bar owner John Matassa, was an eighteen-year-old chemistry major at Tulane University. He hated school, and soon dropped out. His father gave him an ultimatum: he could join the army or get to work. The war in Europe had just ended, and shiploads of soldiers were coming home. Cosimo opted to go to work.

John Matassa ran a side business with his partner, Joe Mancuso, called the J&M Amusement Company (since they shared the initials *J* and *M*). The company put jukeboxes in bars and restaurants on a commission basis. Cosimo joined the business and made extra money selling used records from the jukeboxes. Seeing a solid demand, and the need for a good record store in New Orleans, Cosimo and Mancuso opened the J&M Music Shop at 838 N. Rampart Street, on the corner of Rampart and Dumaine.

"What happened [was] the war ended," remembers Matassa, "[and] we decided to fix up a little shop to sell records and appliances. During the war you couldn't buy appliances, so there was kind of a backlog, and we figured we would be good with that. And my partner said, Why don't we put a little room in the back where people can make records? And it fell to me to operate it. I was a little more technically oriented, I guess."

Just like selling appliances, it would be a quick way of making money: sell records in the front of the store, make records in the back. Simple, except it wasn't so simple. First of all, since the only recordings made in New Orleans up until that time were the rare sessions done at radio stations, there was no old, used equipment lying around to buy. And there was no one around to ask where to get some, no one to ask how to work it or how to fix it.

Those were the days before tape recorders were commonly available. Studios used disc recorders that looked a lot like regular turntables, only bigger. The heavy recording arm had a cutter head on the end that literally cut a groove into an acetate disc. This disc was used as the master from which the actual records were made. One of Cosimo's first quests was to acquire one of these machines. He ordered one from up north.

"Yeah, it was a Duo [Duo Press recorder] made by a company in New Jersey called Presto. And it had cutter heads, Presto cutter heads. At some time along there, I had a friend who was an engineer on a super tanker. Today it would be a tugboat by comparison, but . . . he went to the North Sea and back and he got three cutter heads in England. Grampion cutter heads. The Grampion was no heavier than the Presto cutter head—five, six, seven ounces, you know. About the size of a pack of cigarettes, a little squarer and a little squattier, but it was a feedback cutter head. . . . It was like night and day better than the Presto.

98

"I wanted to buy the driver amplifier that a company in New York called Gotham Audio [sold]. Well, Gotham Audio was run by a guy named Timmer, and he was a strange guy. He knew his stuff and he sold great equipment. He sold Telefunkens [microphones] and things like that, but he wouldn't sell me the driver amplifier because I wouldn't buy the cutter head from him. If I wanted to pay him the price for the cutter head, you know [he would have sold me the amplifier]. And he was the only game in town. . . . So I talked to a guy who was an engineer in Chicago and he said, 'Well, hell, build one!'"

That guy was Bill Putnam, who owned and built Universal Recording Studios, and he went on to build United and Western Studios in Los Angeles, designing his own custom mixing boards and eventually creating his own line of recording equipment. "He was one of the early people I really admired," says Cosimo. "Not just for his recording, but because he was a thinker." Over the phone, Putnam talked Cosimo through the design of a makeshift driver amplifier, and later the construction of a vacuum to pick up the acetate chips made by the cutter head as it bit a groove into the disc.

Though he had to scramble a bit to get his equipment together (originally, he used the three-input mixer that came with the Presto recorder as his control board and used the bathroom upstairs as his echo chamber), the room itself was fairly sophisticated for the time.

A view of Rampart Street in New Orleans in the late 1940s includes a large sign for the J&M Music Shop on the corner of Dumaine, near the old site of Congo Square.

Inset: This sign—the original from 1948—remains etched in marble on the corner of Rampart and Dumaine.

99

"[It] was about sixteen by seventeen and a fraction," recalls Cosimo. "It was a tiny room. The control room was about the size of two really good-sized phone booths. In fact [to accommodate], the rack for the Presto gear, I made a hole in the wall. It was a full-length rack, a seventy-two-inch rack. And I stuck it in the wall so that you could operate it from the control room, but to work on it you had to go out into the hall and open the back.

"[The studio] was air-conditioned. The room was state of the art, and the reason was because the architect made some effort to get the very latest. The floor was floating, there were double walls, staggered studs. They put noise reduction in the ducts. It had some bass tuning.

"The room wasn't bad at all. It was tiny, which meant that the primary resonance was high enough so that it wouldn't destroy the low end. It was carpeted, so you didn't make a lot of noise. It was at the back of the building, which meant you had the front wall, the building itself [to help shield street noise]. Then there was two solid wood doors, and the inner one had solid lead sheeting on it."

After nearly a year of design and construction, the J&M Recording Service was finally up and running and . . . nothing much happened. Cosimo's earliest recording sessions were of individuals or glee clubs making records for their family and friends. But then, in 1947, DeLuxe Records, an independent label based in Linden, New Jersey, came to New Orleans looking to find some authentic, undiscovered jazz and blues musicians. They soon learned about Cosimo's little studio. Instead of taking their discoveries up north to cut a record, they could save money and record right in town. Plus, Cosimo charged only fifteen dollars an hour.

They had a studio. They had a plan. Now they just needed to grab the talent.

A lot of this talent could be found hanging around a near-mythical club called the Dew Drop Inn, known by local musicians and hipsters as simply "the Drop." Situated in midtown at 2840 LaSalle Street, the Dew Drop Inn was primarily a nightclub, with tables in front of the bandstand and a small dance floor in the back. Upstairs there were rooms for rent where out-of-town acts often boarded during their stay. Owned by a Creole named Frank Pania, it was New Orleans's primary stop on the "chitlin' circuit," and on the weekends it was where the hottest black acts in the country performed. However, during the week, it hosted a bawdy all-male drag revue.

More than just a place to hear great music, the Drop served as unofficial headquarters for many of New Orleans's finest black musicians. Many of them were recruited to play at white clubs, sometimes hidden behind a curtain when on stage with white women. After the gig was over, the musicians were asked to leave—immediately. With pay in hand, they headed straight to the Dew Drop Inn.

Writer/producer/performer Allen Toussaint remembers hanging out at the Drop when he was just a kid. "We would see the older guys [musicians] get through with their gig somewhere downtown and they would all stand on the outside of the Dew Drop talking and jiving around, and we were the younger guys. We hadn't acquired the rite of passage yet. So we would stick close by and watch them interact with each other and it was quite a learning process. We were just wide-eyed and joyed to be there. We saw how it goes. And we noticed all the mannerisms when the guys listened to music, how they would shake their heads and all. 'Cuz they were the guys who were *there!* And we wanted to *go there!* And it was a great place to be. . . . It was just a paradise."

One night in early 1947, singer Roy Brown made what would become an eventful visit to the Drop. Just days before, Brown had been playing at a club in Galveston, Texas, where he penned a little ditty called "Good Rockin' Tonight." He sang the song live on a local radio broadcast, and the station's phones began to light up. A few days later, however, Brown had to get out of town after being caught with a club owner's girlfriend.

He made a beeline to his birthplace, New Orleans. Flat broke and in need of some instant cash, Brown headed straight to the Drop, where the handsome blues shouter Wynonie Harris was playing. Brown wrote the words to "Good Rockin' Tonight" on a paper bag and tried to get Harris to buy the song from him. Harris passed, but his band let Brown perform the song at the show's intermission. It went over well, and a band member suggested he take the song to another club, where a musician named Cecil Gant might be interested in it.

When Brown sang the song for Gant, Gant flipped for it. He called one of the owners of DeLuxe Records at four in the morning and had Brown sing it over the phone. Gant was told to give Brown one hundred dollars and a room at the Dew Drop Inn; they'd be down to record him later that week. On the day of the session, Cosimo was having a problem with one of the microphones. Brown had to crouch and sing his vocal into the piano mic.

The record quickly blew up in New Orleans, and it soon caught fire throughout the South. Ironically, Wynonie Harris wound up covering it and actually had the bigger national hit. Perhaps the most legendary version was cut seven years after the original by Elvis Presley up at Sun Studio in Memphis.

Enjoying good success, DeLuxe Records continued to scout for talent around New Orleans. Their next big "discovery" was the group many considered the best band in town. Trumpeter Dave Bartholomew's group featured the hard-driving drummer Earl Palmer and sax man Alvin "Red" Tyler. A talented arranger and prolific writer, Dave Bartholomew led his band through many hot sessions for DeLuxe at J&M.

Then, in 1949, Bartholomew met Lew Chudd, head of L.A.-based Imperial Records. Chudd was looking to get more R&B acts on his label, and he recruited Bartholomew to head this effort. Though Imperial was still a relatively small independent, Bartholomew's position as an A&R man was a rare opportunity for a black musician.

One of Bartholomew's first discoveries for Imperial was Antoine "Fats" Domino, a shy kid who made the rounds of different clubs in town playing boogie-woogie piano. In late '49, Domino sat at J&M's baby grand piano for the first time. Cosimo had just gotten a new piece of equipment, an Ampex 600 tape recorder. Though listed as a portable machine, it weighed about three hundred pounds. This was the first session Cosimo used it on, and (literally), right out of the box, he recorded a hit on it. The record Domino made that day, "The Fat Man," caused a sensation and went to number one on the R&B charts, launching Domino's incredible career. Matassa was at the board to record Domino's easy-rolling rock and roll for more than a decade.

With "The Fat Man," plus other early Imperial hits, like Jewel King's "3 x 7 = 21" and Archibald's (Leon Gross) loping version of "Stack-a-Lee," the new "sound of New Orleans" was making noise in the record world. The J&M studio was hot, and suddenly it was the music shop and appliances that became secondary. Matassa and Mancuso had a disagreement over business and parted company. But Cosimo didn't miss a beat. He was in the studio engineering sessions practically around the clock.

Dave Bartholomew "supervised" most of these early recordings (*producer* wasn't a term used at the time). He handpicked many of the best musicians in town for his sessions, including drummer Earl Palmer, bassist Frank Fields, sax players Red Tyler and Lee Allen, and pianist Huey Smith. To this day, Cosimo fondly remembers working with this talented group.

"Sessions with those guys were gorgeous. Absolutely gorgeous. . . . And Dave Bartholomew was a great guy to work with. You gotta remember, New Orleans musicians do tend to be laid back, especially back then. So you needed somebody to keep them focused [to remind them] that this really is a job and something you had to take seriously. Dave was great at that—to the extent that if you goofed with him, you missed sessions for a long time. He'd hit them in the pocketbook."

The success DeLuxe and Imperial Records were having in New Orleans was noted by other R&B independents, including Atlantic Records in New York and Specialty Records in Los Angeles. In 1950, Jerry Wexler and Ahmet Ertegun, who headed Atlantic Records, came down to J&M to record Roy Byrd, better known as Professor Longhair. "Fess" played with a Caribbean-inflected style that influenced a whole generation of New Orleans piano men, including James Booker and Allen Toussaint. His first Atlantic session included an early version of his original "Mardi Gras in New Orleans."

Longhair had a habit of kicking the fronts of the upright pianos he played in clubs, and more than once he had to pay for the holes he'd made in them. When he came to J&M, there was nothing for him to kick beneath the studio's baby grand. So Cosimo nailed a board behind the pedals to make Fess more comfortable.

Another legendary New Orleans character, Guitar Slim (Eddie Jones), had at least two memorable recording sessions at J&M. Slim lived at the Dew Drop when he wasn't on the road. In fact, the Drop's owner, Frank Pania, was his manager. Everyone knew when Slim was back in town, because he would regale the neighborhood with his playing at seven in the morning, his P.A. (he never used an amp) turned up to peak volume, waking the locals some three blocks away.

Specialty Records recorded Slim at J&M in 1953. He arrived in typically resplendent fashion, sporting a lemon-and-lime-colored suit with a fuzzy felt hat and tie to match. He had four songs to do, but it took him take after take to get them down. As the session ground on—from day to night to nearly day again—everyone involved was drained, especially the pianist and arranger, a young and barely known Ray Charles.

They call him the Fat Man: A young Antoine "Fats" Domino plays boogie-woogie piano at J&M, ca. 1950.

Charles was in town playing gigs at several of the local clubs and enjoying daily meals at the Drop. He had yet to score a hit of his own and hadn't developed the soulful style that would soon make him a star. Many believe that his stay in New Orleans during 1953 was a turning point in his quest to find himself as an artist, and some even claim this marathon session at J&M—observing the all-out blues ramblings of Guitar Slim—went a long way toward helping him make that discovery.

Cosimo remembers Charles being totally in charge of the session, rehearsing the band, stopping and correcting wrong notes, making sure Guitar Slim himself stayed on his toes for take after take after take. The grueling record date concluded with the testifying blues "The Things That I Used to Do." As the horns take the tune out, Charles is clearly heard shouting "Yeah!" in the break. It was nearly dawn.

Producer Johnny Vincent sent the tape to Specialty Records owner Art Rupe, who pronounced it the worst piece of shit he'd ever heard. But "The Things That I Used to Do" would

103

be Slim's biggest record, staying at number one for six weeks on the R&B charts. In many ways, it was Ray Charles's first studio triumph as well.

Slim would return to J&M three years later, this time recording for Atlantic Records. Jerry Wexler remembered the studio sweltering at around 103 degrees, but Slim came to the session decked out in an overcoat, a doo-rag, and a wide-brimmed fedora. Sipping mineral oil from a bottle to clear his throat, he complained that the room was *too cold*. Another marathon session ensued, and this time, not only did Slim keep muffing words and skipping entire verses, he repeatedly turned up the gain on his guitar, blowing out tubes in Cosimo's tape recorder and the lights in the studio as well.

However, when it comes to the wildest, most historic session at J&M, there's absolutely no contest. It took place over two days, September 13 and 14, 1955. That's when Richard Penniman, a.k.a Little Richard, walked into that studio for the first time.

Art Rupe and Specialty Records had already found success at J&M. Lloyd Price recorded "Lawdy Miss Clawdy" there in 1952, and, of course, Guitar Slim cut "The Things That I Used to Do" there in 1953. (In 1956, Rupe would send Sam Cooke to the studio to make his first secular recordings.)

Little Richard's first session for Specialty was produced by bandleader Bumps Blackwell, whom Rupe had just hired as an A&R man. Rupe saw Richard as possible competition for Ray Charles, who had come into his own with the record "I Got a Woman" in 1954 and was now a hot property for Atlantic. The pressure was on Blackwell to come back to L.A. with a hit. Blackwell recounted his version of what happened in Charles White's biography *Little Richard: The Quasar of Rock and Roll*.

"When I got to New Orleans, Cosimo Matassa . . . called and said, 'Hey, man, this boy's down here waiting for you.' When I walked in, there's this cat in this loud shirt, with hair waved up six inches above his head. He was talking wild, thinking up stuff just to be different, you know? I could tell he was a mega-personality."

They started recording the blues. Huey "Piano" Smith, who later wrote and performed on the New Orleans hits "Rockin' Pneumonia (And the Boogie Woogie Flu)," "Don't You Just Know It," and "Sea Cruise," was seated at the piano. His playing was light and precise. On "Lonesome and Blue" and "Wonderin'," the first two songs of the session, Richard's vocal seemed to mirror the piano: light, tasteful, reserved. "All Night Long," another nondescript blues, hinted at Richard's power. A midtempo "Kansas City" was somewhat promising, though the vocal wasn't nearly as kickass as the version he would record months later.

The first day, Richard and Blackwell left the studio with four pretty-good sides: well sung, but nothing special. They certainly weren't hits. Blackwell wasn't worried—yet. He had another day and four more songs to go.

But the next day the results were no better. Richard did his four songs, and though there were glimmers of magic, there was nothing that even whispered "hit." Blackwell was plenty worried now. In fact, he was scared. "So I'm thinking, Oh, Jesus. . . . You know what it's like when you don't know what to do? It's, 'Let's take a break. Let's go to lunch.' I had to think. I didn't know what to do. I couldn't go back to Rupe with the material I had."

So they took a break. Blackwell says they went to the Drop. (Drummer Earl Palmer says this is impossible because the Drop was too far away.) "We walk into the place. . . . There's a piano, and that's his [Richard's] crutch. He's on stage reckoning to show [saxophonist] Lee Allen his piano style. So *wow!* He gets to going. He hits that piano, didididididididididi . . . and starts to sing 'Awop-bop-a-loo-mop, a-good-goddamn—Tutti Frutti, good booty . . . ' I said, 'Wow. That's what I want from you Richard. That's a hit!'"

Richard had performed the song for a couple of years. He claimed he wrote it while washing dishes in a greasy spoon in his hometown of Macon, Georgia. It had a driving rhythm, but those lyrics: "Tutti Frutti, good booty/If it don't fit, don't force it/You can grease it, make it easy . . ." What radio station would play that?

Fledgling local writer Dorothy La Bostrie was at J&M earlier that day because Blackwell had Richard cut one of her songs, "I'm Just a Lonely Guy." Blackwell called Cosimo to see if she was still hanging around. She was. He told her to come down to the Drop right away. He needed her to write some lyrics to this tune Richard was playing. Suddenly it looked like there was light at the end of the tunnel. Then the train appeared.

"Well, Richard was embarrassed to sing the song and she [Dorothy] was not certain that she wanted to hear it. Time was running out, and I knew it could be a hit. I talked, using every argument I could think of. I asked him if he had a grudge against making money. I told her that she was over twenty-one, had a houseful of kids and no husband, and needed the money. And finally, I convinced them. Richard turned to face the wall and sang the song two or three times and Dorothy listened."

The musicians hustled back to the studio and quickly took their positions. Richard manned the piano (aural evidence suggests he'd been playing most of the day). His muscular style wasn't as "clean" as Huey Smith's, but it could drive a nail into a block of wood. They had fifteen minutes of session time left. Take one—no good. The second take sounded sloppy. Richard seemed unsure of all the words, and the arrangement needed cleaning up.

Five minutes of session time left. Take three: "Awop-bop-a-loo-mop, a-bop-bop-bop! Tutti Frutti! Aw-rooti!" From the opening line, take three was a monster. The hint of uncertainty in Richard's voice was gone. And after Lee Allen's brief sax solo, Richard came back strong, his playing and singing shifting the song into high gear. Like a hot rod with no brakes. The session wrapped with two minutes to spare. No sweat.

The result was perhaps the first true rock and roll record from beginning to end. With its nonsense lyrics, Richard's volcanic vocal, his pile-driving piano, plus Earl Palmer's whiplash drums (stripped down to match Richard's pounding left hand), it was like nothing put on record before. And even with the lyrics cleaned up for the radio, the record was still chock-full of rock and roll's not-so-top-secret ingredient: sex. As New Orleans' own Dr. John (Mac Rebennack) says, when he first heard "Tutti Frutti," he knew they weren't talking about ice cream.

Cosimo remembers getting goose bumps during Richard's sessions. "He was phenomenal. . . . He had what I call a 'Queen of the May' syndrome [meaning], he wanted to be the best. So he drove himself. He *drove* himself. . . . He bled on those records. And you can hear it."

By the time "Tutti Frutti" came out, J&M was making a name for itself—and to some, it wasn't necessarily a good one. Many whites referred to it as the "nigger studio," but Cosimo didn't care. As far as the musicians were concerned, Allen Toussaint remembers, "We were around the people we wanted to be around, and we were having a marvelous time. . . . As far as the racial thing, it never dawned on us when we got to the studio that Cosimo was white or anything like that. It just didn't feel like that then."

Not long after Little Richard's first session at J&M, there was a police raid on a bookie who lived above the studio. The cops were thorough and tore out the phones. Cosimo started looking for another place. He found it at 523 Governor Nicholls Street. This room was about twice as big as the first. But in a couple of years, he moved again, into the building right next door, at 525 Governor Nicholls. This room was huge—and the building even had parking in the back, a luxury in the densely packed French Quarter. Instead of J&M, the new studios were known simply as "Cosimo's."

"It was a cold-storage room for avocados," Cosimo recalls. "So here it is with three inches of real cork on the walls, on the floors, the ceiling, everything else. And it's thirty-five feet wide. It's about eighty feet long, and it had about a sixteen, seventeen-foot ceiling.

"All I did was put a room in at an angle. Build a control room. Never got to have air-conditioning. Used to bring in two tons of crushed ice and a window fan to cool the place down. Shut the window fan off while they're doing a take, then turn it back on. But if they're real close on the mic, sometime you'd leave the fan on." Coz laughs at the memory.

It was in the Governor Nicholls studios, sometimes under sweltering conditions, that New Orleans R&B reached its hit-making zenith. "Rip It Up," "Ready Teddy," "Lucille," and "Good Golly Miss Molly," by Little Richard. "I'm Walkin'," "I'm Gonna Be a Wheel Someday," "I'm Ready," "Walkin' to New Orleans," by Fats Domino. "Let the Good Times Roll," by Shirley and Lee. "Don't You Just Know It," by Huey "Piano" Smith and the Clowns. "Sea Cruise," by Frankie Ford. And these are only some of the records that took off before Allen Toussaint produced a string of hits that started a whole new era in the New Orleans sound.

Actually, Toussaint had been around for a while, first recruited by Dave Bartholomew to play piano on a Fats Domino track while "the Fat Man" was out on the road. He and Mac Rebennack (Dr. John) were only in their teens when they were picked to sit in on sessions at Coz's studio. "I'd become a session guy around seventeen and a half years old," says Toussaint in his formal, elegant fashion. "Mac [was there] around the same time. He was mostly guitar. Well, when *I* was there he played the guitar."

Both Cosimo and Dave Bartholomew would call Toussaint for session work. In 1958, RCA held open auditions at J&M, and Cosimo asked Toussaint to accompany the talent. Hopefuls were lined up around the block. At the end of three days, only one person got a contract—the piano player. RCA quickly released *The Wild Sounds of New Orleans* by Al Tousan (RCA execs decided "Toussaint" was too exotic). The album didn't do that well, although today it's a coveted collector's item, but it did produce a hit . . . for Al Hirt. He would record Toussaint's "Java" four years later.

In the meantime, Toussaint continued doing sessions at Cosimo's and leading jam sessions with his neighborhood friends, including Aaron Neville and Irma Thomas, in his parents' living room. In January 1960, a new local label called Minit Records held auditions at a New Orleans radio station. Aaron and Irma were each auditioning and wanted Allen to come down and play for them. He agreed, but once he got there, he wound up playing for everyone. Unlike RCA, Minit signed several of the singers who tried out, including Neville, Jesse Hill, Joe Tex, and Benny Spellman. And they also hired Toussaint to be their writer and arranger.

Now Cosimo's studio was filled with a new blend of loose, jivey rhythms, the musical creations of Allen Toussaint. And radio stations from coast to coast ate up the new platters coming out of the Crescent City. "Ooh Poo Pah Doo," by Jesse Hill. "Mother-in-Law" and "A Certain Girl," by Ernie K-Doe. "I Know," by Barbara George. "I Like It Like That," by Chris Kenner. "The Fortune Teller," by Benny Spellman.

"Baby, don't you wish your man had long hair like mine?" Don't mess with Little Richard, 1956.

107

J&M: Cosimo's Factory

"[Those sessions] were very live. Very red beans. Very meat and potatoes," remembers Toussaint. "We would congregate in my parents' living room and I would write a song for an artist and they would sing it. And whoever was around would sing backup. And then I'd write another song. Another song became four. . . . We'd do that in the living room and get up to a frenzy and have a good time and laugh with it and drink a Coca-Cola"—Toussaint smiles slyly— "and we would take that [energy] to the studio.

"I never knew that something was coming that would be called great later. I remember great feelings, how we felt at the time, but not as far as commercial success. Just didn't know about that. But I remember feeling good about Chris Kenner sessions, like 'Something You Got.' When we first did that, that just felt so good and funky. Just felt like this is who we are and where we should be."

To Cosimo, Toussaint was a creative wonder, making the most of the talent he had to work with. "He had a great ability to write good songs, great lyrics. I even wanted him to do a book of his songs. . . . But to me the most interesting thing was he almost always, with a few exceptions like Irma Thomas, picked people who were just ordinary singers. He would wrap them up in an arrangement that was just right for them." Coz kidded Toussaint, saying he could make a chicken out of a feather and a wishbone.

Toussaint reserved some of his best work for singer Lee Dorsey, who was the perfect vessel for Toussaint's musical brews. "Holy Cow," "Sneaking Sally through the Alley," "Ride Your Pony," "Yes We Can-Can," and "Working in a Coal Mine" were playful, wry songs that captured the humor and joy of both men.

"He was such a high spirit," Toussaint says of alter ego Dorsey. "A smile came with him. And not only was his face smiling, his whole movement, his whole attitude. . . . His voice had this kind of slight, almost a yodel in it. And it wasn't a debonair voice. It wasn't a crooner. It had some humor in it. Some fun. Let's laugh. And some blues. And I wrote things for him that I wouldn't dare write for most people, because most people think that they're too cool for most things. Lee Dorsey was cool but he was cool with a high spirit of freedom [so] that I could write 'I Took a Little Trip to Mexico' . . . he or I had no reason to think about Mexico. Or 'Working in a Coal Mine.' Me and Lee Dorsey? Working in a coal mine? *Please*."

But sadly, 1966, the year "Working in a Coal Mine" came out, was the last great year for Cosimo's studio. By then, many of the labels that had thrived on New Orleans music (Imperial, Specialty, Ace, Aladdin, Minit) were either out of business or in decline. With a sudden shortage of sessions, Cosimo started his own label, Dover, which quickly backed two big hits: "Barefootin'," by Robert Parker in 1966, and Aaron Neville's first smash, "Tell It Like It Is," in early 1967.

"Tell It Like It Is" was recorded at Cosimo's last studio—a converted warehouse at 748 Camp Street that Coz dubbed "Jazz City." Ironically, the success of Neville's huge hit spelled disaster for Cosimo. He fell deep into debt trying to keep up with supply and demand.

Distributors sent urgent requests for more copies of the record, but were predictably slow in paying Cosimo his royalties. At the same time local banks refused to lend Cosimo more money to press the records until he could start paying them back. He wound up losing just about everything, including the studio. The IRS closed it down, and the contents were sold at a sheriff's auction in 1969.

Until then, Cosimo's was so successful, and Cosimo himself was such a popular figure, that he remained the only real studio in town for more than twenty years. When he was shut down, Allen Toussaint and his partner, Marshall Seahorn, were forced to build their own studio, Sea-Saint, in what was once an old paint and lumber shed at 3809 Clematis Avenue. For a short while, Cosimo freelanced there, engineering sessions.

"Cosimo's was *the* studio," Toussaint insists today, "and if it wouldn't have been for him going out of business, we wouldn't have built one. Everyone was always satisfied with Cosimo's . . . I would be satisfied with Cosimo's today.

"Cosimo and Dave Bartholomew are the trailblazers. It all starts there. I can't imagine it all without Cosimo. And I don't mean 'a Cosimo,' but *him* in particular."

Toussaint's Sea-Saint Studio has an illustrious history of its own. For years, the Meters served as the house band. Paul Simon cut "Kodachrome" there. Paul McCartney came over to record the album *Venus and Mars*. It's where LaBelle wailed the original "Lady Marmalade." Toussaint continues to write and produce, mainly for NYNO Records, a label he co-owns, a label dedicated to the advancement of indigenous New Orleans music.

Cosimo Matassa, in spite of the incredibly low note that ended his career as a studio owner and engineer, is a happy man. A sparkle dances in his eyes. He smiles when he says he has no regrets. You know he means it. Today he runs two small markets in the French Quarter, where people come in to get their po' boys, some dessert, and maybe something to wash it all down. It's the same business his father was in. It's a good business.

Today, 838 N. Rampart, where it all began, is Hula Mae's Tropic Wash and Beach Café— a Laundromat that serves food. In the area of the actual studio at the back of the store, there's a counter where you can fold clothes. On the walls are pictures of Cosimo, Fats Domino, and others who played a part in the J&M story. Outside, locals who need to get their clothes clean step over the store's original marble skirt with "J&M Music Shop" written in bold '40s-style script. And on the outer wall by the front door there is a plaque designating the building as a landmark of New Orleans and Louisiana. It was put there on December 10, 1999, fifty years to the day after Fats Domino recorded "The Fat Man" back where the dryers now steadily hum.

Chess
RECORD ROW ROYALTY

On the South Side of Chicago, there are two seasons: dirty gray February, and greasy hot August. Tonight, it's the latter. Upstairs at 2120 South Michigan Avenue, at the tail end of Record Row, there's a session going down. It's 1957, and it is a typical evening for the dysfunctional Chess family.

Sonny Boy Williamson is set to record. The day before, he crawled through the sliding-glass partition—just like a damn dentist's office—over the secretary's desk, and proceeded to shout that he was looking for that motherfucker Leonard; he needed dough. Leonard Chess came out, like some bantamweight rooster with a polio peg. Threats and promises volleyed like gunfire.

Tonight both are back, with the usual cast of codependents. Fred Below on drums, Luther Tucker and Robert Lockwood, the youngun' and the old pro, on guitars. Otis Spann on piano. The one in the family who always holds it together, musically and emotionally, the chocolate Buddha, Willie Dixon, is on upright bass. All are stone Chess legends.

Sonny Boy, hip flask in hand, is in good form: "He got to the place where he could perform better by having a few drinks than without having a few drinks," related Dixon in his autobiography, *I Am the Blues*, "because I think his mind worked better."

Sonny Boy is telling Dixon and anyone else who cares to listen, "Keep them goddamn Chesses away from up here where I am! I'm going to record, and they ain't going to do nothing but make me mad."

"The first time I heard him sing, I thought the mic was busted": Howlin' Wolf at Chess, 1966.

Phil Chess, the good cop, the soft-touch brother, looks almost worried, but Leonard just waves his hand dismissively and chortles out cigarette smoke.

Engineer Malcolm Chisholm, behind his Bill Putnam–designed Universal console (Putnam was the owner/designer of both Universal and United Western studios, both considered among the best built studios ever, acoustically), is checking his levels on all eight inputs feeding the Ampex 350 two-track machine. There are some crickets in the basement's echo chambers; he sweeps them out and comes back. He and Leonard are in the cramped control room, about ten feet above the killing floor.

Sonny Boy is lubed and ready. Leonard is stoking his engine with Parliament cigarettes. Malcolm states: "We're rolling. Take one—"

Leonard cuts in on the talkback mic: "Whattsa name of this?"

Sonny Boy tries to stay composed, but this is just the kind of shit he was talking about.

"Little Village," he says. He stares that dead-man stare up through the glass where his nemesis sits, and waits for the reaction he knows is coming, which is stone silence.

"A Little Village, motherfucker, Little Village!" says Sonny Boy, losing it.

"There's nothin' in that motherfuckin' song about a village, you sonofabitch," Leonard retorts over the talkback.

The drummer, below, punctuates his laughter with the bass drum at the rear of the pitched-ceiling room.

Leonard continues, on a roll: "Nothing in that song that has got anything to do with a village."

"Well, a small town!" says Sonny Boy.

"I know what a village is—"

"Well, all right, goddamn it! You don't name it no town, you son of a bitch! When I get through with it, *you can name it your mammy!*"

Leonard has got to laugh.

The take starts and then stops. Too fast, all agree.

They try it again, slower. "Sonny Boy was pretty high," said Dixon years later, "and he was leaning against the isolation booth—it must have been seven feet tall, four inches thick, and rolled on wheels. Sonny must have fell against the booth; it sounded like the whole house was coming down—*bram!* They finished recording this thing with him on the floor."

The Chess story is such an American story. It's the story of the Illinois Central Railroad, and of the slaughterhouse. A story of switchblades and bankrolls, poets and shylocks.

It's a story of two idiosyncratic cultures—in an ongoing American experiment—fighting it out every day, and, in the process, making some of the freshest, most scathingly original music of the latter twentieth century.

The characters are sometimes noble and occasionally tragic, but always complex. The time and place, like Paris in the 1920s, are inextricable. This wasn't Paris, however.

Postwar Chicago was an interesting place. Always pragmatic, insular, the city was a place of contrasts. Nowhere was this contrast more evident than at Chess Studio, where the migrant communities of African Americans, who formed Chicago's own "Little Mississippi" village, were juxtaposed with the Jews from "the White Russia" of Motol, Poland.

These two discrete tribes fled plantation and pogrom for something—anything—better. The people who made records at 2120 South Michigan Avenue, records that continue to inspire and influence, were not slick people. This was the first generation, together in the city in a funky new age of discovery.

Chess Records, for all intents and purposes, was the fruit of six geniuses: Willie Dixon, Leonard Chess, Muddy Waters, Howlin' Wolf, and, later, Bo Diddley and Chuck Berry. What these very strong-willed individuals would create—however improbably—at Chess Studio in Chicago would provide the ultimate sonic bridge between acoustic blues and electric rock.

If these elements are reduced further, the two central protagonists become Chess and Dixon, as far apart as two Chicagoans, or, for that matter, *Homo sapiens*, can be. This colliding and collaborating of Jewish and African American cultures is at the core of the Chess story. For decades, both Jews and blacks—arguably America's two most persecuted communities—have been circling each other warily. Each suspicious, each covertly trying to gain from the other. Boxing fans witnessed this dance in the relationship between boxing legend Muhammad Ali and the late sportscaster Howard Cosell. They certainly used each other. Less easily understood was their mutual love for each other.

It's a struggle fraught with artistic wins and personal losses. Throughout recent history, deep wounds have been inflicted, specifically in the form of litigation. In the case of the families Dixon and Chess, both South Side Royalty, these wounds have yet to heal. The enmity that persists to this day is the blues version of the Montagues and the Capulets: the Chess story *is* Shakespeare, filtered through the pen of August Wilson.

It would be facile and condescending to say that Leonard Chess was the heavy, and that the black artists were innocent lambs led to their own financial slaughter. Facile, but maybe pretty damn close to the bone. (Charges of shady accounting practices have been leveled at virtually all the major labels of this era—from Atlantic to Motown. At Chess, it allegedly was not unusual for an artist to be given a Cadillac in lieu of publishing percentages.) What should be kept in mind, however, is that when talking about Chuck Berry, Bo Diddley, Leonard Chess, and Howlin' Wolf, one is invoking the names of the most elusive psyches in music. That's saying a lot.

The Chess brothers came to Chicago in 1928, settled on the West Side, and started their journey in the scrap business. They soon moved to the thriving South Side and opened a couple of liquor stores. They parlayed their revenues into a nightclub, the upscale Macamba Lounge, where musicians such as Ella Fitzgerald, Billy Eckstine, and Louis Armstrong performed. The Cottage Grove neighborhood, at 47th Street, was the heart of a swinging scene

that was more jazz than blues. This part of town became known as Bronzeville, and it was Chicago's Harlem. Clubs like the Macamba, the Club DeLisa, the Palm Tavern, the Triannon Ballroom, the Pershing, and perhaps the two most mythical of all, the Regal and the Savoy, were jumping, filled to capacity with sharply dressed denizens. The brothers were astute, watching the crowd for anything that was popular, meaning anything that made money.

They were into something good, and they wanted more of it. They saw the success that record labels such as Modern in Los Angeles were having with what was then called "race music," essentially, embryonic R&B. They saw the all-black crowds respond to certain types of music. They saw an opportunity and reached for the next level—recording hot new artists on their own label. The label that provided the "in" was Aristocrat, one of several small local labels that catered to a niche market. Leonard and Phil bought into—and, after a short while, gradually bought out—the original owners. Some Chicago labels, such as Mercury, were recording blues, but these acts were more national, as opposed to local blues artists, like Big Bill Broonzy, Memphis Minnie, Tampa Red, and Sunnyland Slim, all of whom were being recorded with modest success. (Blues records at this time were relatively well-produced affairs, more jump than grit, but that would change.) The Chess brothers moved somewhat desperately to acquire the contract of their first artist, Andrew Tibbs, before, they feared, he signed with Modern.

From the get-go, the records that Leonard and Phil released were challenging and fresh, to say the least. The very first single, by Tibbs, almost a half century before NWA would record "Fuck tha Police," was a hopeful ditty called "Bilbo's Dead," about the segregationist politician from Mississippi, Theodore Bilbo. It was banned in the South.

"Got My Mojo Workin'": Muddy and friends play cards between takes at Chess, mid-1960s.

The club scene flourished in these heady postwar years. Trains on the Illinois Central continued to deliver Southern blacks from Delta hamlets such as Glendora and Helena, Arkansas, and especially Clarksdale, Mississippi, to Chicago. These new migrants were lured by the stories they'd read in the *Chicago Defender*, the nation's premier black newspaper, about steady, well-paying (if brutal) jobs in Chicago's steel mills, stockyards, and slaughterhouses.

Occasionally, there was a specific breed of migrant who came north to Chicago. Not because it was the "Hog Butcher for the World," but because, in the tight-knit communities of the Delta, especially those who grew up on, or near, Colonel William Howard Stovall's plantation in Clarksdale, Chicago was seen as a promising place for blues musicians to play in the city's clubs and lounges. Or perhaps make a record.

One such migrant from Stovall's, a disciple of Son House and Robert Johnson, was McKinley Morganfield, a.k.a. Muddy Waters. Like so many others from Stovall's, including Pops Staples and B.B. King, Muddy grew up listening to the legendary radio broadcasts from Helena's KFFA of *The King Biscuit Time* shows, featuring Sonny Boy Williamson.

115

Chess: Record Row Royalty

Smithsonian folklorist Alan Lomax had ventured to Stovall's with his recording gear on more than one occasion, and he even got a couple of sides on Muddy in 1941. These recordings gave the twenty-six-year-old Muddy the confidence to take his acoustic guitar north to Chicago. The Delta had come to the City.

In his classic book *Deep Blues*, the late Robert Palmer described the intricacies that distinguish Delta blues:

> It seems simple enough—two identical lines and a third answering line make up a verse, there are no more than three chords and sometimes only one, melodies are circumscribed, rhythms are propulsively straightforward. Yet countless white musicians have tried to master it and failed, and Delta bluesmen often laugh among themselves, remembering black musicians from Alabama or Texas who just couldn't learn to play acceptably in the Delta style. Delta blues is a refined, extremely subtle, and ingeniously systematic musical language. The fine points have to do with timing, with subtle variations in vocal timbre, and with being able to hear and execute, vocally and instrumentally, very precise gradations in pitch that are neither haphazard waverings nor mere effects.

In a matter of weeks since disembarking the Illinois Central in May of 1943, Waters was playing at "rent parties," where a small entrance fee was paid to help the host defray housing expenses. He graduated to small clubs on the West Side where, for the first time, he was fronting a band. But there was a significant change in his sound. He still used the bottleneck, a signature of the Delta bluesmen, for a slide effect, but Muddy, who had rapidly assembled a killer band, had to forgo his acoustic guitar. It wasn't getting heard in the smoky, noisy clubs of the city. So Muddy electrified his sound, the band got tighter, and the mournful, suspicion-and-sex-soaked music from the Delta was forever changed.

"All of the musicians that came to Chess were always by recommendation," said Malcolm Chisholm, engineer for Chess from 1957 to 1960, and again from 1967 to the early 1970s. "The Chess brothers were unique; they trusted the endorsements from their artists. That was good enough for them." Sunnyland Slim told Leonard about Muddy. A few years later, Muddy would tell Leonard about Chuck Berry. From Muddy Waters, Chess's favorite son, on down to the end of the line in the early '70s, this would be the rule.

In the spring of 1948, Muddy's first smash for the Chess brothers (released on the recently acquired Aristocrat label) was "I Can't Be Satisfied," a slashing bit of sexual chest thumping that served as the clarion call for other blues performers. The word was out—Chess was the shit, the label for this new, juiced-up Delta sound. Everyone wanted in, and the brothers, refashioned as record men, kept adding more pawns to the Chess set.

Little Walter was typical of the first era of Chess recording artists. A man who was restlessly creative—"he always be thinkin', thinkin' new ways to do things"—Muddy related to

116

Robert Palmer years later, he got off the train in Chicago and immediately headed for the legendarily funky flea market on Maxwell Street, or "Jewtown," as it was, and is, known in the black community. He busked his first day, making "three cigar boxes full of money." He joined up with Muddy and provided an innovation that was as startling as Muddy's newfound electricity. He had amplified his harmonica, but that was no big deal: Willie Dixon had seen Sonny Boy amplify his harp as early as the 1930s. What created a sensation in the blues clubs wasn't merely Walter's cranked-up harp, but the fact that it was becoming a lead instrument in the band, à la Louis Jordan's saxophone. This pairing of Muddy's electric and Walter's distorted harp would be the blueprint of the sound that the world has come to recognize as Chicago Blues.

This electric, distorted, defiantly sexual music has proliferated so much that virtually all rock music made today contains traces of these Chess masterpieces from half a century ago. It can be heard in tracks from Steely Dan to Led Zepplin, but it has most strongly affected Eric Clapton and the Rolling Stones, the latter having made a lucrative and storied career out of anglicizing the Chess records made in the 1950s and 1960s. In fact, were it not for the zeal with which Keith Richards, Mick Jagger, and Brian Jones absorbed and assimilated these Chess records, it is unlikely that 2120 South Michigan Avenue, or Chicago Blues in general, would be as universally known today.

In the early days, from 1948 through 1956, Chess recorded almost exclusively at Universal, first at the Civic Opera House location and, finally, the great Universal A studio that Bill Putnam had built in the North Side's Rush Street district. Leonard Chess, always mindful of the bottom line, realized he needed to vertically integrate, meaning he wanted a cool studio of his own where the artists could make music without the clock ticking so loudly. And he knew just the spot: Record Row, the area on South Michigan Avenue that was becoming the center of all things music.

"Record Row was the scene," says Jerry Butler, one of the first soul singers who recorded for Vee-Jay, Chess's only real rival on the Row. "[It]went from just south of the Loop [12th Street], all the way down to [23rd Street] where Chess was. There was always something happening, and we threw the best parties."

Labels, distributors, coffee shops, rehearsal spaces, and studios merged in a swirling mocha of music machinery. The labels with ties on the Row were not only the big boys, like Mercury or Capitol, but also the indies, such as One-Derful, Brunswick, King, Constellation, and Vee-Jay. Everyone had a scam or a hit. If you had a hit, you didn't need a scam. If you had a scam, you might wind up owning that hit.

"Guys would go up and down the aisles of the coffee shops, pitching their songs. They might sell the same song two or three times over," chuckled Phil Chess in the wonderful documentary *Record Row*.

For Chess people, the hangout where deals got done—whether it was it was a publishing deal, gambling debt, or girlfriend dilemma—was Batts Restaurant ("Next to Home . . . it's Batts"), where a buck thirty-five got you the Mama Batts's special: meat blintzes with apple-sauce and fries. This was directly across the street from 2120, at the New Michigan Hotel. The food from Batts would be the solid sustenance that fueled these artists.

In the summer of 1957, Chess opened its own studio. The records made there in the decade from 1957 to 1967 are the cornerstone of the Chess legacy. And although Chess is famous for electrifying the sound of the Delta, blues was, in reality, only one aspect of the Chess juggernaut.

It is indisputable: there is no one label that had as much impact on the development of rock from the 1950s to the 1970s as Chess. Rock and roll was, if not created at 2120, certainly nurtured there into the music that gave anyone under twenty a reason to live. If only for the legacy of Bo Diddley, whose "shave and a haircut" groove has served as one of the rhythmic touchstones of rock, and Chuck Berry, whose witty lyrics and country-boogie guitar riffs remain unequalled, Chess's place in rock history is secure.

Under the Chess umbrella, subsidiary labels such as Argo, Aristocrat, Checker, and Cadet made seminal records in jazz (Ramsey Lewis's "The In Crowd" continues to score in movies); pop (Fontella Bass's "Rescue Me" contains the most recognizable bass line this side of Motown); gospel (the Reverend C. L. Franklin was a mainstay, and his baby girl, Aretha, actually started out recording with Chess); doo-wop (the Dells' "There Is" is widely consid-ered a masterpiece of the genre); comedy (Moms Mabley and Pigmeat Markham); and hard soul, epitomized by the mighty wailings of Etta James.

Once again, the shadow of Bill Putnam looms. Leonard, from the days at Universal, had gotten to know Putnam's staff of gifted young engineers. Two of them, Malcolm Chisholm and Jack Weiner, would figure prominently in the overall design of the Chess space and the sound of its records.

Built in 1911, the edifice at 2120 was long and narrow, approximately 25 feet wide and 125 feet deep from Michigan Avenue to the alley behind. The building was vacant and in need of repair, just the investment property that Leonard had been looking for. Weiner was only twenty-two when he was charged with the task of building the new studio. He had never done that sort of work before; prior to this, he was the in-house mastering engineer at Universal. He had learned whatever room design he knew from—you guessed it—Bill Putnam.

"Weiner was a nice guy, and he did a not-bad job with the space," Chisholm recalls. "But at first I looked [at the space] and thought, 'Ye gads, it's too bloody small!'"

Weiner, who passed away in the mid-'90s, was reportedly less than thrilled with the new digs, but the studio space, roughly twenty by thirty-seven, would have to do. Remembering the job Putnam had done with Universal, Weiner covered the original wood on the second floor with two inches of cork, over which he laid concrete. The walls were "floated," or spring mounted, to better insure against vibrations from the street. Also similar to Universal were

the nine variable panels on the south wall that could be opened for a more absorptive, dead sound, or closed for a reflective live feel. Weiner also put two echo chambers in the basement. Guitar, vocals, or harmonica signals from the Universal console upstairs would feed the chambers via RCA 77 ribbon microphones, giving the records being cut upstairs an open, smooth feel.

Although the Chess stable boasted the world's greatest blues harpists, here the Wolf proudly blows his own, ca. 1965.

Today, Malcolm Chisholm takes another drag on his cigarette and says, "You cannot live without ribbon microphones. We had lots and lots of them at Chess, along with some nice Altecs and some Telefunkens [very expensive and sought-after German microphones]. Chambers are notorious for sucking up [using] too much top end; once you rolled off the low end it [the reverb] sounded quite nice."

One unusual design feature was the staircases leading up to the studio. From the reception area on the first floor, the stairs leading to the studio split off in two directions, one leading to the studio itself, the other to the control room. In years since, the myth has been that Leonard wanted this split so that the musicians (mostly black) and the technicians (white) would have minimal interaction. Like many Chess myths with racial overtones, this has been debated down the years.

The first floor was gutted and given a new exterior in keeping with the times: the storefront was swathed in aluminum and recessed at an angle, with the words *Chess Producing Corp.* emblazoned across the front. Inside, a ribbed-glass reception area with sliding glass panels

119

Chess: Record Row Royalty

revealed secretaries who announced visitors to the inner sanctum, which included the California redwood–trimmed office of Leonard.

The first sessions at 2120 were by the old hands who had put Chess on the map: Bo Diddley with his rap precursor, "Say Man," and Howlin' Wolf's "Sitting on Top of the World." On the outside looking in—as a freelancer—was the man who would be more responsible for Chess's legacy than anyone: Willie Dixon.

Dixon, like so many others, had made the journey up from the Delta. He traded in his boxing gloves for a bass that was made for him out of a washtub, broomstick, and string. From these scraps, Dixon, who would in time buy a proper upright, played bass on recordings by everyone who would become a Chess legend: the Wolf, Muddy, Chuck Berry, Bo Diddley, and on and on. In the cases of Muddy, Wolf, and others, he was even the composer of their biggest hits. However, Dixon not only wrote and played on many of these records, he was also de facto producer, although credit for producing and sometimes even authorship was allegedly given to the Chesses.

Willie Dixon was unique not only because he was so utilitarian, but because among Chess artists, he alone rebuked Leonard's penurious practices. He had gone to a small label, Cobra, for the latter half of the 1950s, then begrudgingly returned to Chess, but he refused to kiss any behinds, least of all Leonard's.

That Dixon is not well known outside of the blues community, let alone mentioned in the same breath as Armstrong or Ellington, is a damn shame. The author of more than five hundred songs, covered by everyone from Cream to Rod Stewart to Bonnie Raitt, he was to Chess Records what Brian Wilson was to the Beach Boys.

"Leonard died not knowing how smart Will Dixon was," Malcolm Chisholm says today. "Will didn't act or sound like a producer. He was very low key in dealing with the musicians, but they always listened to what he said because of the immense respect they had for him."

One common misconception is the idea that the Chess sound was raw and gutsy. Along with the view that Chess made mostly blues records, this is myth more than truth. In fact, not only are there many genres of Chess records, there also are a few different types of sounds. Most longtime engineers and producers will tell you that the studio, in fact, doesn't affect the sound of the recording nearly as much as the players and the arrangement do. This was also the case at Chess, but then again, most engineers are too modest to acknowledge the significance they assume. With the same arrangement, players and room can sound vastly different depending on who is at the board. The Chess releases can be stratified into roughly four categories: the early years of 1948 through 1957 (mostly, if not all recorded at Universal); the early 2120 days of 1957 to 1960 (mostly engineered by Chisholm); the years between 1960 and 1967; and, finally, those records done at the wane of Chess in its new space, around the corner from 2120 at the 321 East 21st Street studio.

The records made at 2120 between 1960 and 1967 are not only not raw, they are among

the most high-fidelity recordings of the era. Credit for that must go to an engineer who has not received his due, the late Ron Malo. "Ron Malo was an exceptional engineer," says colleague Chisholm, "but he was a total control freak." Most great recording engineers are, in truth, total control freaks.

Muddy, Willie Dixon, and young turk Buddy Guy, laying down a track for Muddy's back-to-basics album, *Folk Singer,* 1963.

The early Chess recordings, including those done by Chisholm between 1955 and 1960, are gut-bucket raw, aurally akin to the sound Sam Phillips produced at Sun. Whereas Phillips's tiny storefront studio worked as a compressor to make the music feel more explosive, the Chess era of the mid to late '50s feels very plug-in-and-go. There is no attempt at anything artful; the amazing songs of Bo Diddley, Chuck Berry, and the rest do all the work.

After Chisholm left in 1960 to join Putnam at United Western, the man who had designed 2120, Jack Weiner, was left to record the music. This arrangement lasted only briefly, however, and the reasons—artistic, philosophical, or financial—for his departure from Chess remain, like so many other instances, a matter of speculation. What cannot be disputed is the detail, depth, and imaging of the tracks that Malo cut starting in 1960.

There are two records that demonstrate the sonic excellence that Malo achieved. The first is by Chester Burnett, known as Howlin' Wolf. The Wolf's records are almost more rock than blues in feel. His music is the sound of razor blades, fierce and cutting. On "Killing Floor," his own composition from 1964, the sound is spacious and wide, with Buddy Guy's

121

acoustic guitar perfectly balanced with the amazing Hubert Sumlin's fluid ax. Anchoring the track is a solid low end of bass and drums, with the midrange covered by two saxes along with legend Lafeyette Leake's piano. Right in your face is the always menacing voice of the Wolf ("The first time I heard the Wolf sing, I thought the mic was busted," says Chisholm). The sound is clean, driving, and fresh as this morning.

By 1963, the times they were a-changin', and Chess released an album that was regarded as something of a novelty at the time, *Muddy Waters Folk Singer*. (Chess, trying to compete in the new frontier of the '60s, would brazenly stamp records with the stylistic trend du jour. As incompatible as Muddy and folk appeared to be as bedfellows, try *Twistin' with Muddy*, or even the bad acid trip that was *Electric Mud*. Ouch.) Regardless of the title, *Folk Singer* displays perhaps the most empathetic rhythmic support ever heard on record, with Dixon on upright bass, young turk Buddy Guy on acoustic guitar, and yet another Chess giant, Clifton James, on skins. The cover of the LP features photos where Dixon, Guy, and Waters are seen leaning in the same direction, eyes closed, beatitude on their faces. Muddy Waters had come home.

From the opening track, "My Home Is in the Delta," to the end, this is a marriage that lasts. It's the sound that records have when everything—the lighting in the room, the material, the players, the engineer—are in perfect alignment. Never will a listener hear so much heavy space on disc. On a few tracks, Muddy simply and eloquently plays his acoustic and moans, sounding not unlike what Alan Lomax had documented back on Colonel Stovall's plantation.

This was, in a sense, the swan song for Muddy and Willie at Chess. Rock was taking over via the Rolling Stones and the Beatles. Muddy would ironically record less and less while becoming more and more famous. Willie, with classics like "Spoonful," "Back Door Man," "The Red Rooster," "I Just Want to Make Love to You," and dozens more tunes being covered by rock bands, would also become an international blues legend, but his nonelectric bass and his refusal to do anything musically trendy kept him from getting first call for sessions.

Shortly after *Folk Singer* was finished, the Stones began making pilgrimages to 2120. Among the more prominent tales of Chess, Keith Richards relates: "We walked in and there was this guy up on a ladder, painting the ceiling. We looked up, and it was Muddy! Here was the guy who made Chess records, and they had him painting—what a disgrace."

The Stones recorded the better part of the *12x5* album at 2120, which, fittingly, had an instrumental titled simply "2120." They would also record basic tracks of a song that would catapult them from blues cover band into rock icons, "(I Can't Get No) Satisfaction," a tip of the hat to the guy they saw on the ladder painting, the man who had started the Chess express an epoch before with a song called "I Can't Be Satisfied."

In 1969, Leonard Chess, the life force behind his namesake, died. The company, now run by brother Phil and son Marshall, became rudderless. As one musician said, "Without Leonard, there ain't no Chess." In a few short years, the incomparable Chess catalog of blues, jazz, gospel, doo-wop, comedy, soul, and rock would be sold to the GRP consortium.

Today, after decades of neglect, ownership of 2120 has been taken over by Willie Dixon's widow, Marie, who has restored it to its original splendor. The Blues Heaven Foundation, a not-for-profit organization designed to educate the world about the blues (and, more to the point, to educate musicians on legal and financial issues), is headquartered there in a particularly sweet example of poetic justice.

Universal
WINDY CITY SOUL

Imagine a long, fluid tracking shot, like the one in *Goodfellas*, or better yet, the great opening shot in *Touch of Evil*. It's the ring-a-ding-ding '60s, Chicago style.

We start out at the Playboy Mansion (pre-Viagra Hefner, back when orgies meant something), then zoom up the Glitter Gulch, where State hits on Rush. There's Mr. Kelly's. We see a nebbish comic from New York, named Woody (whose new flick, *What's up, Tiger Lily?* is a gasser), he's opening for Miss Sarah. Across the way, there's Ramsey Lewis, in with the in crowd at the Happy Medium. Pan over there—we see the Jazz Unlimited, the Gate of Horn, Hotsy Totsy, the Zebra Lounge, the Domino Lounge. Wiseguys and sophisticates cross on cue. Downstairs, next to Bragno's Liquors, it's the original Playboy Club, tonight featuring Skitch Henderson. Finally, we track upstairs, to Putnam's new house on the corner of Rush and Walton, the Magnificent Universal Studio A. The players are in place; we start the scene.

The smoothest soul anyone ever heard is being laid down up there by a boxer named Major Lance, who can dance but not really sing. It doesn't matter, he's in the best of hands. The track, a Spanish-tinged thing called "Monkey Time," was written by local boy wonder Curtis Mayfield. The arranger is the venerable Johnny Pate, who does all of Curtis's stuff these days. Producing is the man with the big ears, the one who hears hits where others don't, Carl Davis, the steward of Chi-Soul. Behind the board, naturally a custom Universal console, is the young kid from Minnesota, the Swede called Swedein.

Another night, another dance craze, another effortless smash.

Universal Recording, in the belly of Chicago's swingin' Rush Street scene, was the right place at the right time, built by the right guy. This wasn't some old factory or church reconfigured. This was one of the first modern studios designed from the ground up to record music. The music that was recorded in this room would provide an aural bridge in the evolution from swing to soul. Universal is where Bruce Swedein cut his teeth. It's where he would join forces with Quincy Jones to form one of the greatest producer/engineer combos in recording history. But it was his mentor, the man he calls "the father of modern recording"—driven, garrulous, chain-smoking Bill Putnam—who created what Swedein calls "the most magnificent room ever."

Of all the legends interviewed for this book, one man is mentioned repeatedly, whether by Cosimo Matassa in New Orleans, Sam Phillips in Memphis, or Phil Ramone in New York. When it came to audio, when it came to sound, there was nothing Bill Putnam couldn't do, and do better than it had ever been done, be it mixes, console design, speaker and EQ innovations, acoustic design, client relations . . .

"He smoked cigarettes and, like me, he was a night owl," says the affable Swedein. "Very, very gregarious. Open. Did not believe in secrets. Would tell you anything. He knew who he was, but Bill was, oh, man, I just can't say enough. He's my mentor. He gave me the kick in the ass," he gushes years later.

Unlike today, when the recording industry has spawned billion-dollar sales as well as millions of dollars via recording schools, back in the day, most of the engineering pioneers were autodidacts, guys who had glommed on to all things audio/electronic at an early age. Bill Putnam was one of these guys. He was born in 1920 in Danville, Illinois, to a heritage that seemed to predestine his future. His father was a businessman who also produced a top-rated country music radio show. As a boy, he built his own crystal radio sets and a one-tube radio. He got his ham radio operator's license (wouldn't it be interesting if today's up-and-coming engineers had to get certified in this stuff?) and was soon building and repairing equipment. His music, business, and technical interests flowered while he was in high school, when he sang in local dance bands and rented out P.A. systems he had repaired. Technical college, work at radio stations, and a stint at radio engineering for the army during World War II preceded his entry into studio ownership. He dreamed of developing new recording techniques and designing highly efficient modern audio gear for a new age of recording. With staggering swiftness, he would become the singular force in modern recording technology. Putnam, who passed away in 1980, said simply, "We started from scratch in the good old American tradition: with an idea and a will that it become a reality."

Putnam started the Universal Recording Corporation in 1946 in Evanston, Illinois, birthplace of the Hammond organ. It was around this time that Universal Audio (which later crystallized into UREI, the now legendary line of audio equalizers, speakers, limiters, etc.)

126

was formed to provide studios with new solutions to old problems. Within a year, he relocated his business to Chicago, a few miles south, where he set up his first studio in a most unlikely locale: the top floor of the august Civic Opera House. Like the rest of America, Chicago had no facilities in which to record modern music properly. A line of demarcation between old and new was being drawn, and the stick in the sand was held by Putnam.

Most great engineers have that one "moment," that one record that catapults both the studio and its operator into the stratosphere. In the case of Putnam and Universal, which would record many of the greatest pop and jazz musicians of the twentieth century, that moment arrived not with a musician possessing a horn, guitar, or golden voice. It was three fellows with harmonicas. This sonic epiphany occurred in 1947, on a recording that was so different, so gorgeous, it simply slapped the ears of those early pioneers, such as Ramone, Matassa, and Phillips. The record was by a group that has since retreated into obscurity, the Harmonicats, three Chicagoans who played chromatic harmonicas. The song was their version of "Peg o' My Heart." It was pleasant enough, as instrumentals go, but it was the sound–specifically, the heavenly, lush sprawl of the reverberation–that grabbed the listener. One such listener was a young Minnesotan.

"That record, you see, was the first time that anyone used reverb artistically," says Swedein. "Up 'til then, people used reverb only to re-create the sound of the studio; they tried

Putnam's custom Universal console at rest, ca. 1950s. The room and console combo was a pinnacle of recording innovation, heard in the swing of records by the Count Basie and Duke Ellington big bands and in the Chicago soul of Curtis Mayfield and the Impressions.

127

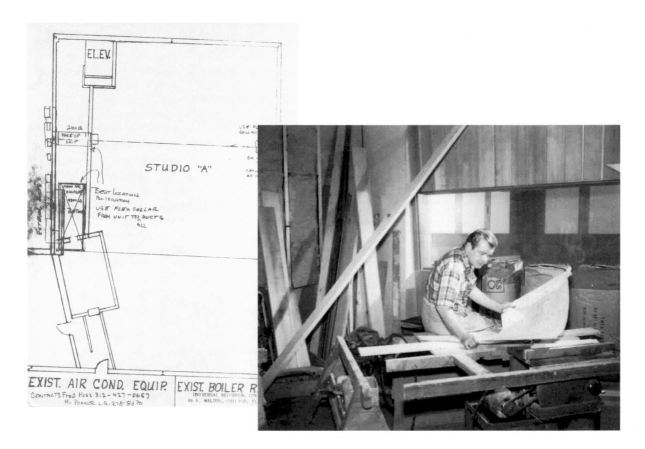

CONTRACTS FRED MOSS 312-427-0657
M. POENER L.A. 278-5370

UNIVERSAL RECORDING CORP.
46 E. WALTON, CHICAGO, IL

The man with the plan. Putnam goes over blueprints for Universal A, perhaps his greatest studio, 1957.

to use it in a 'natural' manner. Bill changed all that. That record sounded unlike anything on the radio at that time. I was just a youngster in Minneapolis when I first heard it, and I wore out many, many copies of that record."

"Peg o' My Heart," which sold well over a million copies, was a first. For the legendary echo, Putnam had utilized neither a high-tech plate nor an acoustically designed echo chamber. Instead, Putnam, soon to become the most revered name in audio innovation, went to the bathroom at the Opera House.

"Bill would put up a sign saying Wet Paint or Men at Work outside the rest room, so they could use it as a chamber," says Swedein. "Sometimes they'd be recording, with a speaker and a mic in there, and people would ignore the sign, and you had the sound of a flushing toilet on a take." On "Peg," the remarkably smooth, natural decay of the rest room's marble tiles, coupled with the comb-filter cotton candy of the chromatic harmonicas, combined to transport the listener into the ether. This recording spurred the youngster to meet its maker. "My parents were tired of hearing 'Bill Putnam this, Bill Putnam that,' so when they went to Chicago for a business trip, they decided to give Bill a call at Universal. Well, Bill took my parents, who were total strangers, right in to the session, introduced them to Patti Page. They got to sit in on a session with Bill!" he says, still incredulous.

As Putnam's credits grew, Universal was garnering serious buzz. The bank book also grew, as Putnam's business acumen helped fill the coffers. He financed the recording of "Peg"

128

for a nice piece of the profits and even had a million-dollar record, Al Morgan's *Jealous Heart*, on his short-lived Universal Records label. This shrewd business sense would become a Putnam hallmark just as surely as his technical achievements would.

Patti Page, Dinah Washington, and the fabulous Vic Damone were followed into Universal by names so big only one was required: Muddy, Ella, Count, Nat, Dizzy, Sarah, Duke. With this level of record making and a stunning list of technical firsts, such as the use of tape repeats, half-speed mastering, and vocal booths, Putnam and Universal were on the map big time. By the mid-'50s, Putnam had set his sights on building the greatest studio in the world.

"Lemme tell you something: that's a world-class studio," says Swedein, significantly still using the present tense. "Those studios were built with some incredible technology. For instance, the studios were built on four or five inches of cork. A cement slab was then floated [suspended] inside the building that did not touch the walls of the building, and then the wall of the studio was supported by that slab. There was no physical contact between the outer walls and the inner walls. This was all Bill's design. I think [famous acoustic architects] Bolt, Brannick, and Newman, 'borrowed' his designs. A huge studio, about eighty feet by sixty feet, with a thirty-foot ceiling, it had variable acoustics with rotating panels. Magnificent room.

"The console was, of course, custom-made. At the time, you couldn't go out and buy a

129

console, so we literally went out and built them all. The consoles that Bill Putman [built], well, we all worked on them. It had twelve inputs, with rotary faders, and was designed around mono. Prior to that, there were [only] two channels—stereo—and, In 1959, when we were doing this, there was no release medium for stereo, no wide release. There were a couple of labels just messing around. Bill Putman, to me, is truly the father of recording, because many of the techniques, and, indeed, the way [modern audio] equipment is made, began in his mind. Stuff we take for granted, like the design of modern consoles, how the components are laid out and how they function, cue [headphone] sends, echo sends and returns, multitrack switching—this all came out of his imagination."

With Universal and the burgeoning UREI both growing fast, Putnam needed help. Swedein recalls, "Bill called me up in 1957, and told me he was building a new facility in Chicago, at 46 East Walton. He told me he needed a mixer, a young guy, for Studio B. Studio A was a gigantic room, but B wasn't finished yet. He got me a job with RCA for eleven months doing things like the Chicago Symphony Orchestra with Fritz Reiner. Finally, in 1958, I got the job at Universal. In those days, Chicago was a real center for recording; every major band or musical act in the late '50s recorded in Chicago."

When the young engineer from Minnesota, at Putnam's suggestion, casually threw up a rough mix during a tour of Universal, the clarity of sound emanating from the control room simply floored the staff who heard it. Putnam, who would mentor and train perhaps more great recording engineers than anyone, had found his first acolyte.

"I think Bill must have believed in me, but Studio A was finally built and my job was kind of following Bill around, helping and learning. I would do part of a session and he would sit in the back and smoke a cigarette."

Unbeknownst to Swedein, the baton was being passed—along with Putnam's golden Rolodex of clients. But every engineer who has ever assisted a mentor has endured that baptismal moment when they must fly solo. Legends have legendary baptisms.

"[Putnam] started one song, this was with Stan Kenton and the band, and he must have worked this out with Kenton beforehand. He started to sit down and [track the] song, and he gets up and says, 'Okay, Bruce, you finish this one. I've got to go pee-pee.' I was terrified. He left the control room at Studio A and I didn't see him again for five years."

For Swedein, the guy who would go on to engineer the biggest-selling album in history, Michael Jackson's *Thriller*, the guy who has worked in every studio one could care to name, his first and most enduring love, it seems, is Universal A. Back in Chicago, back in the day: "Universal was right in the middle of it [Rush Street]. I would record them [great musicians] during the day, and then [my wife] Bea would come to meet me, and we would go out for dinner and go to Mr. Kelly's and hear them at night. I remember with Basie's band, probably more than others, there would be these . . . I used to call them 'band flies' . . . these people who would come from the club [with the band]. When we did this particular album, *Nothing but the*

Blues, the idea was to have the band play the club date and then come to the studio. So the sessions didn't start until 2 A.M. and lasted 'til dawn . . . and a lot of the people from the club just came with the band. So what I did was set up chairs around the outside of the studio and I thought to myself, 'Oh, shit, now I'm in trouble.' But you know, it's funny, I don't remember one instance where anyone [was] making a noise or creating a problem. People would be carrying on with jokes and everything, but Basie would raise his hand, and say, 'Let's do it,' and there would be absolute silence. Dead silent. And we'd do a take.

"This was 1960, and it was coincidentally the first [recording] that I did on three-track [Ampex 300]. What I wanted to do was to have myself, or my personality, be a part of the sound field. So there was this piece of music, 'The Nighttime Is the Right Time.' Joe Williams sang. Count Basie starts out with an intro with muted trombone playing close to the mic, and then Joe Williams does a verse, then there's a trombone solo, and I thought, 'Wouldn't it be great'— and it was very open, the Basie sound was very, very open, lots of space—'Geez, why don't we put this trombone solo outside the orchestra.' So what I did was, I told [trombonist] Penny Reed, 'OK, when it comes time to play your trombone solo, get up, tippy-toe over to the corner of the studio.' It was a huge room. Remember, it was seventy-five or eighty feet long with a thirty-foot ceiling. A big, big studio. I said, 'Tippy-toe over there and play your solo into the corner of the studio away from all the microphones,' and everybody said, 'What?' It ended up coming out all right, though; that's still one of my favorite albums.

"I would do those sessions, and I'd drive home just as the sun was coming up over Lake Michigan. What a feeling."

Most of the music being recorded at Universal at this time could be divided into these camps: the major labels such as Mercury/Verve (Sarah Vaughan, Oscar Peterson), Chess (Muddy Waters, Little Walter, Bo Diddley), the late great Vee-Jay (Jimmy Reed, Gene Chandler, Jerry Butler, the Four Seasons), and the indies, as personified by the Okeh and One-Derful labels. Not counting the Chess studio, which by the late '50s started its own historic room at 2120 South Michigan (built and staffed largely by Putnam protégés), Universal was it. Chess, Vee-Jay, and all of the indies lined South Michigan Avenue, which became known as "Record Row."

From the stomp of Kenton, Basie, and Ellington to the standards by Sarah Vaughan and Nat Cole, from the teen pop of Lesley Gore and the Four Seasons to the blues of Jimmy Reed and Muddy Waters, the room on Rush Street heard it all. But it's a sadly forgotten genre of music that would be born and raised there, the singular beauty known as Chicago Soul.

"You see, there is a Philly sound, but with Chicago, it's *sounds*," says Jerry Butler, who was credited in *Rolling Stone* as having the first soul record ever, 1959's *For Your Precious Love*. "We [Chicago] have a whole variety of influences. You've got the gospel of the Staple Singers [indeed, the man called the "father of gospel," Thomas A. Dorsey, is from Chicago], you got all those cats like Muddy and Willie Dixon and Jimmy Reed coming up from Mississippi,

131

doing that Delta Blues stuff, and then you've got this strong jazz influence. So it isn't just one sound, or any one arranger or producer."

A sea change was occurring in Chicago's demographics. In 1940, for example, there were approximately 220,000 blacks in the city. By 1960, this number had swelled to 887,000, with most migrating from five southern states: Mississippi, Tennessee, Alabama, Georgia, and Louisiana. In music circles, Chicago became known as "Little Mississippi." This demographic shift would result, musically, in two fresh new schools of American music: the cranked-up electric blues of Chess Records, and Chicago Soul. Practically every guitarist worth his or her weight in stomp boxes can tell you about Chicago Blues, and most old-schoolers can identify a Philly sound or a N'awlins sound, but few today are familiar with Chicago Soul.

What is the Chicago Soul sound? It's not as bouncy as Philly, nor as assembly-lined as Motown, but neither is it as gritty as Memphis Soul or as funky as the New Orleans stuff. It's intimate and breezy at the same time, yet smooth as single-malt Scotch. It's the alloy of church, lounge, and Delta. You can hear Chicago Soul in these recordings: "Ooh Child," by the Five Stairsteps; "Woman's Got Soul," by the Impressions; "Turn Back the Hands of Time," by Tyrone Davis; "Oh, Girl," by the Chi-lites; or any "dusty" you choose to hear by sadly forgotten artists like Walter Jackson or the Dells. It's a solid rhythm section where nothing sticks out. There's piano, some guitar, some vibes. The backbeat is no big deal. Neither are the strings and horns, but they're always there, making the bed. No, in Chicago Soul, the whole deal is the singer, really. (In fact, Chicago's legacy of vocalists is arguably as rich as that of any city in the United States. Consider, for example, a list of singers from there: Sam Cooke, Lou Rawls, Mahalia Jackson, Mavis Staples, Johnny Hartman, Dinah Washington, Nat "King" Cole, Anita O' Day, Jerry Butler, Mel Torme, Chaka Khan, Minnie Riperton, Big Joe Williams . . . and, um, R. Kelly and Billy Corgan. Well, you get the idea.)

Jerry Butler, the "Iceman," the sort of man who captures sentiments, whether sung or spoken, with simple eloquence, puts it right: "In Chicago, there are storytellers, not singers. A story is always being told." No storyteller of the '60s is as closely identified with Chicago Soul as Curtis Mayfield. In fact, Mayfield is to Chicago Soul what Allen Toussaint is to New Orleans R&B—an idiosyncratic visionary whose musical juxtaposition causes the listener to suspend their disbelief. If Toussaint, a dapper gent, seems an unlikely candidate to write about "working in a coal mine," equally improbable, and equally delightful, is the case of Mayfield, the chubby kid from the Chicago projects, singing about gypsies, madrigals, and Spanish isles.

"You see, Curtis was always a reader," says Jerry Butler. "His mother got him reading fairy tales and such at an early age. One day I got to Curtis and said, 'Hey man, that fairy tale stuff is cool and all, but you need to write about what is going on in the street.' Next thing you know, songs like 'It's All Right' and 'Keep On Pushing' came out."

Mayfield came of age singing with Jerry Butler in church choirs. The sanctified vocal

132

sound of their group, the Impressions, got the ear of Calvin Carter, A&R man, producer, and life force behind Vee-Jay Records. The story of Carter and Vee-Jay
would itself make for a great book. It would be a sad story, though. Vee-Jay was
modeled after Motown, but at one time, in the early '60s, it was bigger. In fact, it
was the biggest black-owned label in the nation. Instead of exclusively featuring
black artists, however, Vee-Jay had it all—Jimmy Reed, Eddie Harris, Jerry Butler,
the Four Seasons, Betty Everett, and even, for a short while, a band from England called the
Beatles.

Nat "King" Cole
and Bill Putnam
listen for flaws that
perhaps no one else
could hear, late
1950s.

During these halcyon days of the late '50s through the late'60s, most of the hits on Vee-
Jay, like "It's in His Kiss" (a.k.a. "The Shoop Shoop Song"), "Duke of Earl," and "Big Girls
Don't Cry," in addition to Impressions gems such as "I'm So Proud," "Gypsy Woman,"
"People Get Ready," as well as Soul nuggets like "Higher and Higher" by Jackie Wilson, were
recorded at Universal. But, by the '70s, the machinery that crafted the great Chicago Soul hits
of the '60s was being gradually dismantled. Swedein still sounds bitter: "I think Chicago got
fucked up by jingles [commercials]. I mean, Chicago musicians were certainly world class,
some of the best, and when jingles came to town and musicians could work from nine to five,
and get royalties and whatnot, they didn't have to really work. The passion left. That's why I
left. I could not deal with it. I called Bea one day and I said, 'Honey, I just did my last Pizza Hut
commercial.'"

133

Universal: Windy City Soul

The early 1970s were unforgiving to many cities, and Chicago was no exception. Just as Berry Gordy and Motown would leave Detroit, Bill Putnam, Quincy Jones, Vee-Jay, and Swedein, one by one, forsook the snow of Chicago for the tender green landscape of Los Angeles. Bill Putnam, naturally, was ahead of the curve. He had been scouting locations for a new studio in Los Angeles by the late '50s, after being encouraged by pals like Nat "King" Cole, Bing Crosby, and Frank Sinatra to head west. By the early '60s, he had designed and built United Western Recorders in Hollywood, still considered by most studio acousticians to be among the finest live-sounding studios in the world.

It wasn't until the late '70s that Swedein would catch up with his friend and comrade Quincy Jones, whom he'd met in 1959 at Universal while doing a record for Sarah Vaughan. In Los Angeles, in the '80s, they would team up again to make even more historic records, like Michael Jackson's *Off the Wall* and *Thriller*, among many others.

Tainted by scandal, Hugh Hefner, too, fled to the West Coast, taking much of Chicago's ring-a-ding-ding swagger of the early Playboy era with him. Mr. Kelly's closed, to be followed by a high-class hooker-boîte. The original Playboy Club, next to Universal, was no longer the sort of place the sort of man who once read *Playboy* would inhabit. The Chicago sounds of sweet soul and blues were giving way to funk, disco, and then house music. When Vee-Jay, the pride of the South Side's Record Row, moved to the West, communities changed and some hearts broke. ("Calvin Carter was a great person. I was just sorry that he went out after Motown

134

moved. You know, Vee-Jay moved out, and they hung Calvin out to dry. I really think he died of a broken heart out there," says producer Carl Davis.)

Chess Records, after the death of Leonard Chess in 1969, was soon sold and shut down, morphing the once robust Record Row into Desolation Row. It would be thirty years before Rush Street, Record Row, and the Chicago music scene were reanimated.

Universal carried on until the late '80s, occasionally making records, but it wasn't the same after Swedein left. Rising real estate prices required that Universal move from the corner of Rush and Walton to another, decidedly less commercial spot. Once a beacon for the A-list of American recording artists, it had become merely another studio.

Today, Swedein knows that Universal A is gone, of course. Yet he sounds like the married guy who can't help inquiring years later about the one who got away. A love like this is always unrequited. "Is Bragno's [the snazzy liquor store on the first floor] still there?"

How to tell him the most magnificent recording studio ever has been turned into a vapidly trendy retail store. Where they sell lava lamps.

"How about the elevator? Is it still there?"

Opposite: How it used to be done. All the players in the same space at the same time, music bleeding into the mics. Bill Putnam mans the console in the control room [center] with an unknown chanteuse at the mic, ca. 1958.

Above: A typical orchestra setup at Universal, late 1950s.

135

Motown
THE SNAKE PIT

It took a lot of nerve. An ambitious twenty-nine-year-old buys a drafty house in an unassuming, middle-class Detroit neighborhood and hangs a big sign across the front reading "Hitsville U.S.A." In the summer of 1959, Berry Gordy started living out his own version of *Field of Dreams*. If he built it (the studio), they (the hits) would come. Like the onlookers in that Kevin Costner classic, some believed him, while others believed he was crazy.

Stevie Wonder tells Peter Noone of Herman's Hermits that Mr. Gaye is ready to sign his album now, outside the doorway to Hitsville, 1966.

Gordy wasn't totally new to the business. He'd written a string of songs for the great Jackie Wilson that helped the dynamic singer's career blast off: "Reet Petite" in 1957, "To Be Loved" and "Lonely Teardrops" in 1958, and "I'll Be Satisfied" in 1959. He'd also produced a record for a group he was managing called the Miracles. But the meager financial return from these ventures inspired Gordy to demand more from the music business.

When he appealed to his family for an $800 loan to launch his own record company, his sister Esther confronted him with a cold, hard question: "You're twenty-nine years old and what have you done so far with your life?" He was momentarily stumped for an answer. Gordy had quit high school to become a professional boxer, then, lured by his love of music, quit to become a songwriter—something he had no idea how to do. Before he could learn he was drafted into the army and served two years in the Korean War.

When he returned to Detroit in 1953, he pursued his love of music by opening a record store. It quickly failed. In 1954 he got married, and soon had three children. He got a job on the assembly line of the Lincoln-Mercury plant, and wrote songs there in his spare time. After two years he quit the plant to pursue his dream of becoming a songwriter full-time. He sold some songs to Jackie Wilson's managers, but since Gordy wrote the songs with his sister Gwen and another partner, he split the small songwriting royalties three ways. With little money coming in, tensions built up between Gordy and his wife, and she filed for divorce (he wrote "To Be Loved" in his depression after getting served with the papers).

In his upwardly mobile family of hardworking parents and siblings, Berry had earned his reputation as a self-described black sheep. So in the spring of 1958, when he came to them for a loan to back his biggest dream—the dream of owning his own record company—he knew it wouldn't be an easy sell. Five years earlier he couldn't even run a record *store*. Now he wanted to run a record *company*? Esther's question "What have you done with your life so far?" stung like a slap in the face. But Gordy stood up for himself, stood up for his dream. His family lent him the money he asked for.

Pride and Joy

Gordy began recruiting talent. He was already managing the Miracles, with their lead singer and songwriter William "Smokey" Robinson. Marv Johnson, Mabel John, Barrett Strong, and Eddie Holland were also part of this early stable. The very first record to come out of the new company, "Come to Me," by Marv Johnson, was released on Gordy's Tamla label in January 1959. But it became so popular locally that Gordy worked out a deal to have it distributed nationally by United Artists (UA) Records in New York. Two successful Johnson follow-ups, "You Got What It Takes" and "I Love the Way You Love," were also released on UA, but they were the products of Gordy's new company. The Miracles' "Bad Girl" was the first song to appear on the Motown label. Like "Come to Me," it quickly became one of the most popular records in the Detroit area. Once again, since Gordy's company was not yet set up for national distribution, he leased the record to a company that was. This time it was Chess Records out of Chicago.

Until August 1959, Motown was being run out of the cramped apartment Gordy shared with his girlfriend, Raynoma Liles (who was expecting their child), and her son. He put the word out to family and friends that he was looking for a bigger base of operations, and it was Raynoma who found the two-story home at 2648 West Grand Boulevard. It once housed a photographer's studio and had a large picture window in front framed by two separate entrances. Something about the window appealed to Gordy. The house would become his company's headquarters, and there was also living space for him, Raynoma, and the kids on the second floor.

Berry's father, Pops Gordy, was a successful contractor and he, his sons, and various true believers who had hitched their star to Motown worked hard to transform the residence on West Grand into a functional place of business. Upstairs was Berry's office and living area.

138

A reception area, an office for the Jobete Publishing Company (then run by Raynoma), and the studio control room were on the first floor. The control room looked down on what was once the photographer's studio in the basement. Pops Gordy transformed it into Motown Studio A. It was not large, no bigger than an average-sized family room, and it never would be much to look at. But it's here that some of the best-selling and best-loved records of all time were made.

Mission control at Hitsville, ca. 1960s, candy machine at the ready.

One of the first songs recorded in Studio A featured the kind of infectious groove that would soon become a Motown specialty. But unlike most of the precisely crafted gems that were to come, this record had the loose, spontaneous sound of a party. Gordy liked to ask questions to prompt himself to come up with song ideas. "What do people want most?" he asked himself. Love was the easy and obvious answer—too obvious. Everyone wrote about love, he thought. What else? Money!

Janie Bradford, the company's young receptionist and a budding songwriter herself, claims that Gordy was actually asking these questions out loud as he sat down at the studio piano, repeating a simple blues lick over and over. She also remembers that she was the one who shouted "Money! That's what I want!" when he asked, "What does everyone want?" However it started, Gordy came up with two verses; one became the first verse ("They say the best things in life are free . . . "), and the other the third verse ("Money don't get everything, it's true . . . "), and he also banged out a rough version of the chorus. As he played the song for

139

Janie, she laughed at the lyrics. Gordy took this as a good sign. Then, as he continued to play, she ad-libbed a verse of her own: "Your love gives me such a thrill. But your love can't pay my bills." Gordy thought that was the best verse yet, put it in the song, and would later give Bradford half the songwriting credit.

Meanwhile, Barrett Strong, a singer and songwriter who was working in another room, heard the groove and, being a better player, slid in next to Gordy, took over the piano, and began singing along. (Strong claims he was playing the piano when Gordy and Bradford came in and started tossing lyrics around.) Gordy liked how Strong's vocals sounded. Drummer Benny Benjamin, one of the company's very first staff musicians, sat behind his kit and picked up a beat. According to Strong, two white kids walking home from high school heard the music out on the street and wandered into Hitsville. They asked if they could play along, and soon they were jamming on bass and guitar.

By now Gordy was dancing around the room shouting instructions as the groove was getting hotter and hotter. Gordy had a vision of Native Americans around a campfire and told Benjamin to give him a tom-tom beat. Another songwriter, Brian Holland, jumped in with a tambourine and started banging it. The party was on—and they played the song over and over until they got it as tight as they possibly could. Then they were ready to record.

The session was captured live onto a two-track tape recorder, adding to the spontaneous atmosphere on the record. Barrett Strong plays the opening piano riff, a swaggering urban blues figure. The tambourine pops in on the next bar, then the rest of the instruments join in. Strong's faux Ray Charles wail rises above Benjamin's tom-tom drumming: "They say the best things in life are free, but you can give them to the birds and bees. . . ." Then the record is off to the races, with Strong demanding "Money!" and the Rayber Voices, a group Gordy built around Raynoma, chirping, "That's what I want," as the piano, bass, and guitar repeat the funky blues line over and over. Musically it's simple, yet the groove is spit-shined to perfection, which Gordy demanded. Meticulous musicianship would become a Motown trademark. Remarkably, when the session was over, Strong claimed he never saw the two boys who played bass and guitar again.

In the spring of 1960, "Money" became something a lot of people wanted. It went to number two on the R&B charts and landed at a respectable number twenty-three on the Pop charts. Beyond that, this early Studio A recording would go on to become a frat house classic, sharing hallowed ground with other toga-party favorites such as "Shout" and "Louie, Louie."

Months after its release, Smokey Robinson wrote a song that he believed would give Barrett Strong a hot-selling follow-up to "Money." But Gordy convinced Robinson he should cut it with his own group, the Miracles. However, when the Miracles' version of "Shop Around" was released and began getting radio airplay, Gordy heard it and hated it. "Too slow," he thought. Each time it came on the radio, he felt worse.

After four or five days of this he couldn't stand it anymore. He called Robinson at three in the morning and told him he had to cut the song over again—right now. Robinson couldn't believe it, but his boss wasn't joking. Smokey called the rest of the Miracles, and when they all assembled at Hitsville an hour or two later, Gordy was there with the musicians and an engineer. However, the pianist Gordy called must have gone back to sleep, because he never showed up. Gordy took over the piano duties himself, and the session began. Several takes later, they'd produced a version of "Shop Around" that in the fall of 1960 would go on to be number one on the R&B charts, number two on the Pop charts, and become Motown's first million-selling release.

Gordy and everyone at Motown was ecstatic about the song's success. But to the ambitious boss of Motown, having the number-two Pop record in the country was a matter of "close, but no cigar." But Gordy wouldn't have to wait long to see one of his records make it all the way to the top.

After the success of "Shop Around," kids from all over Detroit started hanging out in front of Hitsville, hoping to get discovered or to catch a glimpse of someone famous. In April 1961, four high school girls from suburban Inkster, Michigan, auditioned for the company. They called themselves the Casingettes, a playful name derived from "can't sing yet." But after their very first recording session for Motown, Gordy changed their name to the Marvelettes. That session produced "Please Mr. Postman," which, after its release in October 1961, became Motown's first number-one Pop record. Besides featuring a deliciously raspy vocal by singer Gladys Horton, the record had an irresistible beat provided by the snappy drumming of another recent Motown arrival—Marvin Gaye.

By 1962, groups like the Temptations, the Supremes, Martha and the Vandellas, and Jr. Walker and the All-Stars were added to the Motown lineup along with singers like the sensuous Mary Wells and the eleven-year-old phenom, Little Stevie Wonder. An amazing house band was also being assembled. Along with drummer Benny Benjamin, bassist James Jamerson became an indispensable presence on most Motown recordings made at Hitsville. Jamerson was a master at sight reading—taking music he was seeing for the first time and playing the heck out of it. Songwriters and producers loved him because he took their melodies, quickly began improvising with his bass lines, and instantly made their good ideas sound even better. Some believed that Jamerson contributed so much to the final sound of many records that he deserved songwriting credit.

Gordy regarded Jamerson as a musical genius, but that didn't stop him from showing the brilliant but stubborn musician who was boss when necessary. Most of Motown's house musicians loved playing jazz. And although Gordy was a jazz fan himself, he was not running a jazz label. Jazz didn't sell—a lesson he learned from his failed record store, which featured jazz records. If the music at a session slipped too much into a jazz feel, his buttons were immediately pushed. While producing the rhythm track to "Do You Love Me?," a song he'd written, Gordy felt the band was playing it too much in a jazz style. He wanted pop. He wanted funk.

And after giving those instructions a few times, all of the musicians fell in line—all except for Jamerson. Gordy stepped down out of the control booth and confronted him. In his 1994 autobiography *To Be Loved*, Gordy recalled the showdown:

> The last thing I wanted to do was take him off the session. But I really had no choice because if I let him get away with it, I'd have no control over anybody else.
>
> "Look man," I said. "I've told you over and over again this ain't no fuckin' Jazz session. You've got to stay on the fuckin' downbeat."
>
> Jamerson said nothing, but gave a nod and a shrug, as if to say, "Okay, man, mess up your own session if you want to."
>
> Everybody held their breath. They knew how much he loved to improvise and were waiting for the fireworks.
>
> We started again, my eyes glued on Jamerson. I knew I'd have to kick him out if he deviated from my directions. I held my own breath, hoping he wouldn't. And he didn't—not until I got relaxed and comfortable. Dropping my guard, I had turned my attention to Benny Benjamin on drums; he was grooving like a dog. In that split second, Jamerson hit four or five Jazz upbeats in rapid succession. Reeling around, I turned to let him have it. But before I could say anything he had jumped back on the downbeat so brilliantly I could only smile.
>
> He glanced at me in impish defiance. He knew I loved what I'd just heard and everybody else knew it, too. They also knew he had gotten me.

Is it Frank? Is it Nat? No, it's Marvin Gaye noodling the Hammond, ca. 1965.

Though at the time Motown was only recording on two tracks, rhythm tracks were often recorded before the vocals were added to the mix. Many times this was necessary, because an act might be on the road making live appearances. When they returned, they simply added their vocals to rhythm tracks that were already produced.

But sometimes producers grew impatient and, instead of waiting for the act to return, gave the record to another artist. That's exactly what happened with "Do You Love Me?" Gordy had written it for the Temptations, but he was so excited about the music he couldn't wait for them to get back off the road. So, he gave the song to a group that was hanging around Hitsville without much to do—the Contours. In the summer of 1962, the hard-rocking "Do You Love Me?" went all the way to number-three Pop. Just like that, the Contours had a hit. The Temptations would have to wait two more years before they saw one of their records crack the top ten.

Gordy took what he learned from working on the Lincoln-Mercury assembly line and applied it to his own business. He had a motto for keeping his product moving: create, make, sell. First create something: write, record, and produce the record. Then physically make the record, pressing it at the plant. Then, of course, sell the hell out of it.

Gordy had also learned from Lincoln-Mercury that you had to have a high-quality product for it to sell. So each record out of Motown went through a rigorous quality-control process. First, each mix was submitted to the head of Quality Control who listened to it in her office on a small speaker that simulated the sound of a car radio, the theory being that most people heard records for the first time while in their car. After Motown built its own record-pressing facility in 1963, each mix was transferred from tape to an acetate recording (a cheap test disc) to approximate the sound of the final vinyl product as much as possible. If Quality Control rejected the mix, it went back to the studio for more work. If it was accepted, it was submitted to the Friday morning product evaluation meeting.

These meetings are legendary in Motown lore. They took place in Berry Gordy's office and anyone who got there before 9:05 A.M. could attend. Precisely at 9:05 Gordy locked the door, and no one else was allowed in (although Gordy remembers that one time Smokey Robinson just missed the cut-off time and was outside begging and pleading so pitifully for so long that he finally relented). At the meeting each record was listened to, and those in attendance would vote on whether it should be released or not. Gordy could overrule the vote, but he rarely exercised this option. Instead he would prod his staff with questions. If they liked the record he asked if they would buy it over whatever the current hit was. If they said yes, his next question might be, "If you're hungry and you only had one dollar, would you buy this record or a hot dog?" He knew the answer would almost always be the hot dog, but he would evaluate how long it took for people to think about their answer.

Often more than one record was submitted for an act's next single release. Though Gordy demanded good sportsmanship, the meetings became extremely competitive. To add fuel to the fire, if two strong recordings were submitted, a tie went to the writer/producer who had the last hit with a particular act. In the early 1960s, a battle of sorts ensued between Smokey Robinson and a young writer/producer named Norman Whitfield over "ownership" of the Temptations. Smokey had broken them nationally in 1963 after writing and producing the number-eleven Pop hit "The Way You Do the Things You Do." Then Whitfield took them over with the peppy "Girl (Why You Wanna Make Me Blue)." When it was time for the Temptation's next single, Smokey Robinson came to the Friday morning meeting armed with "My Girl" (an answer song to the number-one hit "My Guy," which he had written and produced for Mary Wells earlier that year). With Jamerson's signature bass line and David Ruffin's star-turning vocal, there was no way anyone could top it. "My Girl" was released on December 21, 1964, and headed straight to number one.

But none of Robinson's Temptations' singles after "My Girl" cracked the top ten. Knowing Gordy wasn't really satisfied with anything that fell too far from number one, Whitfield was ready to snatch back control in 1966. Along with Eddie Holland of Holland-Dozier-Holland, a writing and producing triumvirate (made up of Brian Holland, Lamont Dozier Jr., and Eddie Holland) that was even hotter than Smokey, he wrote "Ain't Too Proud to

144

Beg." With Holland's pleading lyrics, lead singer David Ruffin's agonizing vocal, and his own masterful production, Whitfield believed he'd get the green light at the Friday morning vote.

But Smokey had a Tempts jam, too. The committee heard both records, and Smokey's "Get Ready" was the one that got pressed and released. Whitfield was crushed, and after the meeting he made his feelings clear to anyone who cared to listen (except for Robinson and Gordy, of course, because bad sportsmanship was not tolerated at Motown).

Released in late March 1966, "Get Ready" hit number one on the R&B charts but did a dismal twenty-nine on the Pop charts, spending only a brief three weeks in the top forty. Motown quickly released "Ain't Too Proud to Beg" as a quick-fix follow-up. The song held the top spot on the R&B charts for eight straight weeks, reaching number thirteen on the Pop charts. The tall, talented, terrific Temptations were Whitfield's once more, and he would hold on to them for the next eight years. Teaming up with writer Barrett Strong, the singer of "Money," they guided the group through the heartbreak of "I Wish It Would Rain" (number-four Pop, in 1967), the highs of "Cloud Nine" (Motown's first Grammy-winning song), and the fragile beauty of 1971's "Just My Imagination (Running Away with Me)."

Ain't No Mountain High Enough

The competition between Robinson and Whitfield was just a microcosm of what was consuming every staff writer and producer at Motown. Everybody had an idea. Everybody had a hit. And everybody had to get into the studio to record. Motown Studio A was humming twenty-four hours a day. Bassist James Jamerson gave his fellow musicians, who were on call around the clock, the name "the Funk Brothers," because the instruction they received at nearly every session was "Make it funky!" Jamerson also dubbed the studio "the Snake Pit," originally because of the maze of patches and electrical cords running all over the floor. But it soon became synonymous with the keen competition between producers to cut hit records.

Often the musicians arrived at the studio around 10 A.M. and left at about 7 P.M. Then they'd blow off some steam, jamming at a club and playing their beloved jazz, until 2 A.M., when they might get a call from a producer for an early morning session at 3 or 4 A.M. When they finished at 6 A.M., they'd crash somewhere at Hitsville, then start all over again at 10 A.M.

Staff engineer Mike McLean rigged up Motown's eight-track recorder in 1964, quite an accomplishment, since only Capitol and Atlantic—two much older and established labels—had that capability at the time. Eight-track recorders allowed the engineers and producers greater flexibility to mix a record. Studio A also featured a high-end Studer two-track mix-down machine and a customized Altec console, two of the most legendary names in European and American audio.

After the eight track was installed, a recording assembly line began to take shape. First, the Funk Brothers laid down the rhythm track. Then vocals were added. Strings and horns came next. Additional effects and percussion—something to give a record that extra edge—

usually came last. This last step was not just an afterthought at Motown, and producers would come up with odd and creative ideas while looking for a sound. It could be as simple as an ashtray tapped by a drumstick or black-eyed peas being shaken in a jar. On the Martha and the Vandellas' classic "Dancing in the Street," a heavy bicycle chain whipped against a wooden board on the floor gives the record that extra percussive umph.

By 1966, Motown was the hottest record company in the world. The company's two most successful acts were the Supremes (the top-selling record makers after the Beatles) and the Four Tops, featuring the outstanding lead vocals of Levi Stubbs. These two groups were "owned" (in the Motown sense) by the team of Brian Holland, Lamont Dozier Jr., and Eddie Holland. The string of hits they wrote and produced for these two acts is the very definition of the Motown sound: "Baby I Need Your Lovin'," "Baby Love," "I Can't Help Myself," "You Can't Hurry Love," "Reach Out I'll Be There," "Stop! In the Name of Love," "Standing in the Shadows of Love." And, in addition to these great songs, Holland-Dozier-Holland also wrote and produced "(Love Is Like a) Heatwave" by Martha and the Vandellas, "Mickey's Monkey" for the Miracles, and "Can I Get a Witness" by Marvin Gaye.

Gordy described his studio's sound as "a thin, somewhat distorted sound with a heavy bottom." His description is pretty accurate, especially of the earlier records such as "Shop Around," "Do You Love Me," and "Stubborn Kind of Fellow." In most cases the music was anchored by the bottom of Benny Benjamin's bass drum and tom-tom. James Jamerson's bass percolated over these rhythms, buried deep enough in the mix so that they were often felt more than heard. The guitars of Robert White, Eddie Willis, or Joe Messina often stood out in contrast, picking up the studio's tinny sound. On many of the mid-'60s hits, baritone sax became a lead instrument, adding a gritty sound. There was also plenty of echo on the instruments. At first, the echo chamber was the men's room. Then, after Gordy purchased 2644-46 West Grand, next door to Hitsville, that building's attic was converted into an echo chamber.

The company's success demanded an ever-growing staff. A choreographer helped the groups with their dance steps. A charm school instructor gave lessons to help with the artists' poise offstage. Staff technicians kept the studio up and running. They pressed their own records. They had their own talent agency and publishing firm. To accommodate the growing staff, Gordy bought most of the homes on his side of the street and another across the street.

From 1965 to 1968, few companies on the planet ran more smoothly or enjoyed more success than Motown. Then, from nowhere, a crisis emerged. Holland-Dozier-Holland, the Cadillac team in Gordy's assembly line, abruptly went on strike in 1968 in hopes of being given more money and more power in the company. Gordy sued them for breach of contract. H-D-H left under a very dark cloud. It was an ugly and traumatic experience for everyone. The Supremes and the Four Tops were in near panic. However, Motown's competitive staff of writers and producers were more than ready to jump into the void. At the top of that list was Norman Whitfield.

More than a year before H-D-H split, Whitfield bopped in to a Friday prod-uct evaluation meeting confident that he had recorded Marvin Gaye's next hit record. Although "Pride and Joy," a song Whitfield cowrote with Gaye, had made it to number-ten Pop in 1963, and Holland-Dozier-Holland's "How Sweet It Is (To Be Loved by You)" had made it all the way to number-six Pop in 1964, Gaye hadn't cracked the top ten in the three years since.

The record Whitfield had cut with Gaye was a thing he'd written with Barrett Strong called "I Heard It through the Grapevine." But Whitfield didn't have the only Marvin Gaye record at that meeting. The mighty Holland-Dozier-Holland threw their hats in the ring with a song called "Your Unchanging Love." Both records were played at the meeting. The majority vote went to "I Heard It through the Grapevine." Whitfield had gone up against H-D-H and won! In *To Be Loved*, Gordy recalled:

> Most of the time I gave in to a majority vote, but this time I announced I was overriding the group and going with "Your Unchanging Love." I personally liked "Grapevine" better, but I felt the other record was more in the romantic vein of what Marvin needed.
>
> Norman sprang to his feet to make his case. "This is a smash, a number-one record and I know it. I got those chills I get when I know I got a hit! And you know my chills don't lie!"
>
> "Norman," I told him, "I love innovation, but I'm going with HDH. That's it."

147

Motown: The Snake Pit

Whitfield was hurt and frustrated, but not defeated. A few months later he was back with a totally different version of the same song. It was now a gospel-inflected, Aretha-inspired shouter by a relatively new group to Motown, Gladys Knight and the Pips. This time the record was released, and it went all the way to number-two Pop, and number-one R&B.

With Gladys Knight's version a solid hit, Whitfield confronted Gordy on the steps of Hitsville about adding "Grapevine" onto Marvin Gaye's upcoming album. The songs for the album had already been selected and sequenced. But this time Gordy relented. The album was resequenced, but the song was not being released as a single.

But when Gaye's album came out, DJs around the country recognized the title and went straight to the track. They started playing the song over the air. It was getting a great response. This time, Gordy couldn't deny what was happening. Marvin Gaye's version of "I Heard It through the Grapevine" was released almost thirteen months to the day after the Gladys Knight version. It went straight to number one on both charts and became Motown's biggest-selling single for years to come.

It couldn't have happened at a better time. By then, Motown was reeling from the departure of Holland-Dozier-Holland, and looking for a sign that it could withstand the blow. On the week of December 28, 1968, they got the thumbs-up they needed. Marvin Gaye's "I Heard It through the Grapevine" held the number-one spot. Stevie Wonder's "For Once in My Life" was number two. Diana Ross and the Supremes logged in at number three with "Love Child." In addition, "I'm Gonna Make You Love Me" by Diana Ross and the Supremes and the Temptations held the number-seven spot, and the Temptations' mold-breaking "Cloud Nine," another Whitfield production, held down the number-ten spot. For the week, Motown had five out of the top-ten records in the country. They held the top three positions for an entire month.

Someday, We'll Be Together

In the fall of 1968, Berry Gordy moved to Los Angeles. The company had kept a West Coast office out there for years (as they'd kept an East Coast office in New York), and had even done some recording in town. But now, after the Detroit riots during the summer of 1967, after the departure of Holland-Dozier-Holland, after a phenomenal thirty-eight top-ten hits in eight years (including eleven number-ones), Gordy sensed it was time to move on. The heart of the entertainment world was in L.A., and now he'd earned the right to be a part of that full-time.

Without skipping a beat, Motown's golden age, part two, began in 1969. Though the Jackson 5's "I Want You Back" and follow-up hits were recorded in L.A., the Snake Pit was also churning out hit music. Norman Whitfield cut the Temptations' top-ten multivoiced hits "I Can't Get Next to You" and "Ball of Confusion (That's What the World Is Today)" there. Marvin Gaye cut the single "What's Goin' On" there (and received some of the worst in-house reviews of any song released up to that time).

Yet with these successes, and many, many more, after 1969 much of the original innocence of Hitsville had vanished. More and more artists followed Gordy's lead and moved to L.A. In June 1972, Motown's base of operations officially moved there. Activity at the old studio on Grand Avenue slowed to a trickle. In 1974, Norman Whitfield and the Temptations recorded "Papa Was a Rolling Stone" at Studio A. It was his last great collaboration with his favorite group (Whitfield was now pushing the group so hard at sessions that they refused to work with him again), and it was the last big hit recorded at the original Hitsville.

Today the house at 2648 West Grand in Detroit is a museum overseen by Berry's sister Esther. It looks much like it did in its mid-'60s prime. The highlight of the short tour is "The Snake Pit," Studio A, all set up as in the old days, ready and waiting. The 2002 documentary *Standing in the Shadows of Motown*, by Funk Brother historian Allen Slutsky, actually reunites many of Motown's surviving house band members in the studio. Many appear visibly moved to stand in the room once more, and for one shining moment, it's transformed from a shrine back into an enchanted space where dreams—and funky music—were made. Across town, a large, multimillion-dollar Motown Museum is in the works. It is designed to stand as a monument to one of the most extraordinary stories in the history of recorded music. But there will always only be one Hitsville—a landmark that's as much a symbol of the American can-do spirit as Kitty Hawk or Hoover Dam. Long may it stand.

149

Motown: The Snake Pit

Sigma Sound Studios
THE SOUND OF PHILADELPHIA

It starts with a rumbling piano flourish in the lower register, as if the villain has just entered a silent movie. Then four chords rising upward hang in the air, like the villain's laughter. There's a split second of silence before the drum and bass kick off a groove nailed to the floor by a conga's Afro-Cuban syncopation. The piano rumble is repeated underneath as a guitar picks out a plaintive melody, riding on top of the rhythm. Then a giant wave of strings washes in, picking up the guitar's line. Finally, a wall of fat horns adds an "amen" chorus, marching in line behind the strings. The effect is a slick and soulful swirl, more than half a minute of melodic hypnotism. Then the spell is broken by a series of dramatic stabs straight out of the Tito Puente school of salsa breaks. In an open space between the music, an accusing jury of voices asks, "What they do?" The Afro-Cuban groove kicks back in as the sweet sad reply begins: "They smile in your face /all the time they want to take your place /the back stabbers."

When we were kings: Kenny Gamble, Joe Tarsia, and Leon Huff at the height of their Philly Soul dynasty, ca. 1975.

The introduction to the O'Jays' 1972 number-one smash "Back Stabbers" is the very definition of the "Philly Sound." It's all there: the funk, the sophistication, the message straight from the street delivered by impeccable musicianship, complex yet complementary arrangement, and peerless mixing. It sounds like a long, sleek Cadillac with all the trimmings rolling down South Street in slow motion, everyone's head bobbing in rhythm as it drives by.

Like Rocky, the city's cinematic favorite son, Philadelphia went from unlikely contender to champ of the popular-music world. It happened twice—at the start of consecutive decades.

Both reigns lasted about three years (the first from 1960 to 1963, the second from 1972 to 1975). The hits from each period were vastly different, but the person who recorded most of them was the same: Joe Tarsia.

The seeds for Philly's first stint as music mecca were planted back in 1956, when Dick Clark took over as host of a local TV show. The next year the program was picked up by ABC affiliates across the country. Airing every weekday afternoon, *American Bandstand* was the first nationally broadcast television show devoted to rock and roll. For a full ninety minutes, Clark played the latest tunes as teens danced, rated records, and watched many of their favorite stars lip-synch their hit songs.

"He's the only reason I'm in the business," Tarsia explains. "Because when he [Clark] had a major show emanating from Philadelphia, it was like a window of opportunity. And a lot of people, including the people I worked for, were stimulated by that possibility. Because he was a reachable guy, and if you went up to him and said, 'I have a record,' and he played it, it was worth a thousand promotion guys, because it was heard all over the country."

With *American Bandstand* a fixture in nearly every U.S. household with a teenager, several independent record labels sprang up in Philly to take advantage of the potential national exposure. Dick Clark himself was part owner of Swan Records, until the courts ruled it was a conflict of interest for DJs—or in Clark's case, VJs—to have financial dealings with record companies. Bob Marcucci, the "idolmaker" who discovered South Philly heartthrobs Fabian and Frankie Avalon, released their music on his own Chancellor Records. But the company that may have reaped the greatest benefit from its proximity to Clark was Cameo-Parkway (one company with two labels, Cameo and Parkway).

In 1958, Hank Ballard wrote a song called "The Twist" and recorded it with his group the Midnighters for Cincinnati-based King Records. The song was actually released as a B-side of a 45 and was only a moderate success, but over the next year the dance known as "the Twist" began to catch on. "Kids were dancing to the Twist," Tarsia remembers, "and Dick Clark wanted Hank Ballard to appear [on *American Bandstand*], and apparently twice Hank Ballard did not show up." Kal Mann, co-owner of Cameo-Parkway, saw an opportunity and jumped on it.

In 1960 Mann recorded a note-for-note version of the music track on "The Twist" and had one of his label's young singers, Earnest "Chubby" Evans, recut the vocal. (The affable young Evans worked a day job as a chicken plucker, but he had a great talent for mimicking other vocalists.) Weeks later Evans, renamed Chubby Checker—a spoof on Fats Domino—by Dick Clark's wife, appeared on *Bandstand*, lip-synched his version of "The Twist," and the rest is history. "The Twist" quickly became one of the biggest-selling singles and one of the most popular dance crazes of all time, and it remains the only record to reach number one twice—first in 1960 and again in 1962.

Around the time "The Twist" made its second stop at the number-one spot, Joe Tarsia became Cameo-Parkway's chief engineer ("I had the title 'chief engineer' because I was the only engineer"), but he had been a fixture at various studios in town since 1958. "I went to night school at Temple and I took electronic courses and lucked into a job at Philco," recalls Tarsia. "I got a job in the research department, which was really a fluke. Now I'm working with business engineers and so forth, and it really expanded my horizon. At night, I was always moonlighting at something. I was fixing TV sets, and one day this guy says, 'Can you fix a tape recorder?' and I said, 'Sure!' It turned out that tape recorder was in a recording studio, and I never left."

The tiny studio belonged to Dick Clark's partner at Swan Records (Tony Mammarella), and after this first short whiff of the record business, Tarsia was hooked. He hung around, eventually rebuilding all of the studio's equipment. Word of his expertise got out, and he was asked to make some repairs at Chancellor Records' facility. Then he was hired to do some work at Reco-Art, one of the older studios in town. He studied recording techniques and began to sit behind the console at Cameo-Parkway, engineering sessions. "I guess one of the early records I worked on was the Orlons' 'Don't Hang Up' and Chubby Checker's 'Limbo Rock,' and so I had my foot in the door. I loved it. I was there twenty-four hours a day."

In 1962, when Tarsia became Cameo-Parkway's chief engineer, the Philadelphia music scene had hit a new zenith. By then, *American Bandstand* had become a weekday religion for most teens. Local boys Fabian, Bobby Rydell, Frankie Avalon, and James Darren formed an Italian brat pack, topping the charts with cute pop tunes and forging an image of nice boys who sang rock and roll for now, but dreamed of growing up to become the next Frank Sinatra or Dean Martin. Riding the wave of dance tunes ("Let's Twist Again," "Wah-Wah-Watusi," "Pony Time," "Mashed Potatoes"), Cameo-Parkway grew into the number-one independent record label in the country. Tarsia was hard at work recording a string of top-ten hits designed to ignite *American Bandstand*'s dancers, including "South Street," by the Orlons; "You Can't Sit Down," by the Dovells; "Do the Bird," by Dee Dee Sharp; and "Wildwood Days," by Bobby Rydell.

And then Philly's ride at the top hit a brick wall. Near the end of 1963, Dick Clark pulled up stakes and moved his show to California with an eye toward expanding the opportunities open to his production company. Within months, the Beatles landed in New York for the first time, and musical trends shifted sharply and forever. Suddenly, performers like Bobby Rydell, who was two years younger than John Lennon, seemed old and, worse yet, old-fashioned. By the middle of 1964, Cameo-Parkway couldn't buy a hit.

It was about this time that nineteen-year-old Kenny Gamble finally got his foot in the door of the Cameo-Parkway studio. "I met Kenny Gamble I guess in 1962," Tarsia says. "Kenny was a laboratory technician at Jefferson Hospital, but his insatiable thing was to make music." Gamble would come by Cameo-Parkway to try to get into the studio and peddle his songs, but with little success. He didn't play an instrument and couldn't write music. But he had ideas. He just needed to meet someone with the musical expertise to help him get them out.

In the late '50s Gamble had teamed up with his high school friend Thom Bell to form the

153

A Kenndy-era Joe Tarsia at Cameo-Parkway, 1961, before he knew what he was getting into.

singing duo Kenny and Tommy, making one record together called "Someday." Gamble and Bell went on to form the Romeos. Gamble sang, Bell played piano, and Roland Chambers, later a Sigma Sound Studio session regular, played guitar. On top of writing and performing with the Romeos and working at the hospital, Gamble owned a small record store and also rented space in the Schubert Building, Philadelphia's version of New York's Brill Building—the legendary Broadway address where songwriters and publishers maintained offices, wrote hits, and made deals. Located at 250 South Broad Street, the Schubert Building was more than a place for songwriters to hang their shingles; the building's hallways and even elevators were prime networking territory.

It was in these halls that Kenny Gamble met writer/arranger/musician Leon Huff—a similarly ambitious young man. In 1964, Gamble and Huff collaborated on their first song, "The 81," a dance record that they sold to Cameo-Parkway, where it was sung by a group called Candy and the Kisses. It was a moderate East Coast success. But the next year Gamble and Huff collaborated on the song that gave them their first real national exposure, "(We'll Be) United," sung by the Intruders. The record peaked at number fourteen on the R&B charts in the summer of 1966. Recorded at Cameo-Parkway but released on the duo's Gamble label, "(We'll Be) United" was given a gorgeous arrangement by Bobby Martin, who, along with Thom Bell, would become a fixture on the Gamble-Huff team. With its soaring strings taking off over a bed of vibes and luscious harp fills, it's a wonder this song wasn't picked up by the airline ("We're gonna *fly* United . . .").

As chief engineer at Cameo-Parkway, Joe Tarsia was at the board recording these two early Gamble-Huff records. And he was also there when they cut their first big national hit, "Expressway to Your Heart," in 1966. Tarsia shows off some of his mixing expertise as the record begins with a series of well-timed car horns blending into one of the most recognizable bass grooves ever recorded. Given a hip, Rascal-esque reading by rival "blue-eyed soul"

154

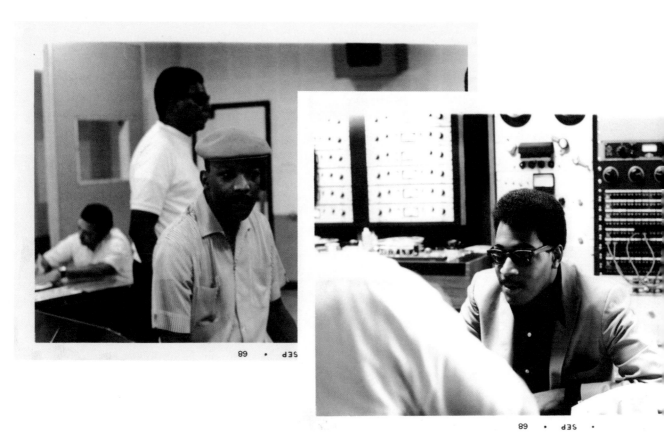

band the Soul Survivors, "Expressway to Your Heart" went all the way to number three on the R&B charts and number four on the Pop.

At this point, Joe Tarsia could tell which way the wind was blowing. Cameo-Parkway was the past. Gamble, Huff, Thom Bell, and Bobby Martin were the future. Reco-Art, a studio he'd done some work for when he was just starting out repairing equipment, was up for sale. It seemed like a now-or-never opportunity. "Literally, I hocked my house and [took] all the cash I had accumulated—everything I had—and got a bank to lend me forty thousand dollars and never looked back. I signed the lease on the place in '67, and when I finally got it open it was August of '68. I did my first session on August fifth." Tarsia renamed the studio, off an alley at 212 North 12th Street, Sigma Sound. (He saw "Sigma" on a place mat at a Greek restaurant and liked its academic sound.) Gamble and Huff, recording a female singer named Ruth McFadden, Stan Watson with a group he managed called the Delfonics, and writer/producer Weldon McDougle III, who had a huge hit with Barbara Mason's "Yes I'm Ready" in 1965 (the record Tarsia credits as the first to have the Philly sound), were among the clients who booked sessions that very first day. All claim they were the very first session. Tarsia says he honestly doesn't remember who was first.

But even before Sigma officially opened its doors, Gamble and Huff began working with their newest client, Jerry Butler. An original member of The Impressions with Curtis

Above left: Leon Huff and arranger Bobby Martin (standing behind) at Sigma one month after the doors opened.

Above right: Kenny Gamble at a very early Sigma session in 1968.

155

Mayfield, Butler sang lead on that group's first big hit, "For Your Precious Love," in 1958. After going solo, he charted with "He Will Break Your Heart" and "Make It Easy on Yourself" on the Vee-Jay label. Though Butler was based in Chicago, it was a Philadelphia DJ who gave him the nickname "The Ice Man"—because of his cool stage presence—in 1960. Butler signed with Mercury Records in 1966 and was assigned to staff producer Jerry Ross, who was based in Philadelphia. Ross introduced Butler to Gamble (the two writers had once shared an office in the Schubert Building). The cool, bluesy singer and the energetic young songwriter hit it off immediately.

The result was a string of five top-ten singles in two years, and two all-time classic soul albums (with equally classic titles), *The Ice Man Cometh* and *Ice On Ice*. For his material, Butler joined forces writing with Gamble, Huff, and Thom Bell. Huff or Bell worked out the melodies, Gamble and Butler assembled the words. They penned "Hey Western Union Man," "Brand New Me," and "Never Give You Up" in a single day, using the piano at Pep's nightclub. And they produced a number-one record with the philosophical "Only the Strong Survive."

The pairing with Gamble and Huff revived Butler's career, but the singer also had a profound effect on his new colleagues. Butler liked to take his songs from real incidents in life. "Only the Strong Survive," a mother's advice to her son after a romantic breakup, was real advice from Butler's mom. After working with Butler, Gamble and Huff became better storytellers and began listening to the street more closely for their musical ideas.

While writing and arranging with Gamble and Huff for Jerry Butler, Thom Bell was also working with a local group called the Delfonics. With William Hart, the group's lead singer, he wrote all of the group's early hits. As a kid growing up in a middle-class Philadelphia home, Bell had listened mainly to classical music, and you can hear this influence in his work with the Delfonics. That group's first top-ten hit, "La-La Means I Love You," from 1968, shows off Bell's mastery with strings. Violins delicately open the song, repeating three soaring, sustained notes. Then, in the song's dramatic, cascading chorus, the strings rise in fragile crescendos, like a small flock of birds taking wing. Equally dramatic is the descending line he uses in the sumptuous "Ready or Not Here I Come (Can't Hide from Love)," using a string quartet to similar effect as the Beatles on "Eleanor Rigby." But perhaps his most inspired classical touch was the French horn "call to arms" that opens the majestic "Didn't I (Blow Your Mind This Time)," which reached number ten in February 1970.

The song was one of Tarsia's favorite recordings because, he says, "it was done all live. The producer, Stan Watson, I thought he was going to punch me, because he said, 'Take the echo off the drums,' because this was a piece with strings in the room and it was not a big room." But Tarsia had learned from his early days at Cameo-Parkway that in their larger sessions (which were recorded at Bell Sound in New York), the full drum sound came through the mics used on the strings. This leakage made the entire room, and particularly the drums, sound bigger. To satisfy the producer, it appears Tarsia turned the mics down on the strings,

156

since they are placed further in the background on "Didn't I (Blow Your Mind This Time)" than on other Delfonics recordings.

Before long, Tarsia's gamble to buy Sigma was paying off with steady work and a steady string of hits by the talented producers, arrangers, and artists who were booking his rooms. Oddly enough, as classy as those records sounded, Sigma Sound was still a pretty funky place.

"Listen. The original studio was very primitive," Tarsia says. Before he bought it, "the owners had rented the place, and the heat was steam. They had those big steam radiators. And when that steam came out you would hear the steam hammer. Bang! Bang! Bang! There was an air conditioner hanging out the window of the control room, so you could hear every time the trash truck or the trolly rolled down the street."

But worse than the trash trucks was another annoyance from inside the studio. Because of a grounding problem, a buzz was heard in the studio every time someone used the soda machine. Tarsia couldn't find the root of the problem, so he put a red light on top of the machine, which came on when sessions were being recorded. Until a take was completed, the light served as a warning not to use the machine.

On the plus side, Sigma had an excellent echo chamber about forty feet long built over a hallway. In addition, Tarsia always had an eye out for the best and latest equipment. The original Sigma console was a custom fourteen-input Electrodyne model built from components. "Electrodyne made equipment for the motion picture industry," says Tarsia. "[This board had] two-band EQ, three selectable frequencies, and one send. One send!"

A "send" sends a signal from the board to a musician's headphones or to an echo chamber. Having only one send meant that all musicians had to hear the same playback. Today, sixteen different sends are not unusual. However, the limited amount of sends was hardly the biggest problem Tarsia had with his board. Like the buzz that came from the soda machine, the Electrodyne created a buzz in the studio every time it was plugged in. Again, the culprit was a wiring problem. Until it was fixed, Tarsia connected his board to a car battery. Another battery was across the street at the gas station getting jumped. The enterprising engineer kept the two car batteries in relay to keep his studio up and running for the first early weeks of operation.

Sigma originally used a Scully eight-track recorder. A Scully four-track was also put into the same cabinet and wired to accommodate twelve-track one-inch tape, but that format never got off the ground. In the early '70s, Tarsia upgraded to a large sixteen-track machine using two-inch tape. This quickly abandoned format was actually the greatest analog recording format ever, since 16 tracks afforded more magnetic real estate per track than the more cramped 24 tracks that took its place.

In 1969, the pieces seemed to finally all be in place for Philly to make its move in the music world. Gamble, Huff, Bell, and Tarsia had all traveled intertwining roads, picking up the professional chops and making key adjustments along the way that would result in the creation of a formula popularly called the Philly Sound. One of the first records out of Sigma to define

this sound was "One Night Affair," written and produced by Gamble and Huff.

The lyrics are street tough and no-nonsense: "Don't want to love you/Don't want to make you my wife/Don't want to see you every day for the rest of my life/All I want is a one night affair . . ." Yet the arrangement, credited to both Thom Bell and Bobby Martin, is a frothy (yet funky) confection. The song starts with a playful touch as a penny slide whistle moves up the scale, like the temperature rising. Then it picks up a galloping pace spurred on by an urgent guitar and bass figure. The proto-disco drums keep the action hot on top of a soft bed of strings, piano, and vibes. Finally a lounge lizard sax steps out to put the subject of the song's macho rap in the mood.

"One Night Affair" made it only to number sixty-eight on the Pop charts (possibly because the lyrics were just a little too direct—and cold—for mainstream radio in the summer of '69). But this record, coupled with the string of Jerry Butler and Delfonics hits, caught the ears of other music insiders.

Though he'd enjoyed several R&B hits, Wilson "Wicked" Pickett hadn't cracked the Pop top twenty for more than two years when Atlantic Records sent him to Sigma in 1970. He walked away with two hot singles—"Get Me Back on Time, Engine Number 9" (number-three R&B, number-fourteen Pop) and "Don't Let the Green Grass Fool You" (number-two R&B, number-seventeen Pop). And from the cackle of laughter heard before take six of the latter tune (included on the Rhino/Atlantic two-disc best-of set *A Man and a Half*), it seems that

158

Pickett had fun, to boot. Tarsia remembers sitting in the control room with Pickett cracking jokes for what seemed like hours before Pickett suddenly stopped and asked, "Hey, who's paying for this?" As a producer, Kenny Gamble liked to wait until everyone was ready and in the mood before cutting a take. The relaxed atmosphere suited Pickett, but it didn't please Atlantic Records very much when they got the bill. Pickett's next sessions were held at Muscle Shoals Sound in Alabama.

Thom Bell practices his special psychology on MFSB at Sigma, ca. 1974.

By the early '70s, soul music remained among the hottest-selling genres in the industry for roughly five years running. During the '60s, soul was the primary domain of Atlantic, Stax, and Motown. Now, at the turn of the decade, some of the older majors like Columbia were starting to take notice. In 1972, CBS, which owned Columbia Records, commissioned the Harvard Business School to conduct a major study on how they could become a force in the booming soul-music market. The study recommended acquiring established companies or developing custom labels with established black artists, writers, and producers. As a result, CBS invested in Gamble and Huff, providing backing for their own label, Philadelphia International Records (PIR).

The result: practically instant success. In his 1974 autobiography, *Clive: Inside the Record Business*, music impresario Clive Davis, then CEO of Columbia Records, wrote, "Not long after signing, Gamble and Huff blew up. Within nine months they sold ten million single records." The year was 1972, and the Philly Sound was making the biggest noise in the music business.

159

PIR had three number-one records on the R&B charts: "Back Stabbers," by the O'Jays, which hit number three on the Pop charts; "If You Don't Know Me by Now," by Harold Melvin and the Blue Notes, another number-three Pop single; and "Me and Mrs. Jones," by Billy Paul, which hit number one on the Pop charts. In addition, Thom Bell, partner with Gamble and Huff in the Mighty Three Productions Company, which handled all of their publishing and business dealings, was also on fire in 1972. He produced three big songs for the Spinners, who were on Atlantic Records ("How Could I Let You Get Away," "I'll Be Around," "Could It Be I'm Falling in Love"), and three more smashes for the Stylistics on the Avco label ("Betcha by Golly Wow," "People Make the World Go 'Round," and "I'm Stone in Love with You"). Every song was cut at Sigma Sound, with Joe Tarsia manning the board.

Adding to the success and the sound of these hits was the motley but masterful combination of street and session musicians, including Philadelphia Symphony string players and seasoned jazz veterans, who constituted the Sigma Sound house band. Calling themselves Mother, Father, Sister, Brother (MFSB), they counted among their group ace drummer Earl Young, top guitarists Roland Chambers and Norman Harris, vibraphone player Vince Montana, and super bassist Ronnie Baker.

Ten years after *American Bandstand* left Philadelphia for sunny L.A., the hottest dance show on television was *Soul Train*. Don Cornelius, the show's creator and host, met Kenny Gamble and asked him to help come up with a theme song for the show. Gamble agreed, and when the date was set, Cornelius flew in from Los Angeles for the recording session. Gamble came up with the basic melody and Huff and Bobby Martin did the bulk of the arranging.

The new *Soul Train* theme made its premiere in November 1973. The response was so overwhelming that Gamble immediately began to bug Cornelius about letting him release it as a single. Concerned about *Soul Train*'s good name in case the song bombed, Cornelius reluctantly agreed, but wouldn't let the song be released as "The Soul Train Theme." Gamble changed the title of the song to "T.S.O.P.," meaning "The Sound of Philadelphia." The single was released in March 1974 and went straight to number one on both the Pop and R&B charts.

The method Gamble and Huff used to write and produce most of their hits was loose and communal and incorporated the ideas of everyone in the studio. Gamble might come in with a few lines of a melody. Norman Harris might add a guitar line. Vince Montana would start to fool around with the vibes. Earl Young, whose drumming was credited for creating the disco beat, would jump in with a tasty groove. Gamble, sitting at a stool at the center of the studio, and Huff, at the piano, would encourage or veto ideas, throw in more ideas of their own, and run the skeleton of a song twenty or thirty times until they finally had something—and often that something was a hit.

160   Joe Tarsia fondly remembers one creative collaboration from a session in the fall of 1973. "Kenny Gamble came in with Anthony Jackson, who was a jazz bassist. Not one of our usual bassists. And he had a wah-wah peddle." Jackson began to play a bass line that Gamble

started to write a song around. To Tarsia's ear, hearing the bass with the wah-wah peddle sounded a bit psychedelic. As a song started to develop in the normal Gamble and Huff way, Tarsia had an idea. "I'd just gotten a new piece of equipment, an Eventide phaser. And as soon as I heard that bass line [Jackson was playing], I plugged the phaser into the bass. But when I recorded him I recorded it two ways—the way I'd normally do it and then using the phaser, just in case Kenny didn't like it."

The phaser gave the bass a spacey, whirling sound. Gamble came into the control room and heard what Tarsia did—and loved it. The effect of the phaser sound with the bass line would become a trademark of the song "For the Love of Money," by the O'Jays. Inspired by some of the experimentation he saw at a Sigma session with Todd Rundgren and his group the Nazz, Tarsia continued his "far-out" contributions to the song, recording the O'Jay's background vocals backward and recording the echo on different tracks, creating a reverse echo—an echo that preceded the vocal.

Gamble got into the spirit and started playing around with the echo on the bass, turning it on and off. When Tarsia suggested that manipulating the echo in that way couldn't be done, Gamble laughed. "Sure it can," he said. "You can do anything you want."

Tarsia freely offered his creative input at all sessions, sometimes even suggesting changes, like pointing out to Gamble when a musician was playing too loud. To this, Gamble

161

might playfully answer, "You're a dickhead!" But as often as not, he'd go ahead and make the suggested change. Everyone grooved off each other at Gamble and Huff sessions.

Thom Bell sessions were different. Instead of it being a communal affair, Bell came in with complete arrangements and wrote every nuance. He rarely accepted changes and didn't like ad-libs, a problem when it came to reining in the Spinners's brilliant but eccentric lead singer, Philippé Wynn. Through 1976, Bell continued to chart with the Spinners with hits such as "Mighty Love," "Games People Play," and "Rubberband Man." But as the hits kept coming, the vocally freewheeling Wynn was becoming less accepting of Bell's iron hand. Bell might let Wynn sing the song his way, but instruct Tarsia not to run the tape. Eventually, Wynn would drop his diva pose and do it Bell's way—as if he ever had a choice.

Joe Tarsia remembers a Stylistics session with Bell. They ran through the music ten times, and each time, drummer Earl Young made a mistake. Finally, after another botched take, Young, who stuttered when he got excited, said, "T-T-Thommy!" Bell answered, "What?" "T-T-Thommy. A fly landed on my paper and I played it."

The incredible success of the Philly Sound had artists beating down the door of Sigma's hit-making factory. In 1975, when David Bowie wanted to make an album that captured the American sound of the moment (Young Americans), he naturally came to Philly and Sigma Sound. But for reasons known only to him, Bowie chose not to use Gamble, Huff, Bell, Martin, or even Tarsia on the project, and, as a result, was widely viewed as an outsider by most of Sigma's regulars who believed he merely wanted to exploit Philly's successful sound. Many of MFSB's best refused to play with him.

Though he wasn't behind the board at these sessions (Tony Visconti, who'd worked with Bowie in the past, did the honors), Tarsia was certainly witness to much of what was going on. And he was around to see a very special moment. "There'd be these kids out there [in front of the studio]; every one of them would have different colored hair. And he [Bowie] would walk right past them and go into the studio. They'd be there since seven o'clock [in the evening]. He'd show up at ten o'clock for a seven o'clock session. And he'd stay until it was about light out. And those kids would still be sitting out there. And he'd walk right by them. But when the album was done, he invited them all into the studio. He bought them beer and he bought them sandwiches and played the album for them." Tarsia thought it was a great gesture.

In 1976, the Jacksons were at Sigma to record their first album since breaking with Motown. Gamble and Huff dispatched the bubblegum sound of "ABC" and "Rockin' Robin" and wrapped the talented brothers in a sleeker, more mature groove, scoring hits with the bouncy "Enjoy Yourself" and "Show You the Way to Go," the sexiest "message" song since Marvin Gaye's "What's Goin' On?" Today on the wall of Joe Tarsia's office hangs a framed letter written by an eighteen-year-old Michael and signed by all the Jacksons thanking the engineer and his family for baking them some cookies. "They were living in a hotel and I said, 'Would you like a nice meal? My wife will cook you spaghetti. Come to the house and have a

162

nice Italian meal.' So they came to the house. Somehow they heard it was my daughter's birthday. They brought a birthday cake. [But before they came over] they called me and said what they'd really like was some cheese steaks. So I called my wife. I said, 'Put away the spaghetti sauce. You're making cheese steaks.' So Michael is cooking. My wife is cooking. Smoke is going up, cooking cheese steaks." And cookies for dessert. The Jacksons came back to Sigma a year later to make their next album, *Going Places*.

By then, Sigma Sound had been producing number-one and top-ten hits for about a decade. From day one, Joe Tarsia had been in the studio almost around the clock, working with Gamble and Huff into the wee hours of the morning. And although Joe's son, Michael, was also clocking time at Sigma, the schedule could hardly have led to a very happy home life. When Gamble's wife, the singer Dee Dee Sharpe, would call him at the studio at night, he'd pick up the phone and say "I'll see you when I get there," and hang up. The line didn't always work (Tarsia remembers, "I tried that on my wife—she went bananas!"). At one point in 1974, during a stretch when Gamble, Huff, and Tarsia were working on thirteen albums together, they each found themselves kicked out of their homes at around the same time.

One of PIR's last great successes was with super-smooth soul singer Lou Rawls, who signed with the label in 1976. At the time, he'd been off the charts for five years. Immediately, Gamble and Huff hooked him up with the shimmering "You'll Never Find Another Love Like Mine." It went to number-one R&B and number-two Pop, and garnered Rawls a Grammy. Other blockbusters followed, including the jazzy "Groovy People," the ice-melting "Lady Love," and "I'll See You When I Get There," the title transformed from it's original half-mumbled put-off into a phrase full of loving anticipation.

Light it up: A Sigma Sound book of matches from the 1970s.

Eventually, the hard work and long hours led to creative burnout for Gamble and Huff. The team also refused to buy into the vapid sentiment of a lot of what disco had wrought (which, ironically, they had helped create). Sigma Sound's golden years, which were also the great musical years for Gamble, Huff, Bell, and MFSB, began to fade. Today Gamble, Huff, and Bell still maintain offices on Broad Street, Philly's Avenue of the Arts. Gamble is also very active in an inner-city revitalization project. Bobby Martin, who'd left the music business years before to become a Jehovah's Witness, died in August 2001.

Joe Tarsia and his son Michael still run Sigma Sound at 212 N. 12th Street. They continue to upgrade the rooms. In fact, Studio A, where most of the hits were recorded, has been totally remodeled and sounds better than ever. Certainly, if Rocky can enjoy four sequels, then it's not out of the question for Philly to explode on the music scene again, perhaps making Sigma Sound ground zero for yet another blast of pure magic.

163

Atlantic
R-E-S-P-E-C-T

It started as just another recording session above Patsy's Restaurant at 234 West 56th Street in New York City. That's where the Atlantic Records offices were, up on the fifth floor, in a small room with a couple of desks on a creaky wooden floor. The walls were covered with plywood paneling, and there was a large skylight in the ceiling. When they had recording sessions they'd stack the desks on top of one another, roll a piano out in the middle of the floor, and set up some chairs, music stands, and mics.

It was May 17, 1953. Crowded into the office's tiny recording booth were Atlantic cofounder and president Ahmet Ertegun; Jerry Wexler, a former writer for *Billboard* magazine whom Ertegun was courting to join the company; veteran writer/arranger Jesse Stone; and freelance engineer Tom Dowd. Out in the middle of the floor, seated at the piano, was the man they were all there to record, twenty-two-year-old Ray Charles Robinson, better known simply as Ray Charles. He had been signed by Atlantic less than a year before. This was only his second session for the company. On this day a backing band made up of three saxophones, a bass, a guitar, drums, and a conga was also squeezed into the small makeshift studio.

Tape was rolling. Charles played and sang the slow blues "Losing Hand," written by Jesse Stone (under his pseudonym, Charles Calhoun). Dowd treated the pianist's voice with an extra tweak of echo, making the sorrowful lyrics sound as if they were coming out of a dark cave instead of a humble office in midtown Manhattan. "I gambled on your love," Charles cried, "and came up with a losing hand." Suddenly, the phone in the tiny booth rang. Dowd picked it up. It was a message for Charles. Bad news. Dowd hung up and repeated the message to Ertegun, who directed Dowd to go and break it to the blind man swaying and moaning on the piano bench.

Charles finished the song. Dowd stopped the tape, took a deep breath, and walked out of the booth. He took a few short steps over to the piano and leaned on it for support.

"Ray, I have a bad message for you," said Dowd.

"What is it?" asked Charles.

"I just got a call. Someone says your mother has just passed away."

Dowd watched Charles's face for the impact of these words. He barely knew Charles, and certainly didn't know his mother, but he felt horrible. Groping in the silence, he asked, "Do you want to stop recording?"

Charles was upset, but not outwardly moved. His mother had been sick for some time. He was paying her hospital bills. After a few more agonizing seconds of silence, Charles finally replied, "It's too late for me to do anything. Let's continue."

Dowd walked back to the booth, somewhat chilled by Charles's response. But it had not been as cold as it seemed. Charles would express all his love and sorrow in an electrifying tribute. If "Losing Hand" had been a shout in the dark, "Sinner's Prayer" truly sounded like a man drowning in his own tears: "Lord have mercy/Lord have mercy on me/Well, if I've done somebody wrong/Lord have mercy if you please." Conversely, "Mess Around," written by Ahmet Ertegun, nearly careened off the record's grooves with maniacal abandon—a barrelhouse romp in which you can practically visualize the keys jumping off the piano, like in a Looney Tunes cartoon. It's the second line coming back from a New Orleans funeral.

The session continued a stylistic progression for young Ray Charles and marked another major step forward in his growth as an artist. For years, he had gotten by with a sound based on his idols, Nat Cole and Charles Brown. But on this day, the day his mother died, he took another leap forward in finding his own voice—a voice that would electrify popular music and help make Atlantic Records one of the most important labels in the industry.

Digging R&B Roots

The story of Atlantic Records starts with a young music enthusiast named Ahmet Ertegun. Son of a Turkish ambassador, Ertegun moved to the United States in 1934, when he was eleven, and immediately fell in love with the country—especially its jazz and rhythm and blues music. He and his older brother, Nesuhi, accumulated an incredible collection of 78s, and they helped organize some of the first racially integrated concerts (both on the bandstand and in the seats) in Washington, D.C.

When Ambassador Munir Ertegun died suddenly in 1944, his wife and daughter moved

166

back to Turkey but his two sons stayed behind. Nesuhi headed to Los Angeles, where he edited a music magazine, ran a jazz record shop, and recorded jazz musicians for tiny independent labels. Ahmet hung around Washington, taking some postgraduate classes at Georgetown, but mainly indulging his passion for black music.

Since he was a kid, he'd met many of his musical heroes: Duke Ellington, Count Basie, Lester Young. But he'd also met some of the men who were recording these giants and found out that quite a few of them knew nothing about music—or even much else. Ahmet Ertegun was fluent in three languages, had been educated in the best Washington schools, and had a serious jones for jazz and R&B. Although he was ignorant about the nuts and bolts of the music business, he felt he was as qualified as anyone to run a record company—and saw it as a way to combine a career, something he had yet to settle on, with the music that had become his obsession.

Around this time, Herb Abramson, A&R man with National Records, an independent jazz and R&B label based in New York, was becoming disillusioned with his job. He believed his boss wasn't the sharpest knife in the drawer and that he could probably do better running his own label. The music business being the small world that it was at the time, it wasn't long before Abramson and Ertegun met, realized they were traveling down the same road, and decided to take the ride together. In 1947 they threw in twenty-five hundred dollars apiece to get a record label off the ground. But it wasn't enough cash. So Ertegun persuaded his dentist to invest ten thousand dollars in a long shot. The investment would soon make the dentist a millionaire.

The first quest for the new label, which they named Atlantic, was to dig up talent. Ertegun spent nearly every night in Harlem—where he probably would have been anyway—with his ears open for someone, anyone, with a great sound or a hot song. By the end of 1953, Ahmet Ertegun's late-night talent prowls had helped Atlantic put together a solid roster of artists, including Big Joe Turner, the Clovers, Ruth Brown, Ray Charles, Clyde McPhatter, and Lavern Baker—a "who's who" of the inventers of rock and roll.

Before the company had its own offices, they recorded at Apex Studios, in downtown Manhattan. At the second session a kid walked into the studio. Ertegun asked him where the engineer was. The kid said he was it. Ertegun was furious and told the studio's manager, "I will not have this child ruin my records."

The "child" was Tom Dowd, a baby-faced classically trained musician and physics graduate from Columbia University who had spent the last four years working on the infamous Manhattan Project, which produced the atom bomb. A lot of people in the music business are called geniuses. Tom Dowd really is one.

Though he would technically remain a freelance engineer until 1954, when he was brought in as staff engineer and producer at Atlantic, Dowd recorded nearly all of Atlantic's sessions right from the very beginning. By 1952 he was recording Atlantic sessions in stereo, a good five years before most of the industry was taking stereo seriously. In 1958 he would order an eight-track recorder for Atlantic, allowing himself and the artists a flexibility they'd never enjoyed before: the ability to record music separately on each of the eight tracks. Ten years later, many professional studios would just be getting their hands on this technology.

The man responsible for a lot of Atlantic's early hits was Jesse Stone, a composer and arranger Herb Abramson had met while working at National Records. Ahmet Ertegun would say, "Jesse Stone did more to develop the basic rock 'n' roll sound than anybody else."

Jesse Stone, served as Atlantic's first musical director and wrote most of their early arrangements—and many of their hit songs ("Shake, Rattle, and Roll," "Money Honey," "Flip, Flop, and Fly"). Stone had made his first record in the late 1920s ("Starvation Blues"), and Duke Ellington had helped him get gigs at the Cotton Club in the '30s. He went on to become staff composer/arranger/comedy writer at the Apollo Theater in New York and is said to have taken songwriting lessons from Cole Porter.

Though Atlantic enjoyed some early hits—such as 1949's "Drinkin' Wine Spo-Dee-O-Dee," by Stick Mcghee (Brownie's brother); 1951's "Chains of Love," by Big Joe Turner; and three number ones, including 1952's "One Mint Julep," by the Clovers—the company seemed to shift into high gear in 1953. That year got off to a flying start when Ruth Brown's "Mama, He Treats Your Daughter Mean" reached number one in February.

Around this time, Atlantic moved their corporate offices. The company's first head-quarters, in 1947, were in the Jefferson Hotel, on 56th Street, between 6th Avenue and Broadway. It was a dump and was legally condemned not long after Atlantic moved in. Ertegun and company then set up shop in a tenement building on 8th Avenue and 54th Street near Stillman's Gym, a famous boxing training ground. Drunks and drug addicts sometimes found the building's lobby a good place to sleep. After about five years they moved again, this time to 234 West 56th Street. On the ground floor was Patsy's Restaurant, formerly a speakeasy called the 23456 Club. Atlantic took over the top two floors, the cramped office on the fifth floor doubling as a studio.

Just weeks after the Ray Charles sessions in May of 1953 that yielded "Losing Hand" and "Mess Around," Herb Abramson was drafted into the army, and Jerry Wexler joined Atlantic. Other than writing for *Billboard* magazine, Wexler had no real experience in the music business, but he was an avid R&B enthusiast, not unlike Ertegun himself when he had gotten into the business. Ertegun and Wexler quickly developed an easy chemistry. Wexler believed that his and Ertegun's shared ignorance of the business actually aided their working relationship. They were both afraid to tell the other that they disagreed with an opinion. They were also afraid of taking much of a stand for their own opinions. Neither wanted to make the mistake that sank the company.

The same month that Wexler joined Atlantic, Clyde McPhatter was signed to the label. McPhatter was the lead singer for Billy Ward and the Dominoes, and his soaring tenor had

168

lifted such hits as "Sixty-Minute Man" and "Have Mercy, Baby." One night Ahmet went to Birdland to catch the Dominoes, and Clyde wasn't there. It turns out he had been fired just days earlier and replaced by another tremendous voice, Jackie Wilson. Ertegun ran to the club's phone booth and found three listings in the New York directory for "McPhatter." The first number connected the frantic record exec to Clyde's dad, a minister, who obligingly put his son on the phone. Ertegun arranged for the two to have dinner the next night; he signed McPhatter on the spot.

McPhatter put a group together that he called the Drifters, and their first session came at the end of June 1953. But Ertegun and Wexler weren't happy with the results, feeling the group didn't have enough "bottom," or bass. So McPhatter put a second group together, and in early August they were back in the studio with more impressive results. One song, Jesse Stone's "Money Honey," became one of the most-played R&B songs on the radio in 1953, sticking to the charts for twenty-one weeks. A streamlined, up-tempo number, "Money Honey" has the feel of what Jerry Wexler called "cat music" but Alan Freed more popularly dubbed "rock and roll." McPhatter gives Stone's humorous lyric a tough, sanctified reading as the Drifters' chorus of "Ah-oom. Ah-oom" in the background gives the song an infectious momentum. Sam Taylor's sax solo threatens to blow the roof off as McPhatter lets out a scream that wouldn't be topped for another two years, when Little Richard would let loose on "Tutti Frutti."

Tom Dowd was recording all of this great music on secondhand portable equipment. The mixing console consisted of two pieces of equipment originally designed for radio: an RCA OP-6 (a four-position mixer) and an RCA OP-7, which was designed for remote radio broadcasts. Among his early arsenal of mics, Dowd used RCA 77s, RCA 44s, Western Electric 639As and Cs, a Western Electric "Salt Shaker," and a pair of Emory Cooke mics made by M. W. Kellogg and Company. With this simple equipment—and in a tiny office—Dowd was getting a crisp, clean sound, with much more clarity than nearly anyone else in the industry. The snap of his drum rivaled the famous Blue Note sound Rudy Van Gelder was recording in the small studio in his parents' living room on the Jersey side of the Hudson River.

In a *Mix* magazine interview, Dowd remembered, "People used to say to me, 'How the hell do you get that drum sound? What mic do you use?' And I'd say, 'I don't have a mic within ten feet of the drums.' I couldn't afford one—the damn drums were leaking in every place else I got. I didn't have any control on what the drums were doing. [Laughs.] But people would try and emulate that and they've got seventeen mics on the drums!"

In 1951, Atlantic went from cutting records direct to disc, to recording on tape. They acquired a state-of-the-art Ampex 400 recorder, which recorded only in mono. But Dowd also had a portable Magnacord that recorded in stereo. Dowd would run the Ampex and the Magnacord at the same time, thus giving Atlantic masters in stereo and mono as far back as 1952. It was strictly a matter of farsightedness on Dowd's part, because Atlantic (and nearly every other record company) wouldn't press stereo records for another five or six years. But

169

he believed that stereo was the future, and he even lugged the Magnacord along to sessions held in more spacious New York studios when there were too many musicians to fit in the 56th Street office.

If an Atlantic artist was touring a lot and couldn't get back to New York to record, sessions were sometimes scheduled on the road. On May 12, 1953, Big Joe Turner was in New Orleans recording "Honey Hush" at Cosimo Matassa's J&M studio, reaping the benefit of a lazy, funky trombone line played behind his own glass-breaking vocal. The song was a smash, reaching number one and becoming another of the biggest R&B records of the year. Nine months later, on February 15, 1954, Big Joe was back in New York at 56th Street, recording a strong follow-up. The song, by Jesse Stone (under the name Charles Calhoun), would be even more up-tempo than the New Orleans record. It starts with a bright playful piano figure played by Stone himself, backed by Connie Kay's driving snare. The rumbling bass plays what would become the quintessential rock and roll line, rising and falling as hand claps provided by Wexler and Ertegun signal the listener that they're about to hear a real "gasser." Turner was at his comical, storytelling best as he stepped up to the mic and shouted, "Get out of that bed/ wash your face and hands / Get out of that bed / wash your face and hands / Well, you get in that kitchen / make some noise with the pots and pans." Stone's lyrics drip with folk wisdom and humor, as if ripped from the pages of a Zora Neale Hurston story. "I believe to my soul / you're a devil in nylon hose," Turner slurs salaciously. "The harder I work / the faster my money goes." Then comes the chorus, a frat-boy sing-along: "Shake, rattle and roll! / Shake, rattle and roll! / Shake, rattle and roll!" with Wexler, Ertegun, and Stone providing the ragged background vocals.

To many music critics, this song was the pistol shot that started the rock and roll craze, which is ironic, because this version, and the even more familiar cover by Bill Haley and the Comets, was recorded by comfortably middle-aged men. Nevertheless, Joe Turner's record, with its original suggestive lyrics ("I'm like a one-eyed cat peepin' in a seafood store") still packs the punch of a heavyweight rocker.

But this wasn't the only historic disc Atlantic would record in 1954. After more than a year on the road working up new material with his band, Ray Charles called Ertegun and Wexler down to Atlanta, where he was playing. They met at the Peacock Club. In his 1993 autobiography, *Rhythm and the Blues*, Jerry Wexler recalled, "We arrived in early afternoon. Except for Ray and his group, the place was deserted. Ray counted off and they hit 'I Got a Woman.' I was staggered."

The song, taken from a gospel tune by Alex Bradford, was unlike anything anyone had heard before. Never had a secular song had this kind of spiritual passion, this kind of downhome fervor, this kind of "home cookin'." A session was quickly put together for the next day at Georgia Tech University's radio station, WGST, in Atlanta.

With "I Got a Woman," Ray Charles had found his voice, his sound. It would later be

called soul. But when the record came out in January 1955, it was called blasphemous by many God-fearing gospel fans who were offended that the Lord's music had been transformed into a shake tune about some woman. In April 1955, at a session in Miami, Charles would do it again, reconfiguring the gospel standard "This Little Light of Mine" into a rhumba-rhythmed "This Little Girl of Mine." It may have hit a lot of churchgoers the wrong way, but there was no denying that Ray Charles had started a revolution. He was soon joined by Sam Cooke, James Brown, and a legion of other "soul men and women" who put some of Sunday morning into Saturday night and let their audiences sort it out for themselves.

Ray's great blues and gospel-tinged records for Atlantic continued on for the rest of the decade: "Hallelujah, I Love Her So," "Drown in My Own Tears," "Lonely Avenue," "The Right Time." The pièce de résistance was the scorcher "What'd I Say," recorded at the Atlantic Studio on July 13, 1959. By then, Atlantic's staff had grown considerably; in 1954 the company had moved its offices to 157 West 57th Street. However, the studio remained on 56th Street, and Tom Dowd was given the entire floor to redesign as a studio. He designed and built a console that made it easier to record in mono and stereo simultaneously, and, in 1957, Dowd proposed that Atlantic add an experimental piece of equipment: the eight-track recorder.

Atlantic's was only the third eight-track recorder Ampex had produced. The first one was in Les Paul's basement studio. The second one went to Mitch Miller's longtime contrac-

Ahmet Ertegun, Big Joe Turner, and Jerry Wexler celebrate the release of "Corrine, Corinna" at the pressing plant in 1956.

171

tor, Jiggs Carroll, in the Woodward Hotel. Owing to Tom Dowd's vision and ingenuity, Atlantic became the first record company to record in eight-track.

The eight tracks came in handy on a Ray Charles session on November 23, 1959, which included Charles's original blues "I Believe to My Soul." The song begins with Ray playing his electric Wurlitzer piano, creating a mood as dark and cool as a lake at midnight. But for some reason, Charles's female backup group, the Rae-letts, couldn't get their parts together enough to please Ray. Frustrated and angry, he sent them home. Tom Dowd recalled: "The girls couldn't get it right, and Ray said to me, 'Hey pardner, you got enough tracks?' I said 'Yeah,' and he did all four female parts on the remaining tracks. One take on each part."

It was a virtuoso performance, and for Atlantic it would be among Charles's last. He was about to sign a sweetheart deal with ABC-Paramount. Ertegun, Wexler, and Dowd took the news hard. They loved Ray, but knew they couldn't match the money ABC had on the table. For Atlantic, it was the end of an era. But even in the midst of this sad time, there was still music being recorded in their tiny studio that everyone could feel good about.

In the mid-1950s, Ahmet's older brother, Nesuhi, joined the company and went about putting together a first-class jazz roster, signing bassist/composer Charles Mingus, the Modern Jazz Quartet, and Miles Davis's tenor player, John Coltrane.

In 1955 Herb Abramson returned from his army stint in Germany—with a pregnant woman whom he said he wanted to marry. There were two problems. One was that Abramson was already married. His wife, Miriam, had been supervising Atlantic's offices since day one and, if anything, had become an even bigger part of the company in his absence. At the time, they had a three-year-old of their own. Miriam gave him a divorce, but things at work were not going to be easy. It was still an intimate workplace.

The self-proclaimed "Hipster Jew" (Jerry Wexler) and the woman he called "Our Lady of Mysterious Sorrows" (Aretha Franklin) confer during a classic 1967 session at Atlantic studios in New York City.

The second problem was that Ahmet and Jerry had become married professionally in a way that Ahmet and Herb never had been. Abramson would not be a partner with quite the same status as he'd had when he left. Eventually, a subsidiary label, Atco, was created for Herb to run. The great R&B clowns the Coasters were signed to the label in 1956, but they were handled exclusively by the songwriting team of Jerry Leiber and Mike Stoller; Abramson had very little contact with them. They made hilarious hit records—many were like mini-radio plays—and pretty much took care of themselves.

Another artist on Atco, Walden Robert Cassotto, was a different matter. Signed away from Decca Records, where he'd been a bust, Cassotto wasn't making any noise at Atlantic either. Plus he was a pain in the ass. After a year, Abramson was ready to pull the plug on him, but Ertegun intervened. He liked this kid, who used the stage name Bobby Darin. Before he would let Abramson cut Darin loose, Ertegun wanted a shot at producing something with the singer himself. In 1957, they went into the studio and in less than two hours had recorded

three sides, including Darin's self-penned million seller "Splish Splash." Soon, instead of Darin, it was Abramson who left the company. He asked to be bought out, was given a generous offer, and left to form his own record company on the West Coast.

In 1959, Atlantic finally built its first large studio. For years, they had been going to other studios in town, usually Capitol and Coastal, when they needed a session with strings and large production. The new studio was built at 11 West 60th Street—and it was plenty big: thirty-two feet deep, forty-four feet wide, and fifteen feet high.

Unfortunately, by the time the studio was ready for business, in early 1960, many of Atlantic's biggest acts were either gone, on their way out, or cold. Their hottest star, Ray Charles, had left at the end of 1959. John Coltrane, who wrote some of his greatest compositions while at Atlantic ("Naima," "Impressions," "Giant Steps") and had a bona fide hit with his version of "My Favorite Things," departed the company in 1961. Bobby Darin, who had become a star with big-band finger-snappers like "Mack the Knife" and "Beyond the Sea," and whom one newspaper called "the greatest natural nightclub talent to come along since Sammy Davis Jr.," abandoned Atlantic for Capitol Records in 1962. After a string of ingenious number-one R&B and top-ten Pop hits ("Searchin'," "Charlie Brown," "Yakety-Yak"), the Coasters' final number one was "Poison Ivy," released in August 1959.

As the Kennedy era dawned, Atlantic's hottest act was the Drifters. Clyde McPhatter had left the group in 1954. After his departure the group continued on and made some good records, but no chart busters. In 1959 the group was reformed around singer Ben E. King. Leiber and Stoller took over their production, just as they'd supervised the Coasters. But when they played their first effort ("There Goes My Baby") for Jerry Wexler in his office, Wexler got so upset he threw the sandwich he'd been eating against the wall. "Get it out of here!" he screamed. "I hate it! It's out of tune and it's phony, and it's shit, and get it out of here!" But Wexler was wrong. The song went straight to number one.

After "This Magic Moment" and "Save the Last Dance for Me," which went to number one in 1960, Ben E. King left the Drifters to go solo. He immediately reached the top ten twice, first with "Spanish Harlem" and again four months later with "Stand by Me." King was replaced in the group by Rudy Lewis, a talented vocalist who sang lead on some of the Drifters' most memorable records: "Some Kind of Wonderful," "Up on the Roof," and "On Broadway." The last song features a guitar solo by "wall of sound" Phil Spector, who learned a lot about the craft from Leiber and Stoller. With the knowledge he gleaned from this apprenticeship—and with his own innovative ideas—Spector went on to become the legendary producer of hits by the Ronettes, the Crystals, and the Righteous Brothers.

In 1964, Drifters lead singer Rudy Lewis died of a drug overdose the night before a scheduled recording session. Everyone was shocked when they came in and heard the news. But the session went on. That day the Drifters recorded "Under the Boardwalk"—a dreamy song of summer romance with a wistful, lilting lead vocal by group member Johnny Moore.

Weighted with loss and remembrance, it would be their last top-ten hit.

During the mid-1960s, Atlantic's biggest sellers came through the company's distribution deal with Stax Records in Memphis, Tennessee. Wexler even sent fiery Atlantic vocalist Wilson Pickett there, who came back with hits "In the Midnight Hour" and "634-5789" in 1965. That year the Young Rascals were signed to Atlantic and given to Tom Dowd to produce. The white soul/pop band scored with the gritty "Good Lovin'" in 1966 and the mellow "Groovin'" in 1967. And though "Groovin'" was a monster hit, 1967 belonged to another artist Jerry Wexler had just signed.

Aretha Franklin was a wunderkind who played an amazing gospel piano and sang like a sanctified angel in her father's Detroit church. In the 1950s she hit the road, performing with touring package shows. Aretha made her first recording in 1956, when she was fourteen, appearing on a live gospel album for Chess. (The label also recorded the sermons of her father, C. L. Franklin, and they were solid sellers.) At eighteen, in 1960, she moved to New York. Family friend and musical idol Sam Cooke desperately tried to get his label (RCA) to sign her, but he had just been signed by the label himself and couldn't pull much weight. Instead she was signed that year by talent scout and producer John Hammond to Columbia Records. Though many at the label recognized her tremendous talent, they were unable to use it to its fullest

The inner sanctum: The Atlantic Records braintrust lend their ears to a playback at an Aretha Franklin session in January, 1969. Clockwise from bottom left: Unidentified (possibly bassist David Hood), drummer Roger Hawkins, guitarist Duane Allman (standing), Aretha Franklin, Cissy Houston, Sylvia Shamwell, Jerry Wexler, Arif Mardin, Tom Dowd.

175

advantage, often draping her vocals in unsuitable arrangements or giving her dated material. In his autobiography, *John Hammond on Record*, Hammond wrote, "When her five-year contract with Columbia ended I was not unhappy to see her go to Atlantic. I knew Jerry Wexler, who would produce her records there, and was sure he would return her to the gospel-rooted material she should be recording."

And that's exactly what he did. Wexler wanted to send her down to Memphis to record at Stax, even offering Stax president Jim Stewart the opportunity of having Franklin on his label if he paid her twenty-five-thousand-dollar advance. Stewart, who was busy with his current artists and growing somewhat suspicious of Wexler, declined.

Wexler still wanted to take Aretha south to record, and he settled on Rick Hall's small but successful Fame Studios in Muscle Shoals, Alabama. Fame was home base for a team of great local musicians—hardscrabble Southern whites who were immersed in black music. In January 1967, Franklin, Wexler, Dowd, and Franklin's husband, Ted White, flew down to Muscle Shoals. Most of the musicians booked for the session had no idea who Aretha Franklin was, but they quickly would get one. She walked into the studio, sat down at the piano, and hit a chord—that's all she had to do. Dan Penn, a songwriter and producer—and one of the few people aware of Aretha's talent beforehand—was on hand hoping she would do a song he'd written with Chips Moman, the lead guitarist on the session. Penn told writer Peter Guralnick,

"When she come in there and sit down at the piano and hit that first chord, everybody was just like little bees buzzing around the queen. You could tell by the way she hit the piano the gig was up. It was, 'Let's get down to serious business.'"

Aretha brought a song along with her called "I Never Loved a Man (The Way I Love You)," written by Detroit songwriter Ronnie Shannon. It was a moaning blues with a somber gospel strut. If the "man" in the title were Jesus, the song might be something a choir would sing as they filed into the church. With Aretha's pew-rattling piano showing the way, the band cut the song in two hours. Penn recalled, "It was a killer, no doubt about it. The musicians started singing and dancing with each other, giddy on the pure joy of having something to do with this amazing record. That morning we knew a star had been born."

But the euphoria was quickly shot down. The musicians took a break as Penn, Moman, and Wexler put the finishing touches on "Do Right Woman." A bottle appeared and was passed around. The trumpet player on the session made a remark to Aretha that offended her husband. The two men started to argue. When Aretha tried "Do Right Woman," she couldn't get it right. Penn came in and sang it—he described it as "screeching"—with the organ and bass playing behind him. That's all that was recorded that day.

That night, Aretha's husband and Rick Hall got in a fistfight. By noon the next day, Franklin and her husband were on a plane home. Session over. Wexler quickly had two dozen acetates of "I Never Loved a Man (The Way I Love You)" made to hand out to key DJs. He wanted to get their reaction. It came back loud and clear. This record was a smash. They had to get

176

their hands on it immediately. No problem, except Wexler only had one side of a record. He had to get Aretha back in the studio to finish "Do Right Woman."

But Wexler couldn't find her. When they got home, Aretha and her husband had temporarily split up, and for about two weeks, she remained out of reach. But when she did come in to the studio in early February, she'd worked out a vocal arrangement for "Do Right Woman" with her sister Caroline. They put her vocal and piano on the tape they'd made in Muscle Shoals, and added the backing vocals of Aretha's sisters Caroline and Erma, and Cissy Houston (Whitney's mom). The rest of the Muscle Shoals musicians, minus the trumpet player, came up to New York and added their tracks to the record.

"I Never Loved a Man (The Way I Love You)" rocketed to number one, as did each of Aretha's first six Atlantic singles—except "Do Right Woman," which got stuck at number two. It was the start of a musical phenomenon not unlike what Atlantic had experienced with Ray Charles more than a decade earlier, using a similar formula of the sacred and the sexual.

The same year Aretha arrived at Atlantic, Eric Clapton also made his debut in Atlantic's studio. He was then part of the English supergroup Cream, along with Jack Bruce and Ginger Baker. While on tour in the United States in 1967, they stopped by the Atlantic studio to record their first album, *Disraeli Gears*.

"I'm a man": Jack Bruce, Ginger Baker, and Eric Clapton of Cream pose at Atlantic studios while laying down tracks for *Disraeli Gears*.

"The first meeting was bizarre," Dowd recalled years later. "Ahmet Ertegun called me up one day and said, 'There's this group that I've signed to Atlantic and they're on tour, but they have to be out of the country by Sunday because their visas expire and I promised that I'd record them. See what you can get out of them.' I didn't know what he was talking about. I went in my studio one morning and there was the road crew setting up double stacks of Marshall amps and two bass drums, and I'm thinking, 'I've got two drummers? What the hell am I looking at?' Then, when the band arrived and started playing, I was flying around the room trying to set everything up and I was thinking, 'Help!'

"We did *Disraeli Gears* in three days. We started on a Thursday, and Sunday at five o'clock a chauffeur came into the studio and said, 'I'm looking for a group that I've got to take to the airport,' and so I looked at the guys and said, 'See you later!'. . . [T]hey had to leave and, when they left, *Disraeli Gears* was in my lap and I mixed it."

Clapton and Dowd would work together a lot in the future, including on the great Derek and the Dominoes sessions that produced "Layla." But by then, Ertegun, Wexler, and Dowd had moved to Miami and most of Atlantic's recordings—including those classic Clapton sessions—were done at Criteria Studio. Finally, there were so few sessions done in New York that the studio was closed in 1989.

Through all of the years and changes in address, Ahmet Ertegun, Jerry Wexler, Tom Dowd, and Atlantic continued a level of recording excellence—great artists, great songs, great sound. For those who were there, and those who merely got to listen, it has been quite a ride.

178

Columbia Studios
TEMPLE OF SOUND

Of all the great recording studios, there is only one literal Temple of Sound. That would be the former Greek Orthodox Church at 207 East 30th Street in Manhattan. Decades after its demise, to say simply "30th Street" is to evoke a flood of memories of a hallowed recording space.

The former church, where landmark albums such as Miles Davis's *Kind of Blue*, Billie Holiday's *Lady in Satin*, and Dave Brubeck's *Time Out* were recorded—in the same year, no less— makes even seasoned engineers wax nostalgic, if not poetic.

"Oh, my God, that's one of the great rooms of all time. The sound of that room was just spectacular, that was just the best. You just opened up microphones . . . and it sounded like cream," says New Yorker and veteran engineer Al Schmitt.

If you were to fantasize about how a vintage recording studio would look and feel, it'd most likely end up looking like 30th Street—cavernous, open, all wood construction, with lots of boom stands holding expensive German microphones. Throw into the mix bona fide musical icons like those mentioned above, plus Tony Bennett, Barbra Streisand, Leonard Bernstein, and Bob Dylan, in addition to a staff of engineers from the shirt-and-tie school, and the result is American Recording History 101.

Old School

Not long after Thomas Alva Edison invented the phonograph in 1877, there emerged the "big three" record labels: Victor (later to become RCA Victor), Edison, and, in 1883, Columbia.

By the mid-1920s, recording went electric, with a microphone and shellac disc replacing the horn and wax cylinder setup. Edison—who never put a name on the labels save his own—failed to realize what consumers wanted: artists whose work they could collect. Just like that, Enrico Caruso and Bessie Smith became recording stars, the record business took flight, and Victor and Columbia began a dance of rivals that would last well into the twentieth century.

Possessing the deepest catalog of recorded American music, Columbia/CBS/Sony is among the most cached brands in U.S. retail history. With a roster of giants in virtually every genre, from blues to Broadway, from Billie to Bernstein, from the turn of the twentieth century to the twenty-first, the simple yet distinctive red label with black lettering has signified a standard of excellence.

To this day, to be a Columbia recording artist carries the patina of pure prestige. If you're on that red label—whether spinning stately on wax cylinder, vinyl disc, or digital compact disc—you are in very good company indeed. Bessie Smith, Robert Johnson, Al Jolson, Bing Crosby, Benny Goodman, Barbra Streisand, Simon and Garfunkel, Johnny Cash, Leonard Bernstein, Bob Dylan, Miles Davis, Thelonius Monk, Charles Mingus, Louis Armstrong, Johnny Mathis, Billie Holiday, Laura Nyro, Ornette Coleman, Dave Brubeck, Tony Bennett and the Boss, the Duke, the Count, the Byrds, Aretha Franklin, and Frank Sinatra are not bad as far as label mates go.

NYC

New York is where the recording business began. Across the Hudson River, in New Jersey, Edison built what would be the very first studio. But the birthplace of most of last century's audio achievements, Bell Labs, was in Manhattan. Long before most cities even had a studio, New York, by the 1940s, had dozens.

In a town of legendary studios, such as Victor's Webster Hall, Vanguard's Masonic Temple, Regent Studios, and Bell Sound, Columbia and its parent company CBS possessed, then let slip away, no fewer than three historic recording spaces.

As far back as 1929, Columbia's 7th Avenue studio was the site for New York's first radio broadcasts. Seventh Avenue, however, wasn't even the oldest Columbia studio. That honor goes to the studio (which recorded acoustically) located in the Woolworth Building, at the time the world's tallest skyscraper. Legend has it that when the Original Dixieland Jass (later Jazz) Band recorded the first-ever jazz session in 1917, traffic stopped as the music came wafting through the studio walls.

Seventh Avenue and 30th Street are the abiding shrines of Columbia Recording. Both have transmogrified into something more earthbound today, serving in the interests of Manhattan real estate developers.

"A [new label] president was there, and, for the first year ever [1980], the studio [30th Street] lost a million dollars and he couldn't tolerate that. He wanted to sell it," says Frank Laico, who engineered for Columbia from 1946 to the 1990s. "He sold it for a million, when he could have gotten God knows how many more millions if he was smart enough. So it became another apartment house." Sadly, that was merely the latest of a trend.

Thirtieth Street was the label's response to the lack of large orchestral space in which to record classical, large jazz ensembles, and the grand-scale Broadway cast albums for which Columbia would be known through the '70s. (*My Fair Lady*, could be considered the *Thriller* of its time, given the fact that the cast album sold an astonishing five million copies.)

In 1946, Harold Chapman, the senior staff engineer in the '40s, went hunting.

"We kept saying to Columbia, 'We've gotta get our own [large room],'" recalls Frank Laico, "and so they finally agreed and a few of them checked out different places. Thirtieth Street originally was an old church that had been laying vacant now for a few years, and they came back and said, 'Boy, we found it, we found it!'

"CBS put up the money, but not before they agreed with [certain] terms: one of them was that nothing was to be done in that studio once we got it as CBS Records, and we determined what we wanted to do with it. Because [Chapman and new pop executive Mitch Miller] didn't want to do anything [to change it]. The sound was there, and they knew instantly that the corporates would get in there and start sanding the floors and waxing them and painting and doing everything.

"When we went in there that church was just the way it had been left. The hanging drapes and everything. Dust, lots of it, and that's the way it stayed until Mitch Miller resigned."

Initially, Laico, who did more sessions in 30th Street than anyone, had reservations.

"I said to myself, 'What the hell are they thinking? My God, this is a big room. What do we do with some of these big surfaces and so forth; how are we going to maintain [control over the reverberation]?' We started off slowly. [The Columbia brain trust] knew what our problems were [from] talking to other guys like myself and [they] booked the kind of people that wouldn't make a big thing out of spending an hour or so rehearsing, having to move around until we found a good spot and then start to record.

"And that's how we started. Did that off and on for about a year. Once we all agreed that it's there, all we had to do now is work it."

From the mid-'50s to the '80s, there were essentially four very talented engineers who worked it at 7th Avenue and 30th Street. These guys are absolutely inextricable from the music made by giants: virtually all of the studio recordings circa 1955 to 1970 of Bob Dylan, Simon and Garfunkel, Miles Davis, Dave Brubeck, Tony Bennett, Barbra Streisand, and Leonard Bernstein. That's quite a lot of good music.

The top guns through most of the '50s and '60s were local boy Frank Laico and Fred Plaut, the foreign-born *tonemeister* who was as skilled in photography as he was in recording. These two got first call on all of the cool sessions, like *Kind of Blue*, *Time Out*, and *Sketches of Spain* (Plaut), or *Porgy and Bess* and *My Name Is Barbra* (Laico). Stan Tonkel and Roy Hallee were two local boys as well. As 1960s record making eased into the more expansive and trippy frontiers of the studio, it would be Tonkel (*Bitches Brew*) and Hallee (*Bridge over Troubled Water*) who did the vanguard releases.

The three local engineers, Laico, Tonkel, and Hallee, are all semiretired and very aware of their place in recording history. Sadly, the German-born Fred Plaut is no longer with us, but it's his legacy that will be hardest to match, in terms of recording critical, commercial, and cultural touchstones. In the space of a year he recorded *Lady in Satin* for Billie Holiday in 1958, and *Kind of Blue* for Miles and *Time Out* for Brubeck—only three months apart—in 1959, all of which were made at 30th Street. All of which are arguably more popular today than when they were made, a pretty cool trick in any realm.

The Columbia Sound, in this era, was the sound of the one-hundred-foot-high, all-wood former church with the old-school echo chamber in the balcony; or the top floor of 7th Avenue, where the stairwells doubled as echo chambers. All recordings featured a massive array of Telefunken(a.k.a. Neumann) tube microphones such as the M-49, the U-47, and the U-67, all routed and processed by a custom-made CBS console and captured by the ubiqui-

tous Ampex tape machines. In addition, the city's best session players knew the engineers and the studios as well as they knew their own homes and families.

With such a high degree of common denominators, it's difficult to get much variety in the sounds, and that was the point. Columbia records meant class and quality—New York style. The recording, mixing, mastering, pressing—the whole lot—were never less than the standard for the day. One can hear greater variances between *Time Out* and *Sketches of Spain*, both engineered by Plaut, than by *Porgy and Bess* and *Sketches*, recorded by Laico and Plaut, respectively. The dictates of the project were more influential, sonically, than the engineer.

"We actually at one time used to have an engineer's rule book," says Laico. "We had all the setups, everything. So, even though Fred [Plaut] and I went about things somewhat differently, within that framework, it all ended up sounding very similar."

The sound that one hears in *Sketches of Spain* and *Time Out*, for example, is very open, with a good-sized window for each instrument in the arrangements. The sense of space is palpable, but the engineers all "cheated"; that is, they didn't merely hang mics up in the air and leave it at that. "We would use the reverb and add it to the performance, especially any time we remixed [approximately 60 percent]," says Stan Tonkel. Laico adds, "I used to return the [sound] of the reverb and record that back through [a] tape [machine]. That was a little secret of mine," he chuckles. "It takes the edge off [the echo], smooths it out."

Opposite: Boyhood friends Simon and Garfunkel during the *Sound of Silence* sessions, ca. 1964.

Above: Art Garfunkel and Roy Hallee listen to playback (with Paul Simon reflected in the glass) during the *Bookends* sessions, 1967.

185

Roy Hallee might have enjoyed knowing that. To this day, Hallee, a multi-Grammy winner, still thinks of Laico as "the man." So, in fact, do the current engineers at Sony.

"Frank was the main guy; he ruled 3oth Street," says Hallee. "Now, the guy who brought me up was Stan Tonkel," says Hallee, his voice growing more affectionate. "He showed me everything, he didn't have any secrets. I learned everything from Stan." This could easily be an apprentice mason talking about his mentor.

The church-cum-studio on 3oth Street was immense. Frank Laico remembers, "It was a big room, one hundred by one hundred by one hundred." This imbued the church with a natural ambience that cannot be bought, and, with real estate prices in New York, won't be. Size alone, however, wasn't all that mattered. The heavenly acoustics were of an era of building that is not to be mistaken for modern construction. "[Thirtieth] just had the old style construction and acoustics," states Laico. "You could hear it as you walked in."

In his excellent book, *Kind of Blue: The Making of the Miles Davis Masterpiece*, author Ashley Kahn quotes Columbia producer Mike Berniker on the unique sonic qualities of the former church: "It had something you don't find in today's studios—it had an identifying sound. There was a grandeur to the sound—a size and scope that you don't find from very close micing."

Frank Laico recalls his mic technique at 3oth Street as "Putting those mics, especially

186

the [vintage] Telefunken/Neumann 49s, way up there in the air. That was the only way to get that sound."

For Hallee, whose working relationship with Paul Simon stretched from "I Am a Rock" in 1965 through *Graceland* in 1995 and *Rhythm of the Saints* in 1996, Studio A at 7th Avenue was his room. Like Laico at 30th Street, he knew what to do with it. Also like Laico, no one else at Columbia knew those particular studios as well: "Frank was the only one who could make 30th Street work," says Hallee. "Everyone else just had all the leakage swimming around. Frank could stick a mic out there in the open, and it would just sound great."

Every great engineer has got that special room: that studio that they've lived in through countless sessions. Although Columbia engineers routinely worked both 7th Avenue and 30th Street, 30th was Laico's room. He *owned* it.

"I had, and I'm not bragging, quite a number of offers from other labels to come to them and *I just couldn't leave that room*. I didn't wanna work in these small studios. I had the best of it and I didn't want to give it up.

"After, when we really got swinging hard down at 30th Street, I very seldom got up to Studio A or B, or D [7th Avenue]. I mostly stayed downtown, at 30th Street. My whole life was in that studio.

"A typical day should have been starting at 9:00 to 6:00, but there were days when I would be in the studio at 8:00 in the morning and not leave until 3:00 or 4:00 the next morn-

187

Miles Davis with flügelhorn and arranger Gil Evans sketching out the charts at 30th Street for the *Miles Ahead* LP, recorded in 1957 by Harold Chapman.

ing—I wish I had a hundred dollar bill for every night I was there until 2:00 or 3:00 in the morning—right straight on through. With an hour between sessions. I never ate very much, but you know, it was so exciting! I wouldn't have traded my job for anybody's."

Seventh Avenue had a longer history, from roughly the late '20s through the late '60s (before being gutted and sold to a "competitor," Phil Ramone; more on that later), with a wider range of musical styles being recorded, while 30th Street, from the late '40s through the '70s, had superior acoustics and tended to feature more of the orchestral and Broadway work.

"Thirtieth Street was where people went to get that '30th Street sound'—very big, open and smooth," said Stan Tonkel, who recorded such divergent yet quintessential Columbia albums as *Bitches Brew* and *The Freewheeling Bob Dylan*. "Solo piano, solo violin, large orchestras, anybody who wanted that specific sound. We had a natural [echo] chamber there, which we had built in [what had been] the balcony of the church. At 7th, we did more contemporary things, more rock and jazz, and we didn't have the natural echo chamber or the space that you had at 30th Street.

"But at 7th Avenue, we made use of the two stairwells. We would hang some [expensive vintage] Telefunken 47s on the top floor and have the sound of the entire stairwell [ten floors high] to use as our reverb chamber. We used that quite a bit, especially when we remixed those

188

Broadway albums that were usually recorded at 3oth. The only problem with the mics in the stairwell was the mics would get stolen. My echo would be gone, and when I went in the stairwell, you'd see the chain that was used to keep the mic secure would be cut!"

Lady in cotton: Billie Holiday sings into a Telefunken M49 mic in one of her last sessions, 1958.

While 3oth Street garnered the reputation as the premier large-scale room in Manhattan, 7th Avenue was getting a different type of rep. "Columbia was not known as a rock label," says Hallee today. "You could not get a rock band to go in there; they all equated 7th Avenue with Johnny Mathis."

Hallee quickly changed all that. He started as a boom operator for CBS television, then worked his way up the ranks to performing edits and remixes for CBS Records division. Finally, Roy got his break at recording. His first session was a track that would forever change what a pop single could be: Bob Dylan's "Like a Rolling Stone."

"I was terrified. I didn't know what the hell I was doing. Dylan didn't help matters—he wanted to record right next to the guitars and drums, no matter how much that stuff bled into his vocal mic. But I got through it.

"Then all the Simon and Garfunkel stuff happened. It became just the opposite; 7th Avenue became the only place in New York that rock bands, like the Lovin' Spoonful, wanted to record. I had so many records on the charts that everyone wanted to work with me there."

Hallee credits Eric Porterfield, head of the tech department, for creating custom CBS

189

consoles that "were built like brick shit houses. Frank Laico never knew how lucky he was *not* to work on the modern consoles of today. Those custom CBS consoles were built to not break down. That's incredible peace of mind when you've got Leonard Bernstein and the New York Philharmonic in the room."

Hallee worked at 7th Avenue pre- *and* post-Columbia. The suits at Columbia decided to let 7th go: "A new president came in and thought 7th wasn't profitable enough," says Laico incredulously. "They let it go. To Phil Ramone. A *competitor*. Smart thinking, eh?"

Phil Ramone's A&R Studios

Phil Ramone was a New York prodigy. At ten, he played violin for Queen Elizabeth. Years later, he decided to satisfy his technical bent and made the switch to the other side of the glass. In 1960, he purchased his own studio, the funky, quaint, A&R on 48th Street. He engineered a score of smash records there, most notably becoming the studio source of bossa nova in the early '60s as a result of two records that are considered classics today: Quincy Jones's *Big Band Bossa Nova*, and the *Stan Getz/João Gilberto* duet LP that spawned "The Girl from Ipanema."

"I think by 1963 or '64 things like the bossa nova records came out of A&R, and that was a huge sound for individual sweetness, and, you know, how things were kept so quiet. I became famous for that sound, and if you listen to *Big Band Bossa Nova*, that's the sound that became, like, this crazy, better than 30th Street"—he quickly corrects himself—"not better, but equal to, this great brass sound."

A&R also became the home for Burt Bacharach and Hal David's incredible string of hit singles with Dionne Warwicke.

"The first thing we did with Burt was *Alfie*," says Phil, who's still actively producing. "We squeezed all those people into that tiny room on 48th Street. But you know, that room wasn't enough. If you're an engineer, you've got that ego; you want your own room. I wanted a *big room*; I wanted to be up there with the big boys."

So in 1969, Ramone, through a consortium of partners, wound up with the studio of his dreams: 799 7th Avenue, former home of Columbia studios.

"We eventually got 799 7th Avenue through the amazing process that Columbia Records decided to give up their 7th Avenue facility, and it was not supposed to be for sale, especially to a competitive independent. But because we were represented by a normal business approach, we looked like a minor-league company. So the Roy Hallees of the world, the great engineers that had been around [New York] said, 'Jesus, you're getting 7th Avenue.'

"They gave it to us without any wiring or anything. They cut all of that out. [Studio] A-1 we called it, became the Temple in itself, because it had a gigantically big ceiling put on it; its peak was forty feet. It was about sixty by sixty-five roughly, and then we built this humongous booth in it so that the performers could work and that kind of isolated you, but you could perform on stage in the room."

Hallee credits Ramone, whom he calls a recording idol, with "taking a good room and making it great. He really worked with the room's acoustics to make the bass sound great."

"Roy, when he found out we had bought 7th Avenue, I convinced him to leave Columbia and caused all kind of mania," says Ramone, "but he loved the room so much that he said, 'That's my home. I want to be in that room.' We had gone way beyond our investment money with banks and I said, 'OK, we've got to make a go of it.' Nobody knew if we could book three studios full time, three music studios, let alone film. We did things Columbia hadn't done and, of course, the biggest picture that first comes out of there is *Midnight Cowboy*, and we have a hit record with (Harry) Nilsson's 'Everybody's Talkin'.'"

The hits for Ramone and Hallee would continue well into the '90s. Owing to the pressure caused by escalating real estate prices, not only would Columbia lose its revered 30th Street shrine, but Ramone would also lose his beloved A&R at 799 7th Avenue.

"Today, I could get the city of New York to preserve some of those places, because of their historical merit. But at that time, you know, in the '70s, they had to change them into office buildings for the IRS. Goes to show you what's *really* important." All the men who worked in these studios spoke of the heartbreak of losing their dream work spaces. Today, in his eighties, Frank Laico perhaps best sums it up: "My whole life was in that studio. That was the best fun I had in my life. I hated to leave, but that's the way it goes."

Van Gelder Studio
JAZZ CASUAL

A warm day in late June, 1965. Soft New Jersey breezes blow off the Hudson, flirt-ing with the sleepy sliver of a town known as Englewood Cliffs. Kids zigzag through the streets on their bikes, still giddy to be on their summer break. On the south-ern border traffic oozes across the George Washington Bridge into Manhattan. The hot exhausts of Chevy Biscaynes, Pontiac Catalinas, Mercury Montereys, and the rest of the road's superwide, electraglide, V8 cruisemobiles muddy the atmosphere, and their constant rumble mixed with the sun's thick honey rays. But a mile or two from the bridge, straight up Route 9W, inside a low-slung concrete-block building with an oddly peaked roof, a tremendous storm is brewing.

It starts ominously as a somber sax intones a simple mournful phrase; then the other players pick it up. A drummer bangs out rolls of thunder. Then, with the overlapping montage of saxes and trumpets, a dissonant tempest threatens to erupt. And soon enough, sheets of sound descend like rain. The drummer becomes a demon with eight arms. Two stand-up bassists duel it out. Piano chords jangle above the mix like shards of glass falling to the pave-ment. Brass and woodwinds screech white hot with tears and prayers. The assault veers out of control as the man in the middle of it turns his horn upward toward the vaulted wooden beams above him and blows his soul through the saxophone. One participant later recalls that the intensity in the room was so great, some of the musicians were screaming.

Then, after nearly forty minutes of in-your-face, shout-your-guts-out blowing, the storm subsides. The man in the eye of it all takes his horn from his lips. His face is a vision of calm—serene, spent. The piano and drum play an ominous coda, like the passing of the last dark clouds.

Behind a thick plate of glass, which seems to provide shelter from this sonic hurricane, a small, bespectacled man starts adjusting levels with hands covered by white cotton gloves. He has carefully taken the measure of the onslaught and prepares to review the results. Take one. John Coltrane and friends have just recorded "Ascension"—and Rudy Van Gelder has just witnessed the making of another masterpiece and committed it to tape.

The Van Gelder Studio should be a national landmark. In this space, giants walked, played, laughed, sweated and, above all . . . never smoked in the control room. That was a strict Van Gelder rule. A short list of those who have recorded at either of Van Gelder's two studios, the first in his parents' house in Hackensack, the second in Englewood Cliffs, is Miles Davis, John Coltrane, Thelonious Monk, Duke Ellington, Sonny Rollins, Wes Montgomery, Coleman Hawkins, Ben Webster, Ray Charles, Bud Powell, Herbie Hancock, Eric Dolphy, Freddie Hubbard, Stan Getz, Elvin Jones, McCoy Tyner, Chet Baker, Horace Silver, Jimmy Smith, Tony Williams . . . and that hardly scratches the surface. Imagine this: Rudy Van Gelder recorded virtually all of the albums made by Blue Note and Prestige Records in the '50s and '60s, a large chunk of the Verve catalogue from the same era, nearly all of the Impulse label's recordings in the '60s, and practically all of the CTI disks from the '70s. And he did it all by himself—placed every mic, tweaked every fader, punched every button, loaded all the tape, set up all the chairs, turned on and off all the lights. And he's still going strong—though as he approached his seventies, he finally took on an assistant. One.

It's hard not to use the G-word when talking about Van Gelder. That's how most of those who have worked with him describe him. *Genius*. But in some ways it's easier to see Rudy Van Gelder as a master chef. He has created sonic recipes that no one else can quite duplicate. And, like a culinary master, his recipes are top secret. He shares them with no one. *No one*. He will not reveal what kind of board he uses, where he places his mics, the dimensions of his studio, or why his wooden cathedral ceiling looks the way it does. He believes that the only things that are really important to know about his place are the sounds you hear coming out of it.

And this much is hard to dispute: Rudy Van Gelder defined the way we listen to recorded jazz. Before Rudy, drums were mushy, pianos sounded dull, and the bass . . . often missing in action. After Rudy, drums snapped and cymbals sizzled, pianos cooked and crackled, and the bass held the bottom like a swingin' ship's anchor. Modern jazz had a modern sound—and it was coming out of a living room in Hackensack.

That's where Rudy's father designed the family home shortly after World War II. It was a modern, U-shaped building with a flat roof and (very impressive for the late 1940s) central air-conditioning. But the elder Van Gelder let his son help design the living room, which made up the middle of the U-shaped house, so it could double as a recording studio. "He let me put a control room in there," Rudy recalls. "There were bedrooms, a living room, a dining room, there was a kitchen, and there was a control room and the control room had a window into the living room. You know, a double glass . . . it's amazing. It still amazes me.

"We had rugs on the floor, lamps, and a television set, and little doodads in the corners. And there were hallways off the edge of it, so it gave a little more acoustic volume. So it was a fairly nice-sounding room. It had a fairly high ceiling, and it was rectangular and pretty well suited for a five-piece bebop band."

Even though the control room was built into the original house design, recording music was strictly a hobby for Rudy at that point. He had been an avid music collector as a kid, and he played trumpet in his school band. He'd bought an early Rek-O-Kut twelve-inch 78-RPM recorder, and he and some of his friends would jam and make records. When he moved into the Hackensack house with his parents, Van Gelder had just graduated from the Pennsylvania State College of Optometry. But the jam sessions continued. The new neighbors complained. The jam sessions continued.

In 1946, Van Gelder was twenty-one. He'd just opened his own optometrist's shop in neighboring Teaneck, and he'd also made his first professional recording. He had not sought this work out, a pattern that would hold for the rest of his professional career. In the first of countless gigs to come, the work had found him.

"What happened is that there was a person, I don't even remember his name, who loved Joe Mooney, and . . . Bucky Pizzarelli, who was the guitar player who was working with Joe at the time, he brought Joe over to my place to record. That was the first commercial record I had ever made. It was called *We'll Be Together Again,* on a label called Carousel. I think it was one of the three records that they ever made. And it was a 78, not an LP. This was before the LP, and it was beautiful. As a matter of fact, there was a disc jockey on WNEW in New York at the time named Al (Jazzbo) Collins. He had a program in the afternoon called 'Collins on a Cloud.' And this [record] was a quiet, beautiful ballad, and [Mooney] played the organ and then sang the vocal, and it was just an absolutely beautiful thing. And [Collins] got on that record and he played it every day. You could turn the radio on about 3:30 or 4:00 in the afternoon and could hear *We'll Be Together Again,* and that went on for a long time. That was the first I had heard anything [I recorded] played on the radio, and you know, that was a thrill.

"Well, from there, of course . . . what happened is the phone started to ring, and kept ringing, and I answered the phone and did what people asked me to do, and mostly it was recording." One of these recordings was by a baritone sax player named Gil Mellé. The recording caught the ear of Blue Note Records co-owner Alfred Lion, who bought the rights to release it.

"Listen to this! Alfred Lion, who didn't know anything about me and [had] never been to Hackensack, he [took the record and] went to the engineer at the place that had been recording for him at that time [WOR], and his name was Doug Hawkins. And Alfred said,

'Look. This is Gil Mellé. I want you to make another record to sound like that.' And the engineer said, 'I can't do that. You'd better take that to the guy who made it.' And that's exactly what he did."

That led to Van Gelder's first recording for Blue Note. Lion was pleased with the results, though there's no record of his first impression of Rudy's "studio." It couldn't have been too bad, because he soon returned to Hackensack with a new task for this gifted young engineer.

"He brought me a master of something he had recorded at WOR and never had success with making a good clean pressing of it. And I believe this was the time when LPs were coming in. And so he gave it to me. He said, 'Here. See if you can make this sound better.' That's what he used to do. He'd give me his problems. And I took that thing and I made it sound better than it ever had. And from then on I did all the masters for him. So those were the first series of events. Those were the first things."

From there, the relationship between Blue Note and Van Gelder steadily solidified. By 1954 Rudy was doing nearly all of Blue Note's recordings, and although the label had existed since the late '30s, it wasn't long before critics began crediting Rudy with creating the "Blue Note Sound."

"Well, Alfred was the foundation," Rudy recalls. "He was the rock upon which I could extend myself financially. I figured no matter what happened, Alfred would be there and that would be enough to keep me [in the music business]. By the way, I also want to emphasize that this whole time span with the original Blue Note included Frank Wolff, because it was the two of them that made it; it wasn't just Alfred. [Wolff] was just as responsible as anyone else for the artistic success of that company, and people don't mention him often enough. They like his pictures, because they were great, but he was very much involved in the musical decisions at every session.

Sonny Rollins in Hackensack, recording *Newk's Time*, 1956.

"And, as a matter of fact, they used to have an interplay that a lot of musicians would make fun of, because they [would be] arguing back and forth and had quite a thing going. Alfred would like a song, Frank wouldn't. Alfred would like a take, Frank wouldn't, and vice versa. And there was a continuing interplay between the two of them. That was the way that thing worked.

"They used to collate the records, putting them in the sleeves before they mailed them. They did every detail, and it was possible then. They were totally involved with the details of the pressing. They used to examine every one to make sure everything was right. I mean, they were totally involved in every aspect of it."

Van Gelder's hobby was becoming a lucrative business. And it wasn't long before his success with Blue Note was noted by jazz fan Bob Weinstock, who ran a jazz record store in New York and started the Prestige record label when he was only nineteen.

Weinstock began recording at Apex studios on 57th Street in Manhattan. Eventually, a young Tommy Dowd, a childhood friend of Weinstock's, took on the engineering chores. But

after Dowd joined Atlantic, Weinstock couldn't find anyone who could make his records sound the way he wanted them to. A flawed recording of an all-star session with Miles Davis, Sonny Rollins, and Charlie Parker—on his second and final recording date playing tenor—so upset Weinstock that he considered abandoning the business. But serendipity prevailed.

"I lived in Teaneck, and I was walking down the main street and I see, 'Rudy Van Gelder, Optometrist.' Right there on the store. A big sign. I said to my wife, 'Go do something for a half hour. I wanna check this out.'"

Weinstock recognized the name on the sign because Alfred Lion had taken the unprecedented step of giving Van Gelder a credit on all of the Blue Note recordings. It would be nearly twenty years before producers were listed on albums with any regularity (and Lion and Wolff never gave themselves producer credits). For an engineer to be given this honor in the early '50s was extraordinary. Weinstock, a big Blue Note fan, was thus familiar with the name. Could "Rudy Van Gelder, Optometrist" be the same guy?

"I went in there and I said, 'Are you Rudy Van Gelder that does Blue Note records?' 'Yeah, that's me.' And we talked, you know. And I asked, 'Are you allowed to do other people's records besides Blue Note's?' He said, 'Yeah. I'm not exclusive to them. I have time open.' And I booked a session with him. A Miles session was the first one I did."

Now Van Gelder had two prolific full-time recording clients. And soon, jazz pianist Marion McPartland would recommend him for work with another major jazz label, Savoy. By 1957, he was one of the busiest men in the business.

A record review in *Audio* magazine from October 1957 includes one of Van Gelder's very first interviews. Even then, at that early point in his career, he skirted specifics about his recording techniques, but he did reveal some of his philosophy and discuss some of his early equipment. He also provided a picture of just how busy he was:

"Mine is a one-man operation, and I don't have time for all I would like to do. I devote a minimum of one day each week to Blue Note, Prestige, and Savoy, my three oldest clients. The jazz labels I have recorded are too numerous to mention. They include Atlantic, Coral, Debut, King, Pacific Jazz, Riverside, and ABC-Paramount. My latest is Signal and I just finished a Lee Konitz date for Norman Granz's Verve label.

"Then I master everything pressed for Westminster by the Abbey Record Manufacturing Company in Newark. Also the Music Treasures of the World, a classical mail-order firm. I do considerable work for Vox. . . . As it is, I am usually busy six days and four nights [a week]."

Rudy goes on to explain his philosophy about microphones, how important it is to learn the sounds each one gives the engineer. He says he chooses a microphone "with the same care a photographer employs in selecting a lens." Though he reveals that he never uses two mics when, in his opinion, one mic will do, he refuses to describe any of his setups "as it might seem to commit me to one particular technique." However, he does include this insightful observation: "Thelonious Monk, Horace Silver, and Mal Waldron all come under the general classification of modern pianists. Yet each has an individual touch, a different sense of the piano in a group. If they are all recorded the same way, an exact comparison of their sound might be provided, but the result would be fair to only one of them. I try to give their separate styles full value, according to the framework of the music. I may also vary my setup from track to track, not treating rhythm numbers and ballads the same way."

The article also quotes Alfred Lion, who noted, "Rudy is more than an ordinary engineer in that his knowledge of jazz, and the way he applies it to the recording of different musicians, puts him, to my mind, in the class of a creative artist."

The article includes a rare description of Rudy's control room and its equipment. The tiny room was equipped to complete a disc from recording through the cutting of a master. The console was new at the time. "It is a real bit of craftsmanship by Rein Narma," said Van Gelder. "He also designed and installed the control console in the home studio of Les Paul and Mary Ford." In addition, the room featured four Ampex tape recorders—two 300s and two 250s—that were interconnected to record in stereo, two portable Ampex 350s used for field assignments, a Scully automatic lathe for mastering, and two bass-reflex cabinets fitted with Altec Lansing 604C speakers for monitoring in the control room. Two backloaded horn cabinets with Jim Lansing (of JBL fame), fifteen-inch woofers, and acoustic lens tweeters were used for playback in the studio.

There are two things to remember about Rudy at this time: First, most of the work done on those "six days and four nights" a week was in his parents' small suburban home, where they all still lived. Second, Rudy Van Gelder still saw himself primarily as an optometrist.

"All during the Hackensack years, I had a practice," Van Gelder recalls today. "I was examining eyes in the daytime and [on] Wednesday[s] I'd be recording Miles Davis."

Van Gelder's parents built a separate entrance in the back of the house so that they wouldn't walk in on the living-room sessions. They never interacted with the musicians. Bob Weinstock remembers meeting them "maybe once." Esmond Edwards, who took over the bulk of the hands-on production from Weinstock, "never saw them. I think I saw his father once, but whether we were recording, morning, noon, or night, they were never there."

One concession Rudy made to his parents—and his neighbors—was that he rarely recorded at night, though he might work on mastering or other postproduction chores after dark. Edwards remembers, "I think the clubs closed at three or something, so realistically you couldn't get anyone in the studio before noon or one o'clock. And of course, I only attended sessions run by Bob Weinstock, and Bob is just a very relaxed guy. He'd kid around and [drummer] Arthur Taylor and Rudy would be cracking jokes back and forth over the microphone and again, of course, just about all the musicians would be high in one form or another. So that led to a very relaxed atmosphere. Sometimes tempers would flare about a musical thing or whatever. But, yeah, the ambiance of the couches and the floor lamps or whatever I think helped to make for a relaxed feeling and it was like jamming in somebody's apartment."

199

One notorious session when tempers supposedly flared occurred on Christmas Eve, 1954, during a Miles Davis session. Thelonious Monk was on piano.

"Monk played very aggressively," Van Gelder recalls, "and so they were rehearsing this tune and it came time for Miles's solo. And the one thing that Monk did say to me during that session was, 'Don't turn me down during the solo.' So, after they did this rehearsal, I guess they must have heard a playback or something. So Miles said to Monk, 'Lay out in back of my solo.' OK. Now, comes the next take, right. So I call the take and they start playing, and they play the opening melody and it comes time for Miles to play his solo. So Miles starts playing and he's sort of hunched over playing into the microphone. So Monk gets up off the piano and stands and looks down at Miles. So Miles says, 'What are you doing?' Monk says, 'Well, I don't have to sit down to lay out!'"

A legend quickly grew that Miles and Monk came to blows—a rumor all parties vehemently denied. But aside from this infamous studio fish tale, what most people remember about recording at Van Gelder's is that sessions were extraordinarily smooth—and fun. Bob Weinstock would tell Rudy who was playing on a given date, and when he walked in, all of the mics and chairs would already be set up. "And it went so good," says Weinstock. "To be honest with you, Rudy had a TV in the living room. And when I came there to record, they had a lot of daytime baseball back then. And I'd put on the TV with no sound and watch the ball games

while he was recording. He and the musicians did everything they had to do and I never had a deep concern. Just listen to the music and that's it. In fact, one day, in the World Series, I saw Willie Mays's famous catch. He went all the way back and made the catch at the Polo Grounds, running away from home plate. And I saw that there. And I started to yell and I ruined the take. They had to stop it. The guys said, 'What's the matter, what's the matter?' I said, 'Boy, you gotta see that catch!' And then finally they showed a replay, thank God!"

Producer Bob Thiele recalled in his autobiography, *What a Wonderful World*, that Rudy's interest in bird watching could also stop sessions. He remembers Rudy running out of the house, "dragging with him as many puzzled and disbelieving musicians as he could entice [to] witness the arrivals of various birds who, it seemed, always made the Van Gelder acreage a requisite stopover in their seasonal migrations." Thiele also remembered Rudy as "more obsessed with hygiene and cleanliness than anyone I ever knew." Van Gelder always wore white cotton gloves to keep oils off the mics.

"And he absolutely forbade smoking in the control room," recalls Esmond Edwards. "So, you know, that irked some of the guys. After they recorded a tune they wanted to go into the control room and light up and listen to the playback and no way! No way!"

Though business could hardly be better, by 1958 Van Gelder was facing a major professional crisis. He was thirty-three years old and had somehow found time enough to get married.

The guilt he felt about taking over his parents' house was weighing on him. Sure, he could find a place he and his bride could move in to, but what about the studio? He was not about to work in a space he couldn't control. And he also didn't want to commute. There was only one solution—and it was risky. He would put up every dime he had—and more—to build a new home/studio entirely from scratch to his own exacting specifications.

First he found a prime piece of real estate in the well-to-do (and convenient to Manhattan) suburb of Englewood Cliffs, New Jersey. It was a wooded plot, and he basically kept it that way, clearing out just enough to build his home/studio and a modest yard. Then he went through two architects. The first design, according to Van Gelder, looked like "an institution." So he contracted another, from a student of Frank Lloyd Wright's, and the result is very much in keeping with the master's latter-period low-slung concrete-block style. On the outside, the building appears modern and modest. Inside, the studio is beautiful and breathtaking.

The most striking feature is its ceiling. The huge wooden beams were transported from the Northwest on flatbed freight cars that went through Canada, where they got lost in a blizzard. Fortunately, they were recovered and completed the journey. The ceiling is a wide, unsupported span, its large beams soaring upward and creating a visual spectacle that brings to mind a cathedral. And like a great cathedral, the dark woods of the ceiling and floor and the warm earth tones of the walls create an environment that is ultimately soothing and introspective—an inspiring space to create great music.

In late 1959, Van Gelder moved to his new digs, ready to record more jazz and make out more eyeglass prescriptions. He recalls: "I actually had my optometry equipment in the back, and that didn't work. I didn't have time. I remember the last lady that came in. . . . She just wanted me to do [her eyes] and I couldn't say no. [But] that was it. I finally gave it up."

With his new dream studio, he could do things he never could back in Hackensack. For one thing, he could record at night. And the large space now allowed him to record big bands and orchestras. But mainly, he didn't have to feel guilty about intruding on his parents any longer. Sadly, after his parents passed away, the Hackensack house was demolished. "I went past the house years later while it was up for sale," Van Gelder recalls. "I saw the sale sign and then one day I went by there and the building was gone. And right in the back there was a white cat sitting in the corner of the property. Wasn't that weird? That actually happened, and I don't understand it. But I remember seeing that thing sitting there and the place was flattened."

The new, larger studio wasn't embraced by all the musicians. "They weren't used to playing in a space like this. They were used to a small kind of Hackensack sound. But Alfred Lion said, 'No. Give it a chance. Give it a chance.' So he was really strong on my side. He foresaw what it could become."

If the '50s were busy for Rudy, they were merely a warm-up for the '60s. Blue Note and Prestige were churning out LPs with astonishing regularity and amazing diversity. Organ-based soul/jazz was coming into its own, a style ushered in during the mid-1950s when Jimmy

Smith hauled his Hammond B3 in a used hearse to Hackensack and toted it into the Van Gelders' living room. (Today, Rudy's own B3 sits gleaming in his studio, and every great jazz organist, including Smith, Baby Face Willette, Jack McDuff, Jimmy McGriff, Larry Young, Shirley Scott, Joey Defrancesco, and even Ray Charles has played on it.)

But the '60s also brought more big clients to Van Gelder's studio. Producer Creed Taylor started Impulse! Records for ABC-Paramount. Then Taylor abruptly left the label to go to Verve, where he continued to shepherd projects to Rudy's place. Producer Bob Thiele took over at Impulse! Over a period of three to five years, Thiele claimed to have made some two hundred albums. Probably 90 percent of those (or more) were recorded at Van Gelder's.

Rudy remembers Thiele was "aware of recording techniques and as a producer, at least, the things I did with him spanned a much wider scope than either Blue Note or Prestige. He was flexible musically and he had very good judgment and [was] also very easy to work for. A heavy smoker, that's the only thing."

In his autobiography, Thiele recalled: "When Van Gelder was once absent and I couldn't stand it, I sneaked a smoke, and perverse destiny caused an errant ash to mark his control room carpet. I desperately (and believed successfully) labored for twenty minutes to eradicate all evidence of my sin, but it was the first thing Rudy angrily noticed upon his return. Our friendship survived that calamity, and I was later invited to experience the ultimate Van Gelderesque privilege: to sit in his prized and seldom-driven 'custom automobile of Italian manufacture' that was enshrined in his impossibly spotless garage. Naturally, he insisted I take my shoes off before I got inside!"

In 1961, Impulse! signed John Coltrane to the biggest contract given any jazz artist up to that time, except for Miles Davis at Columbia. Most of Coltrane's early recordings, including those he made with Miles and others for Prestige, and his one classic recording for Blue Note, *Blue Trane*, had been recorded at Van Gelder's. Then, in 1958, he signed with Atlantic Records. After three profitable years there, recording at the Atlantic studio with Tom Dowd, Trane came "home" to Van Gelder's. "The reason he came back here," Rudy says, "is because Coltrane liked the way I recorded, and he said so. He was comfortable here." His first session back, on May 23, 1961, was a big-band affair (eighteen pieces) for the *Africa/Brass* LP. But Coltrane's next Impulse! release was a live date with his quintet at the Village Vanguard. Van Gelder had done remotes before, but, to paraphrase one of Coltrane's biggest hits, it was not one of his favorite things. "You'd have to sit there one or two nights in a row until three in the morning and you have to be able to listen and have headphones on, and everybody's playing loud and cigarette smoke is filling the place, and it was a nightmare."

Bob Thiele remembered the experience a bit more romantically. "Everyone in the audience was mesmerized: I was so intensely puffing the pipe I smoked in those days it nearly broke in my mouth, and, more incredibly, Max Gordon [the Vanguard's owner] stopped counting his receipts to look up and listen!"

As Coltrane ripped into an impossibly complex and fluid improvisation, Van Gelder grabbed a handheld microphone and ran up to the stage to record it. Thiele would recall that the engineer "became a frenzied blur that mirrored Trane's unpredictable, compulsive choreography . . . continuously and courageously climbing over chairs, tables, waiters, and customers to accurately capture every precious sound." Later, Thiele, Coltrane, and Van Gelder listened to the playback and tried to come up with a title for the song. It was Rudy who came up with the name that described his own physical effort as well as the "sheets of sound" flowing from the saxophone: "Chasin' the Trane."

Other classic Trane sessions followed, including transcendent pairings with Duke Ellington and honey-toned vocalist Johnny Hartman (Van Gelder calls the *John Coltrane and Johnny Hartman* album one of the best things he ever did). Then, on December 9, 1964, John Coltrane recorded *A Love Supreme*, one of the biggest-selling and most revered jazz albums ever. It was recorded in one session. As was often the case, no one had heard the music Coltrane was bringing in that day—not Van Gelder, Thiele, or even the musicians. Rudy remembers, "He would call me . . . and say he wanted to record at 7:30 Wednesday night. And he would come in and assemble out there and he would teach them whatever the song was and they would play it." *A Love Supreme* was Coltrane's gift to God, and it remains among the most sublime performances ever recorded.

A little less than seven months later, Coltrane was back in Englewood Cliffs to record *Ascension*. Many consider it his masterpiece. Less accessible at first listen than anything he'd done before, it was, stated Nat Hentoff in his original review for *Hi Fi/Stereo Review* "his most absorbing success so far." After recording the exhausting forty-minute piece, Coltrane listened to the playback. Then he and his assembled players stepped outside into the warm afternoon. Photographer Charles Stewart, who was documenting the session, remembers that Coltrane walked down the street, bought everyone lunch, and brought it back to the studio. Stewart captures the musicians looking relaxed. Coltrane even appears boyish, horsing around in Van Gelder's yard. Bob Thiele smiles, settled in a comfy Adirondack chair. Drummer Elvin Jones, shirt off, looking thoroughly exhausted, takes a solitary smoke.

After a while, Trane walked over to Jones, put his arm around him, and asked, "Think you can do one more?" Jones nodded, and the musicians joined Rudy back in the studio.

Another intense forty minutes of playing followed. When it was over, Stewart recalls, Jones took his snare drum and flung it across the room—*Bang!* "Well I guess that takes care of that!" he exclaimed, sweat soaked and spent. There were no more takes. When *Ascension* was released, a mix-up occurred and the wrong take—there is now some question as to which take it was—was pressed. Coltrane heard it and alerted Bob Thiele. In the next pressing, the mistake was corrected and "Edition II" was inscribed into the record near the label. As a result, the original release of *Ascension* is quite rare. Both takes appear on the Impulse! two-CD set *The Major Works of John Coltrane*.

Coltrane's was hardly the only challenging music coming out of Van Gelder's during the '60s. A new breed of jazz musician, including Eric Dolphy, Herbie Hancock, Wayne Shorter, Jackie McClean, Larry Young, Rahsaan Roland Kirk, Archie Shepp, Freddie Hubbard, Pharoah Sanders, and Don Cherry was taking jazz into unknown territory. But it was no picnic for one man to get all of these great performances, many of which are now revered as bona fide classics, down on tape. Since his days in Hackensack, Van Gelder had gotten around the problem of booking his many clients by assigning each label a day. "I would never book anybody [else] on that day, and whether [the client] had anything or not—and they usually had something to do—that would be their day. So I was doing five different clients, and each one had their own time slot and there was never a problem."

Except that Van Gelder found himself working seven days a week virtually without a break for many, many years. By the early '70s he'd finally gotten into the habit of shutting down the studio for a month, but by then, many things had changed. Alfred Lion sold his share of Blue Note to Liberty Records in the mid-1960s, and Frank Wolff left a couple of years later after he was diagnosed with cancer. Bob Weinstock sold Prestige to Fantasy Records in 1970. John Coltrane died in 1967, and Bob Thiele left Impulse! a few years later. Rudy kept working, but things certainly weren't the same. Then, as if on cue, Creed Taylor appeared with an intriguing offer.

Between takes while recording *Ascension*, June 28, 1965. John Coltrane (bending down at right) takes a break with friends and fellow musicians at Van Gelder's, including Pharoah Sanders (in the background with his head bent), Archie Shepp (in a hat), Jimmy Garrison (to Shepp's left), and John Tchicai (with his back to the camera).

205

A&M Records was funding Taylor to the tune of one million dollars over five years for his new jazz label, CTI. Following his original vision for Impulse!, Taylor planned to produce great records by great artists with rich-looking, exquisitely designed gatefold covers. George Benson, Freddie Hubbard, Chet Baker, Paul Desmond, and others were signed up, and Taylor needed a full-time studio. Would Rudy be interested, even if it meant dropping all of his other clients? Van Gelder wrestled with the idea—then decided to go for it.

Taylor kept his word and kept Van Gelder busy. The CTI sound was controversial. Some jazz critics found it too slick and too commercial. There were strings, electronic instruments were common, pop and rock songs were routinely covered, and few sessions featured merely the classic jazz trio or quartet. But Rudy loved the challenge of recording the CTI sessions. These were big, lavish productions, taking full advantage of Van Gelder's spacious room. They resulted in handsome albums by Benson, Hubbard, Desmond, Maynard Ferguson, Gato Barbieri, Antonio Carlos Jobim, Quincy Jones, Wes Montgomery, and others. There were even hit singles, most notably Deodato's "Also Sprach Zarathustra (Theme for *2001: A Space Odyssey*)."

But in spite of (and some would say because of) the efforts made by CTI, the late '70s were a nightmare era for jazz. CTI ran into financial troubles. At the same time, Van Gelder was dealing with a crisis of his own: his wife was diagnosed with having cancer. For years, she had sacrificed for his career. In 1977, he closed down the studio to devote all of his energies to her, when she needed him most. Sadly, she died in 1979.

When Van Gelder reopened for business after nearly three years, many of the labels he had worked with, such as Blue Note and Impulse!, were in mothballs. But several independent jazz producers sought him out and kept him going. Then, the Verve label came back in the mid-1980s. Impulse! was resuscitated by Michael Cuscuna. Sony revived Blue Note. New work came Rudy's way. He wasn't as busy as during the '60s, but he was working on some great projects. He remarried.

Then, in the mid-'90s, Sony Music approached him about remastering some of the classic Blue Note albums he'd originally recorded. Soon, beautifully reissued "RVG Editions" were in the record stores. Their success spawned an ever-growing series of RVG remasters. The Van Gelder sound was once again in demand—and sounding better than ever. But what is this sound? Bob Weinstock points out the separation you hear between the instruments. Esmond Edwards chooses the word *scintillating*, noting the bright tone of the drums. Producer Bob Porter simply calls it the standard for all modern jazz recording. And Rudy? How does he describe the Van Gelder sound?

"Well, there is a very obvious, accurate answer to that question, but my problem is, if I describe it, I'm describing what I do. The problem is if I feel comfortable talking about it. The only thing I can say about it is, I do feel that it is unique. I can recognize the difference. I feel comfortable with the difference, and I don't feel that it has [been duplicated] anywhere else."

For the true jazz fan, that's enough said.

When I'm done, turn on Lucy: The incredible Jimmy Smith revolutionized jazz in the '50s with recordings he made in Mr. And Mrs. Van Gelder's living room in Hackensack.

Criteria
STAYIN' ALIVE

Late '50s, Fort Lauderdale. A guy named Jack walks into a hi-fi fix-it shop that a guy named Jeep owns, a place called Music Center, Inc. Jack asks Jeep to listen to a jazz recording his friend made. Jack figures maybe Jeep can help, because his friend, he's desperate.

The desperate guy is Mack Emerman, a Miami jazz nut. Like the great Rudy Van Gelder up in New Jersey, Emerman had started to do jazz recordings out of his parents' home. "The living room was the studio," he recalls, "the garage was the control room." He also did remote recordings in local clubs, places like Herbie's Room on Alton Road, small jazz clubs around town. But there was a problem. Jack knew it too, but he needed an expert opinion on audio. In Fort Lauderdale, 1959, Jeep was the closest thing to an expert.

"He asked me if I would listen to this tape. I listened, and then I told him what the problem was. The music and the mix were fine, I told him, but there was distortion. I explained I had a machine that could measure distortion. I measured, and it was something like 20 percent. That's a lot," says Jeep Harned some forty years later. "Well, next day I went over to Mack's studio for the first time and I saw that he had a custom-made tube console that just wasn't made right. The studio was a good-sounding place, though. I told Mack that the console just was not put together all that well, that I had measured something, again, like 20 percent distortion.

"Well, he was just so upset that he started to cry right there. He told me he didn't have

any more money; he'd already spent every bloody penny on this studio and custom console and everything. I told him, 'Don't worry, I'll fix the distortion problem; you can pay me when you have some success.'"

And so began the story of Mack Emerman and Jeep Harned. Of Criteria Studios and MCI consoles. Of a string of smash hits and audio innovations so extraordinary, for so long, that neither of the young men sitting in the studio on 149th and West Dixie Highway could possibly have imagined it. It was the first time that Jeep helped out. It would not be the last.

Criteria Studios, a recording complex that would amass more than three hundred gold and platinum records in the next four decades, with worldwide smashes like "Layla," "Pick Up the Pieces," "Stayin' Alive," "I Got You (I Feel Good)," "One of These Nights," "Night Moves," "Sweet Melissa," "Could You Be Loved?" "Little Pink Houses," "Rainy Night in Georgia," and "Rhiannon," began as nearly all of the studios of that era began. Without a clue.

The beauty about so many of these studios and their founders is the absolute naiveté that was involved, perhaps required, in the process. By and large, many of these pioneers were making it up as they went along. This wasn't unusual; the people at the labels with whom they worked were doing precisely the same thing. Some of these recording pioneers will occasionally refer to "OJT" or "on the job training." There wasn't a "right way" of doing anything. Stereo was brand new. Multitrack tape machines were new. Modular consoles and their use were being figured and refigured daily.

The recording business was never really about making lots of money; ask any studio owner. For every Bill Putnam who made small fortunes, there were three or maybe twenty who struggled to stay afloat. Some, like Mack Emerman, have had stakes in both camps—they have been flush and bust more than most bookies.

This book starts out in the Golden State, in Hollywood, the land of the happy ending. It ends a few thousand miles away, in Miami, in the Sunshine State. But the ending here is no less satisfying. In fact, it's more satisfying, because it's real.

Mack Emerman was a former trumpet player in the Les Brown Orchestra who decided to pack it in as a musician ("I wasn't a good enough player"). Alternately going to small clubs to record combos and recording tracks for local commercials—and more small combos—out of his parents' home in Hollywood, Florida, Mack honed his chops. He even released three recordings on the Criteria Gold Coast Jazz label.

Why "Criteria"? "My best friend was an architect," Emerman says. "His wife came up with the name Criteria. I didn't even know what it meant. When she told me what Criteria meant, I thought, Yeah, that's OK." He convinced his father to help acquire the deed on a parcel of land in north Miami. A thirty-by-sixty-foot building was erected. "It was where the local television station was. I figured that I could get additional work from them, and if anything went wrong, I could go to them for help. He enlisted the services of one of the television

Opposite: Criteria's original Studio B. By the end of the 1980s, they were through nearly half the alphabet with new studio additions. Above: Jeep Harned's modular console (foreground), which was soon to flood the `70s market, stands at the ready.

211

technicians to help build a tube console for his fledgling operation. The radio tech built Mack's custom console out of his garage. In 1958, the Criteria Recording Studio was open for business.

Even as relatively recently as 1958, smaller markets such as Miami did not have recording studios per se. If a recording was done, it was most likely on a radio station console at a radio station by a radio technician. Jeep Harned was an ROTC civil engineer who had an affinity for all things audio: "My ears were my life," he says. When he decided to help Mack out, rebuilding the tube console, he did so organically, starting with the microphone pre amps, then the line amps, finally the power amps. Soon the console was sounding great. Mack could now make records in his own studio that were sonically equal, or superior, to what was being done in New York.

In those days Miami was still a major tourist and nightclub mecca. Lots of bands came through town. "My father had a favorite phrase," says Mack. "In life, timing is everything." Mack's timing for a recording studio was on the money. Slowly, he built up a clientele of jazz bands, commercial work, and small film work. Sometimes, a real name would come to town. "I had been a collector of Benny Goodman 78s. One day, Benny Goodman came to my studio. He said he heard about my place. So we did a few sessions and he took the tapes with him. I was thrilled, but that was the last I heard of him."

Inspired by recording his hero, Mack sensed he was on the right track. In 1960, Miami Beach became the home of the *Jackie Gleason Show*, a Saturday-night variety show on CBS. ("Miami Beach audiences are the greatest audiences in the world," said the Great One each week to thunderous applause.) Criteria soon landed the production gig for the show's music. By 1965, Criteria was ready for the first of its many expansions.

"In '65, we opened what became known as A, says Mack. "We had partnered with a company called Tel-Air Interests, a local film company. We built a projection room right above the control room in the new studio, which was where the Jackie Gleason TV stuff was done." Timing was again in Emerman's favor. Syd Nathan, owner of King Records in Cincinnati, was in town with his hottest act, James Brown. The Godfather of Soul had just scored his biggest hit with a track that—just like that—created the genre known as funk: "Papa's Got a Brand New Bag." Nathan and Brown booked into Criteria for their next smash single, the equally funky "I Got You (I Feel Good)." Nathan was blown away by the sound of the Harned-modified console. Soon he would be the owner of the first ever Jeep Harned built-from-scratch console. He installed it in the King Studio in Cincinnati. "Those early consoles didn't even have model names or anything," says Harned, looking back on the era with the bemused detachment that comes with decades of perspective and millions of dollars in profits. "I had no idea what I was doing. I knew nothing about retail. I was like the kid who opens a lemonade stand."

This was some kick-ass lemonade he was cranking out. Taking the initials of his audio repair shop, Music Center, Inc. ("I kept on getting too many phone calls to repair musical

212

instruments"), Jeep was now MCI, as Mack had become Criteria. Whatever the moniker, they continued making it up as they went along.

"I used to run up to Cape Caneveral, because they had surplus transports, similar to the Ampex 300 tape machines," remembers Harned. MCI was the first company in the pro audio world to feature not only audio consoles, but also the tape machines to go with them. Both MCI and Criteria were on to a good thing, but neither anticipated the fortunate breeze that would blow their way.

Atlantic

Some studios, like Capitol and Columbia, are, of course, tied to the label that owns them. Occasionally, some independent studios are de facto "label" studios in that they produce the overwhelming amount of projects for a particular label. Such was the case with United Recorders and the Sinatra-driven Reprise label in the early '60s. For Criteria, the label that would be linked with their success, their exponential growth in the '60s and throughout the '70s, was Ahmet Ertegun's Atlantic Records.

By the mid-'60s, Ahmet and his alter ego, producer Jerry Wexler, were living quite large. They signed the artists they dug and practically invented the lifestyle of jet-set bohemia. They had been successful in the '50s, then they co-opted the hook-filled grit of Stax and Muscle Shoals in the '60s. By the latter part of that decade, the world—America at least—was their spicy oyster. Ahmet and Wex began spending more playtime in sunny Miami Beach, where Jerry purchased a huge comfy fishing yacht. They decided the third member of the Atlantic triumvirate, engineer whiz kid Tom Dowd, should check out this whole Miami scene. After all, Dowd and Wexler had struck gold with Otis Redding, the Wicked Pickett, and Sam and Dave in Memphis, and Aretha in Alabama, so why not see what was shaking in South Beach?

The meeting between Tom Dowd and Jeep Harned was the beginning of a polygamous marriage between the record label, the studio world, and manufacturing that was a precursor of the merge-happy 1990s. "Tom is brilliant, absolutely brilliant," says Jeep, echoing a sentiment heard time and again. Harned, though, remains loyal to Emerman to this day as the guy who came first. "Mack was the only one. Then Syd [Nathan]. Then finally, I started getting the phone calls."

One of those calls came from Tom Dowd in New York. "Frankly, I was amazed to see guys from Cincinnati and New York show any interest in what we were doing down here," says Jeep. For his part, Dowd is equally magnanimous about Jeep, calling his plug-in modules "years ahead of the game."

"Mack got me started, Syd Nathan picked it up, and then Tommy Dowd accelerated MCI," says Harned. Dowd and Harned spent several intense days together going over the console that would become an industry standard for the next two decades. Before too long, Atlantic's New York studios would become the third studio to feature MCI gear. And, in the

213

bargain, Atlantic encouraged its artists to work at Criteria. In 1971, Aretha recorded her *Young, Gifted and Black* album there. The year before, an itinerant soul singer named Brook Benton scored the biggest hit of his career with "Rainy Night in Georgia," a threnody of rhythm and blues heartache that captured in three minutes what some novelists spend lifetimes trying to achieve.

"'Rainy Night in Georgia'" put Criteria on the map; that record was huge for us at that time," says staff engineer Ron Albert, who along with his brother Howard would go on to engineer some of the biggest-selling albums to ever come out of Criteria. How Ron Albert came to be a staffer at Criteria was indicative of how Emerman ran things.

"I was just a kid, still in school, but I really wanted to work in a studio, and Criteria was the only place around," says Albert. With more cojones than a man twice his age, he decided to ask Emerman for a job.

Mack was suspicious; the kid looked really young. "How old are you?" he asked the kid.

"How old do you have to be to work here?" came the reply.

"Sixteen."

"I'm sixteen," said the fourteen-year-old.

"Can you type?" asked Emerman.

"Yep," said the boy.

"I was so excited to get that job, I went home and told my mother, 'You have to teach me

how to type, and you have to teach me by tomorrow,'" Albert says now.

Those were heady days for Albert, who quite literally grew up at Criteria. "I remember sitting up in the duct work, above Studio A and looking out over the studio floor. That was all I did; that, and get stuff for Mack." After a short time, his brother Howard would join the growing staff, along with former singer/producer Steve Alaimo, Don Gehman, Karl Richardson, and Albhy Galuten, each of whom has multiple platinum records to his credit. This band of local boys would develop its own way of doing things, such as multimiking drums, in addition to providing a testing ground for the ever-expanding product line of MCI consoles and tape machines. Ron in particular became the chief beta man for Jeep and his growing staff of designers and engineers. "Ron was a genius with consoles," says Mack.

For the Albert brothers, Richardson, and the rest, this was an invaluable time. MCI was leasing consoles to Criteria, with the agreement that they would keep a console for six months before selling it. The influx of new gear, new artists, new hits, and new studios was astonishing. By the early '70s, hits were as pervasive as aqua on 149th Street. Tom Dowd was bringing acts in as quickly as Jeep was bringing in cutting-edge gear. The records being made from 1970 through 1977 include the Allman Brothers' *Idlewild*, Derek and the Dominoes' *Layla and Other Assorted Love Songs*, Eric Clapton's *461 Ocean Boulevard*, the Crosby, Stills and Nash album entitled *CSN*, Lynyrd Skynyrd's air guitar anthem "Freebird," Elvin Bishop's "Fooled

215

Criteria: Stayin' Alive

Around and Fell in Love," and the Average White Bands seminal white-boy soul classic *AWB*, featuring "Pick up the Pieces."

To a man, the Alberts, Richardson, Alaimo, and Emerman himself credit the family feel that they generated at Criteria with their success. "We just cared about the people we worked for," says Emerman simply. "If it was someone's birthday, we made a cake. We'd have a party, and everyone would go," he says, so earnestly you want to work for him right now, today. But this was, after all, the record business. In the '70s. In Miami. It was major party time, right?

"Look, we're just a bunch of guys who love to record music and fish," says Howard Albert. "We would rather put all our money into fishing boats than drugs."

Make no mistake; the men who worked on these tracks at Criteria witnessed the high life. But, according to them today, their tag-team method of working was a distinct advantage.

"We had all grown up together at Criteria, and we all developed the same engineering style," says Ron. "So, what would happen is, sometimes the artists would be going strong for days. But we would not be indulging, so at the end of twelve hours, a fresh new body would come in at, like, eight in the morning, work until seven or eight at night, and the morning guy would have come back fresh, and replace him. And the artists didn't care, 'cause it would be the same sounds, but fresh ears."

For all the hits to come out of Criteria, probably none exemplified the times and the culture so perfectly as the music that migrated from New York in 1975. Barry, Robin, and Maurice Gibb, a.k.a. the Bee Gees, were floundering. The early '60s success of their Beatles-esque pop began to sputter; by the mid-'70s the brothers were casting about for a new sound. Ahmet Ertegun paired them with the hottest new producer/arranger at Atlantic, Arif Mardin. After years of middling tracks, the Brothers Gibb shook the dust off radio with the R&B-flavored LP *Main Course*, featuring timeless cuts "Jive Talkin'," "Nights on Broadway," and "Fanny." The sound of the '70s had hit, and Criteria was the club that artists waited in line to enter.

As popular as *Main Course* was, the streak was only just starting. The Gibbs then teamed up with Criteria staffers Karl Richardson and Albhy Galuten to coproduce their next three albums, which were recorded in the new Studio D. "Stayin' Alive," "How Deep Is Your Love," and "More Than a Woman" were three of the biggest songs that provided a soundtrack for the disco era. It is a testament to all involved that those tracks have emerged as more than guilty disco pleasures, but in fact classic records on their own musical merit.

One of the concepts for any healthy business is the yin-yang mantra, "Expand, stabilize." Criteria, and Mack, got half of that mantra down cold. By the early '80s things had gotten sticky. Disco and the Bee Gees were passé, album budgets were shadows of their former bottom lines, and Mack had leveraged himself to a near financial death. A decision to open a Criteria West had been an accountant's nightmare. "New people" were brought in. The Criteria of the previous decade was but a dream.

With Studio E, in the '80s, Criteria appeared poised to go through half the alphabet with

216

new additions. Spelling was not a problem. Addition and subtraction were proving to be harder. Mack was in over his head. Today, he says, "Quite candidly, I wasn't a very good businessman. I couldn't make the payments. I could see the end was coming, and I didn't handle it very well." These were dark times for Mack. "I got off the page for a couple, three years."

Beset with a mountain of financial stress, Mack suffered a small stroke. This gentle man, who really only wanted to make jazz albums, was out of the box. He had even lost touch with the man he calls one of his best friends, Jeep Harned. He was, frankly, in awful shape.

Full Circle

Miami Beach will never be confused with Frank Capra's Bedford Falls, but Mack was George Bailey to a lot of folks. "Wally Heider [a successful L.A. studio owner/engineer] once told me, 'The industry needs guys like Mack,' says Jeep. I said 'Yes it does.'" One day, Mack tracked down Jeep, who by this time was living the good life as a wealthy man in Colorado. Mack told Jeep he was going to be out west for a wedding. Harned saw his chance to step in once more.

"Jeep said, 'Tell me when you are going to be landing, and I'll be there.' Well, when I landed, Jeep was there with his private jet. He took me back to his home in Colorado and he sat me down and gave me a talk. He told me that what I was doing was wrong. He put me on a diet of what to eat. Told me how to exercise. He saved my life," he says simply. "Now," says the seventy-eight-year-old Emerman proudly, "I go to the gym three times a week."

Criteria changed hands repeatedly until the mid '90s, when the Hit Factory concern out of New York took over. The fit seems to be a good one, with the studios completely refurbished and fighting trim for a new millennium. It's currently the scene of the hits spewing out of the Miami Latin music explosion.

As for the boys who became men at Criteria in the '60s, '70s, and '80s, they are still together, still making music and still fishing. Karl Richardson, Ron and Albert Howard, and Steve Alaimo are currently partners in a studio just across the street from their old haunt, which they call Audio Vision. They won't come out and say it, but they love their former boss, the guy who hired them all when they were just kids. Like Jeep, they look out for him in their own way. They made him a partner.

"Audio Vision took me in," says Mack. "I still go around the town, recording jazz groups that need a record. Now I take the tapes to Audio Vision to mix them." Decades later, they are all back together. Still doing it.

Temples Essentials

A dozen classic recordings from each of the Temples of Sound

Capitol Studios
1. Nat "King" Cole, "Nature Boy"
2. Nelson Riddle, "Theme from Route 66"
3. Nat "King" Cole, *After Midnight Sessions*
4. Frank Sinatra, *Songs for Swingin' Lovers*
5. Frank Sinatra,
   Frank Sinatra Sings for Only the Lonely
6. Tennessee Ernie Ford, "Sixteen Tons"
7. *Nancy Wilson and Cannonball Adderly*
8. Lou Rawls, "Dead End Street"
9. Dean Martin, "That's Amore"
10. June Christy, *Something Cool*
11. Peggy Lee, "Fever"
12. Glen Campbell, "Wichita Lineman"

United Western Recorders
1. Beach Boys, "Wouldn't It Be Nice"
2. Ray Charles, "I Can't Stop Loving You"
3. Frank Sinatra and Antonio Carlos Jobim,
   Francis Albert Sinatra & Antonio Carlos Jobim
4. The Mamas & the Papas, "I Saw Her Again Last Night"
5. The Turtles, "Elenore"
6. Bing Crosby, Sammy Davis Jr., Frank Sinatra,
   Dean Martin, *Robin and the Seven Hoods Soundtrack*
7. Gary Lewis and the Playboys, "This Diamond Ring"
8. Nancy Sinatra, "These Boots Are Made For Walkin'"
9. Dean Martin, "Everybody Loves Somebody"
10. Ricky Nelson, "Hello, Mary Lou"
11. Hoyt Curtin, William Hanna, Joseph Barbera,
    "*The Flinstones* Theme"
12. Beach Boys, "California Girls"

Sunset Sound
1. The Doors, "Light My Fire"
2. James Taylor, "Fire and Rain"
3. Prince, "Controversy"
4. The Turtles, "Happy Together"
5. Led Zeppelin, "Stairway to Heaven"
6. Brasil '66, "Fool on the Hill"
7. Louis Armstrong, "Jungle Book"
8. Randy Newman, *12 Songs*
9. Buffalo Springfield, "For What It's Worth"
10. Love, *Forever Changes*
11. Neil Young, "Cinnamon Girl"
12. Annette Funicello, "Monkey's Uncle"

RCA B
1. Roy Orbison, "Running Scared"
2. Skeeter Davis, "The End of the World"
3. Elvis Presley, "It's Now or Never"
4. Everly Brothers, "Cathy's Clown"
5. Jim Reeves, "He'll Have to Go"
6. Chet Atkins, "Boo Boo Stick"
7. George Hamilton IV, "Abilene"
8. Floyd Cramer, "Last Date"
9. Charlie Pride, "Is Anybody Goin' to San Antone?"
10. Sgt. Barry Sadler, "Ballad of the Green Berets"
11. Bobby Goldsboro, "Honey"
12. Al Hirt, "Java"

Stax
1. Booker T. and the MGs, "Green Onions"
2. Eddie Floyd, "Knock On Wood"
3. Carla Thomas, "Gee Whiz (Look at His Eyes)"
4. Sam and Dave, "Soul Man"
5. Sam and Dave, "Wrap It Up"
6. Otis Redding, "I Can't Turn You Loose"
7. Otis Redding, "Dock of the Bay"
8. Rufus Thomas, "Walking the Dog"
9. Booker T. and the MGs, "Soul Limbo"
10. William Bell and Judy Clay, "Private Number"
11. Wilson Pickett, "634-5789"
12. Johnny Taylor, "Who's Makin' Love?"

Sun Studios
1. Carl Mann, "Mona Lisa"
2. Billy Lee Riley, "Red Hot"
3. Jerry Lee Lewis, "Great Balls of Fire"
4. Jackie Brenston and Ike Turner, "Rocket 88"
5. Elvis Presley, "Baby Let's Play House"
6. Elvis Presley, "Blue Moon"
7. Johnny Cash, "I Walk the Line"
8. Junior Parker, "Mystery Train"
9. Howlin'Wolf, "Moanin' at Midnight"
10. Jerry Lee Lewis, "Breathless"
11. Bill Justis, "Raunchy"
12. Carl Perkins, "Blue Suede Shoes"

J&M

1. Fats Domino, "The Fat Man"
2. Benny Spellman, "Fortune Teller"
3. Little Richard, "Tutti Frutti"
4. Irma Thomas, "It's Raining"
5. Lee Dorsey, "Working in a Coal Mine"
6. Ernie K-Doe, "Mother-in-Law"
7. Jesse Hill, "Ooh Poo Pah Doo"
8. Guitar Slim, "Things I Used to Do"
9. Professor Longhair, "Mardi Gras in New Orleans"
10. Lloyd Price, "Lawdy Miss Clawdy"
11. Chris Kenner, "Something You Got"
12. Barbara George, "I Know (You Don't Love Me No More)"

Chess

1. Howlin'Wolf, "Killing Floor"
2. Chuck Berry, "Johnny B. Good"
3. Ko Ko Taylor, "Wang Dang Doodle"
4. Etta James and Sugar Pie De Santo, "In the Basement"
5. Fontella Bass, "Rescue Me"
6. Bo Diddley, "Say Man"
7. The Dells, *There Is*
8. Muddy Waters, "My Home Is in the Delta"
9. Little Walter, "Mellow Down Easy"
10. Sonny Boy Williamson, "Little Village"
11. The Rolling Stones, "2120 South Michigan Avenue"
12. Billy Stewart, "Sitting in the Park"

Universal

1. Count Basie and Joe Williams, "The Night Time is the Right Time"
2. The Impressions, "Woman's Got Soul"
3. Walter Jackson, "It's All Over"
4. Eddie Harris, "Exodus"
5. Jackie Wilson, "Higher and Higher"
6. Four Seasons, "Walk Like a Man"
7. Gene Chandler, "Duke of Earl"
8. Chi-Lites, "Have You Seen Her?"
9. Young-Holt Trio, "Soulful Strut"
10. Tyrone Davis, "Turn Back the Hands of Time"
11. Dee Clark, "Raindrops"
12. Betty Everett, "The Shoop Shoop Song (It's in His Kiss)"

Motown

1. Barret Strong, "Money"
2. The Supremes, "Love Is like an Itchin' in My Heart"
3. Marvin Gaye, "Stubborn Kind of Fella"
4. Stevie Wonder, "Uptight"
5. The Temptations, "My Girl"
6. Mary Wells, "My Guy"
7. The Temptations, "Psychedelic Shack"
8. Marvin Gaye, "What's Goin' On"
9. The Four Tops, "Standing in the Shadows of Love"
10. Smokey Robinson and the Miracles, "Tears of a Clown"
11. The Supremes, "Reflections"
12. Martha and The Vandellas, "Dancing in the Street"

Sigma Sound Studios

1. O'Jays, "For the Love of Money"
2. Lou Rawls, "Lady Love"
3. Billy Paul, "Me and Mrs. Jones"
4. Spinners, "Games People Play"
5. Laura Nyro and Labelle, "Bells"
6. Harold Melvin and the Blue Notes, "I Miss You"
7. David Bowie, "Young Americans"
8. O'Jays, "Back Stabbers"
9. The Jacksons, "Show You the Way To Go"
10. MFSB, "MFSB" (Soul Train Theme)
11. Joe Simon, "Drownin' in the Sea of Love"
12. The Delfonics, "La La Means I Love You"

Atlantic

1. Clyde McPhatter, "Money Honey"
2. Ray Charles, "What'd I Say"
3. The Drifters, "On Broadway"
4. Ben E. King, "Stand By Me"
5. The Coasters, "Charlie Brown"
6. John Coltrane, "My Favorite Things"
7. Bobby Darin, "Splish Splash"
8. Big Joe Turner, "Shake, Rattle and Roll"
9. Aretha Franklin, "Respect"
10. Lavern Baker, "Tweedlee Dee"
11. The Rascals, "Groovin'"
12. Cream, "Strange Brew"

Temples Essentials

Columbia Studios

1. Miles Davis, *Kind of Blue*
2. Dave Brubeck, *Time Out*
3. Barbra Streisand, *My Name is Barbra*
4. Bob Dylan, "Like a Rolling Stone"
5. Simon & Garfunkel, *Bookends*
6. Miles Davis, *Porgy & Bess*
7. Cast Recording, *My Fair Lady*
8. Laura Nyro, "Eli's Comin'"
9. Barbra Streisand, *A Christmas Album*
10. Tony Bennett, "I Wanna Be Around"
11. Johnny Mathis, "Misty"
12. Billie Holiday, *Lady in Satin*

Van Gelder Studio

1. John Coltrane, *A Love Supreme*
2. *John Coltrane and Johnny Hartman*
3. Deodato, "Also Sprach Zarathustra"
   (Theme from *2001: A Space Odyssey*)
4. Miles Davis, *Relaxin' with the Miles Davis Quartet*
5. Eric Dolphy, *Out to Lunch*
6. John Coltrane, *Ascension*
7. Lee Morgan, *The Sidewinder*
8. Oliver Nelson, *The Blues and the Abstract Truth*
9. Etta Jones, *Don't Go to Strangers*
10. Quincy Jones, *Walking in Space*
11. Jimmy Smith and Wes Montgomery, *The Dynamic Duo*
12. Freddie Hubbard, *Red Clay*

Criteria

1. Bee Gees, "How Deep Is Your Love?"
2. Derek & the Dominos, *Layla and other Assorted Love Songs*
3. James Brown, "I Got You (I Feel Good)"
4. Aretha Franklin, *Young, Gifted and Black*
5. Eagles, "Hotel California"
6. Allman Brothers, *Eat a Peach*
7. Brook Benton, "Rainy Night in Georgia"
8. Gloria Estefan, "Rhythm Is Gonna Get You"
9. Elvin Bishop, "Fooled Around and Fell in Love"
10. Average White Band, "Pick up the Pieces"
11. Eric Clapton, *461 Ocean Blvd*
12. Hank Ballard, "The Twist"

Photo Credits

Acknowledgments

We dedicate this book to our fathers and to the "father of modern recording," Bill Putnam.

Jim Cogan acknowledges

Chess: Malcolm Chisholm, Tim Samuelson, Robert Prouter; Columbia Studios: Frank Laico, Phil Ramone, Roy Hallee, Stan Tonkel, Marc Kirkeby, Matt Kelly, Lo Anne Rios-Kong, Phoung Baum; Criteria: Mack Emmerman, Jeep Harned, Tom Dowd, Ron and Howard Albert, Steve Alaimo, Karl Richardson, Trevor Fletcher; RCA B: Bill Porter, Gordon Stoker, Bob and Kittra Moore, Buddy Harmon, Harold Bradley, Denny Adcock, Marc Neil; Sun Studios: Sam Phillips, Sally Wilbourn; Sunset Sound: Bruce Botnick, Tutti Camarata, Paul Camarata, Ray Manzarek, Barney Hoskyns; United Western Recorders: Allen Sides, Al Schmitt, Candace Stewart, Kelly "Sammy Sinatra" Erwin, Gary Meyerberg-Lauter; Universal: Bruce Swedein, Bill Putnam Jr., Scott Putnam, Jerry Butler, Carl Davis, Ryan Null.

Special thanks to: Hank Neuberger at the Chicago Recording Company, for cool contacts and unstinting support throughout the project; Bill Piekarz, for thirty-plus years of data and inspiration; Bob Cogan, for a lifetime of loving support; and lastly and mostly, to William "Bob" Clark, for being such a gracious partner and such a doggone cool friend.

William Clark acknowledges

Atlantic: Ahmet Ertegun, Jerry Wexler, Tom Dowd; Capitol Studios: Michael Frondelli, Maggie Sikkens, Tommy Steele, Frank Bowen, Charles L. Granata; J&M: Cosimo Matassa, "Sir" Allen Toussaint, Fats Domino, Rick Coleman, Randy Lowman, Roger Branch, Jeff Hannusch, NYNO Records; Motown: Art Stewart, Johnny Bristol, Billy Wilson (Motown Alumni Association), Eddie Willis, Weldon McDougal III, Alan Slutsky, Don Waller; Sigma Sound Studios: Joe Tarsia, Michael Tarsia, Leo Sacks III; Stax: Deanie Parker, "Play It" Steve Cropper, Joe Mulherin, Rob Bowman; Van Gelder Studio: Mr. Rudy Van Gelder, Bob Weinstock, Esmond Edwards, Ashley Kahn, Mr. Chuck Stewart, Dan Skea, Charles Lourie, "The Incredible" Jimmy Smith, Joey Defrancesco.

Special thanks to: Nancy Rosenthal, for helping us make the connection that got this project rolling; Virginia Saxton, for her hard work transcribing our interviews; Wayne Jones and Bob Dunphy, for being old, dear, and faithful friends and lending a big hand at crucial times in the process; Jean Redmond, for support and friendship; Jim Clark, for being a great big brother and cheerleader; my children, Carmen and Jordan, for joy and inspiration; my wonderful wife, Maria, for love, trust, understanding, wit, and always good advice; my mother, for everything; and finally, to a true "pardnah," my great friend, drinking buddy, and fellow writer and dreamer, Jim Cogan.

We would both like to express our gratitude to Chronicle Books and designer Michael Hodgson of Ph.D for helping make this book come to life. We want to thank our editors, Alan "Bruthah" Rapp and Steven "Mr. Mock" Mockus, for guiding us on this fabulous journey.

Index

222

Temples of Sound

224